# Victoria's Blue Jackets & Marines

AFTER THE JUNKS THEY PULLED WITH MIGHT AND MAIN

# Victoria's Blue Jackets & Marines
## The Royal Navy During Queen Victoria's Reign 1839-1901

W. H. G. Kingston

revised and expanded by
G. A. Henty

*Victoria's Blue Jackets & Marines: the Royal Navy During Queen Victoria's Reign 1839-1901*
by W. H. G. Kingston
revised and expanded by G. A. Henty




Leonaur is an imprint of Oakpast Ltd

Material original to this edition and
presentation of text in this form
copyright © 2010 Oakpast Ltd


ISBN: 978-1-84677-974-9 (hardcover)
ISBN: 978-1-84677-973-2 (softcover)

http://www.leonaur.com

**Publisher's Notes**

The views expressed in this book are not necessarily those of the publisher.

# Contents

| | |
|---|---|
| Our Sailors | 9 |
|     The Capture of Aden | 10 |
| War on the Coast Of Syria | 11 |
|     Bombardment of Beyrout | 11 |
|     Capture of Sidon | 12 |
|     Attack on the Castle of D'jebel | 13 |
|     Bombardment and Capture of Acre | 14 |
| Warfare in Chinese Waters | 16 |
|     Capture of Chusan | 18 |
|     Capture of Chin-Keang-Foo and Nankin | 21 |
|     A Timely Rescue | 26 |
| Capture of a Venezuelan Squadron | 28 |
| Suppression of Piracy in Borneo | 31 |
|     Rajah Brooke | 31 |
|     Attack on Sarebus Pirates | 32 |
| Warfare on the Rivers La Plata Battle of the Parana | 36 |
|     Engagements With the Batteries of San Lorenzo | 39 |
|     Gallant Exploit of a Rocket-Battery | 42 |
| Expedition to San Juan De Nicaragua | 49 |
|     Capture of Fort Serapaqui | 49 |
| The Destruction of Lagos | 53 |
| The Burmese War | 59 |
|     Capture of Pegu | 62 |
|     Expedition Up the Irrawaddy | 63 |
|     Attacks on Mya Toon | 66 |
| The Crimean War | 69 |
|     Bombardment of Odessa | 70 |
|     Operations in the Baltic | 71 |
|     A Spirited Action | 71 |
|     An Unsuccessful Venture | 73 |
|     Bomarsund—21st June | 74 |

| | |
|---|---|
| A Capture of Despatches | 76 |
| Attack on Viborg | 77 |
| Bombardment of Sveaborg | 80 |
| The White Sea Squadron | 81 |
| Action on the Danube | 82 |
| Bombardment of Sebastopol | 84 |
| Crimean Naval Brigade | 87 |
| A Live Shell Among the Powder | 89 |
| Edward Saint John Daniels | 90 |
| Bravery of Five Seamen at Inkermann | 90 |
| Commander Roby | 90 |
| Dashing Service of John Shepherd | 91 |
| Expedition to Kertch | 94 |
| Proceedings at Taganrog | 96 |
| Gallantry of S. Trewavas, Seaman | 96 |
| Lieutenant G.F. Day at Genitchi | 97 |
| Closely Pursued | 98 |
| Capture of Kinburn | 99 |
| **The Indian Mutiny** | **101** |
|    The "*Shannon's*" Brigade in India | 101 |
| **The Second Chinese War** | **111** |
|    Battle of Fatshan | 114 |
|    Capture of Canton | 118 |
| **The Slave Trade** | **120** |
|    Capture of Brazilian Slaver *Firme* | 121 |
|    Voyage of A Prize from Accra to Sierra Leone | 122 |
|    Capture of an Armed Slaver | 127 |
|    A Pinnace Attacks a Slaver | 128 |
|    Adventure of HMS Wasp | 129 |
|    Capture of a Slaver | 131 |
|    An Attempt to Recapture a Prize | 132 |
|    Attempt to Retake a Prize | 134 |
| **The Recapture of the Emily Saint Pierre** | **136** |
| **Arctic Exploring Expeditions** | **141** |
|    The North-West Passage | 141 |
| **Voyage of the Fox** | **163** |
|    The Fate of Sir John Franklin's Expedition | 166 |
| **The Expedition to the North Pole** | **171** |
| **Memoir of Commodore James Graham Goodenough** | **181** |
| **The Abyssinian Expedition** | **185** |

| | |
|---|---|
| The Ashanti War | 196 |
| Spirited and Gallant Exploits | 209 |
|     A Remarkable Rescue | 209 |
|     Two Courageous Swimmers | 214 |
|     Rescue of a Boat's Crew | 220 |
| Gallant Deeds | 233 |
|     Humanity of Lieutenant Breen, RN. | 233 |
|     Gallantry Exhibited in Preserving Life | 234 |
|     Gallantry of Lieutenant Boyle, RN. | 236 |
|     Lowestoft Lifeboat | 238 |
|     Bravery of Joseph Rogers, a Maltese Seaman | 239 |
|     Remarkable Instance of Endurance | 240 |
| A Brush With an Ironclad | 243 |
| Gallant Deeds Performed by Naval Men | 245 |
|     Death of Captain Brownrigg | 245 |
| The Egyptian Campaign | 249 |
|     Campaign Against the Mahdi | 255 |
|     Battle of El Tab | 256 |
|     Battle of Tamanieb | 260 |
| Wars in South Africa | 262 |
| The Zulu War | 266 |
| The Boer War | 270 |
| The Boer War | 274 |
|     The Siege of Ladysmith | 274 |
| Fighting in China | 277 |
|     First Attempt to Relieve the Legations at Peking | 277 |
|     The Capture of the Taku Forts | 281 |
|     The Capture of Tientsin City | 284 |
|     A Young V.C. | 290 |
|     The Siege of Peking | 291 |
|     The Relief of Peking | 295 |

CHAPTER 1

# Our Sailors

Let fall the topsails, hoist away—up anchor, round goes the capstan—sheet home—haul taut the braces! and away we glide, to prove to our countrymen that British sailors have not been sleeping on beds of roses for the last quarter of a century since her gracious Majesty Queen Victoria came to the throne.

So wrote our original author some forty years ago. "Up anchor, full speed ahead," is, we suppose, the modern equivalent for his nautical simile, and very prosaic and commonplace it sounds; but we shall find that the romance of the Navy did not go out with the last of the sailing frigates, and that the age of steam and electricity, of enormous ironclads and rapid cruisers, affords as great a scope for individual daring, resource, and heroism as the days of sailing frigates and boarding parties; and that though in recent years our sailors have not had many chances of using their weapons on the sea, the Naval Brigade has taken its part in many an expedition, on land, and on all occasions the British tar has proved himself a worthy successor to the heroes of Trafalgar and the Nile.

During the earlier years of the Great Queen's reign her sailors had little to do in the fighting line, though on the West Coast of Africa the slave traffic gave occasion to many a lively skirmish, and on other seas various events from time to time afforded an opportunity for showing that their weapons were as effective as of old.

## The Capture of Aden

Somewhat of that character was the capture of Aden, an Arab town on the entrance of the Red Sea. A former sultan or chief of Aden had by treaty given up the place to the British; but his successor, not approving of the bargain, refused to submit to it. As it was important for the English to hold the place, to facilitate the navigation of the Red Sea, an expedition, under Captain Smith of the *Volage*, was sent by Sir Frederick Maitland, then Commander-in-Chief on the East India Station, to bring the Sultan to reason.

It was not a big affair, though unhappily it cost several lives, but its result was important and lasting. Captain Smith's expedition comprised, besides HMS *Volage*, three smaller vessels and some transports. On the 19th of January 1839 he bombarded the town and landed his troops, who after a short resistance overcame the Sultan's army, and hoisted the flag on its walls, and Aden became a port of the British Empire, as it has remained ever since (1900).

From early times it had been a very important centre for the trade between Europe and the East, but when the Portuguese opened up the route to India by the Cape it lost its advantage. In the hands of the British its prosperity has returned, and the return of the Eastern trade by means of the Suez Canal to the Red Sea has raised it to a far higher position than ever it possessed in ancient days; it is now the great coaling station for the British fleet and merchantmen in the East. The trade passing through it to and from Southern Arabia exceeds five millions a year, and it is also a strongly fortified naval station.

CHAPTER 2

# War on the Coast Of Syria
## 1840

The next affair in which our bluejackets were engaged was the war on the coast of Syria, in 1840. The causes of this were as follow. Mehemet Ali, Pasha or Governor of Egypt, wished not only to make himself altogether independent of the Sultan of Turkey, who claimed to be his sovereign, but also to hold possession of Syria. Into that country he sent an army under the command of Ibrahim Pasha, who was everywhere successful, and was approaching Constantinople itself. This so alarmed the Sultan, that he was about to ask for assistance from the Russians. On this, England, France, and Austria thought it high time to interfere; for had the Russians once taken possession of Constantinople, it would have been a difficult matter to turn them out again. Accordingly, those three powers sent to the Turks to promise them assistance if they would hold out, and immediately despatched a large number of ships-of-war to the coast of Syria. Sir Robert Stopford was Admiral of the British fleet, and Sir Charles Napier, having his broad pennant flying, commanded a squadron under him.

### BOMBARDMENT OF BEYROUT—SEPTEMBER 1840

The first place attacked was the town and fortress of Beyrout. The English had thirteen sailing ships and four steamers. There was a Turkish squadron of seven ships, under Admiral Walker, who was then in the service of the Sultan, and three Austrian ships. Though cannonaded for several days, the place still held out. However, on the 2nd of October an Egyptian gunner, who had deserted, came on board the *Hastings* at Beyrout, and gave information that a train had been laid along the bridge to the eastern castle, where a large quantity of powder was concealed; and he undertook to guide a party to cut the train and seize the powder.

Commander Worth at once offered to perform this dangerous service, and numbers volunteered to follow him. He embarked in one of the boats of the *Hastings*, protected by the launch and pinnace of the *Edinburgh*, and covered by the fire of the ships. Dashing on in the face of a heavy fire of musketry, he landed on the bridge, cut off the train, and then forced his way into the castle, over the walls of which he threw some sixty or seventy barrels of powder, and succeeded in bringing off thirty-one barrels more.

Unfortunately, in this service, Mr Luscomb, a midshipman of the *Hastings*, was killed; the Egyptian, and two seamen of the *Hastings* and one of the *Edinburgh*, were wounded.

### Capture of Sidon

While the fleet lay off Beyrout, it was considered important to drive the Egyptians out of Sidon, a strong and important place. Commodore Napier undertook to perform the work, and be back off Beyrout in three days. With two steamers and five other ships, having on board 750 English and 800 Turkish marines, he appeared off the place on the 26th September. The town having been summoned to surrender, and no answer being given, was cannonaded for half an hour. Captain Austin, at the head of the Turkish battalion, landed, but was very warmly received, and several of his followers were killed. The fleet again accordingly opened fire, and battered down a number of houses, after which the commodore, at the head of the main body of the British marines, and Captain Henderson at the head of another, in the most spirited manner broke open the gates, fought their way in, and took possession of the castle. Numberless acts of gallantry were displayed. Among others, there was a complete race from the spot where they landed between Mr James Hunt, a midshipman of the *Stromboli*, and Signor Dominica Chinca, a midshipman of the Austrian frigate *Guerriera*, who should first plant their colours on the walls of the town. All now appearing quiet in the town, the commodore left a guard in the castle, and descended into it. No town was ever taken where less blood was unnecessarily spilt, or disorders more speedily put a stop to.

## ATTACK ON THE CASTLE OF D'JEBEL

A strong body of Albanian troops being posted in the Castle of D'Jebel, Captain Martin was despatched in the *Carysfort*, with the *Dido* and *Cyclops*, having on board 220 marines and 150 armed mountaineers, to turn them out. As soon as the marines were prepared for landing, the ships opened their fire on the castle, which was returned by musket-shots.

After the fire had been continued for an hour, the marines, commanded by Captain Robinson, accompanied by a large party of armed mountaineers, pushed off from the *Cyclops*, and formed on the beach to the south of the town, their landing being covered by the ships, which again opened on the castle. The fire from the ships and the launch's carronades having cleared the gardens in front of the castle, the signal was made to push on. The marines on this advanced with their invariable gallantry to the assault; but when they got within thirty yards of the towers, a destructive fire was opened on them from a crenelated outwork, having a deep ditch in front, which was completely masked from the fire of the ships, and numbers fell killed and wounded. In vain Captain Robinson and the other officers looked for some part of the castle wall which might prove practicable. No gate was accessible, and they were therefore compelled to abandon the enterprise. The ships again started firing on the castle, but it was so stoutly built that no impression could be made on it, and at half-past five the firing ceased and the landing party re-embarked.

As the force was retiring it was discovered that an English flag, which had been planted on a garden wall by the pilot of the *Cyclops* as a signal to the ships, had been accidentally left there;

it could not be suffered to fall into the hands of the enemy, and therefore had to be recovered, whatever the cost. It was a dangerous undertaking to run the gauntlet of the enemy's guns and bring it back, but Lieutenant Grenfell and a seaman from the *Cyclops* volunteered to attempt it. Their progress was watched with much anxiety. They crept along from cover to cover, and at last reached the flag, which they hauled down, and hastened back again with their prize. Loud cheers greeted them as they returned to the ships uninjured and successful.

Although the attempt to take the castle by storm had not been successful, it was not found necessary to renew it on the following day, for when morning came it was found that the steady fire from the ships had proved too much for the nerves of the garrison, and that rather than face it another day they had vacated the position and stolen away under cover of the night.

## Bombardment and Capture of Acre
### —3rd November 1840

Ibrahim Pasha, who had taken Acre in 1837, had commenced to strengthen it greatly; but the fortifications he had designed were not completed when the allied squadron of twenty ships, mostly line-of-battle ships, appeared off it, 2nd November 1840. Towed by the steamers, the ships the next morning speedily took up their positions, and opened their fire in the most spirited manner.

After the ships had hotly engaged the batteries for nearly two hours, the grand magazine blew up with a most tremendous explosion, whether caused by a shell or by accident it is difficult to say. A large number of the garrison were blown up, and many probably were buried alive in the ruins or in the casements. The guns, however, notwithstanding this catastrophe, kept up their fire with great spirit to the last. About sunset the signal was made to discontinue the engagement; but the commodore kept the fire up some time after dusk, lest the enemy should be tempted to re-man their guns. The flag-lieutenant then brought the orders to withdraw.

In the middle of the night a small boat brought off the information that the Egyptian troops were leaving the town, and in consequence, at daylight, 300 Turks and a party of Austrian marines landed, and took unopposed possession of the place. The havoc caused by the guns of the squadron on the walls and houses was very great, though, notwithstanding the hot and long-continued fire they had been exposed to, the ships escaped with little damage, and the amount of casualties was very small, being fourteen English and four Turks killed, and forty-two wounded.

An entire battalion, which had been formed near the magazine, ready to resist any attempts to storm, was destroyed. The appearance of the dead and wounded, as they lay scattered about the town, was very dreadful, but they seemed to excite but little sympathy in the breasts of the Turks. Every living creature within the area of 60,000 square yards round the magazine had ceased to exist, the loss of life being computed from 1200 to 2000 persons. Certainly two entire regiments were annihilated, with fifty donkeys, thirty camels, twelve cows, and some horses.

This was the first occasion on which the advantages of steam had been fully proved in battle, by the rapidity with which the steamers took up their positions, and the assistance they rendered to the other ships; as also by the destruction caused through the shells thrown from them.

On the 4th another explosion took place, by which a marine was killed and Captain Collier had his leg fractured.

The garrison being placed in a state of order, was left under the command of Sir Charles Smith, with 3000 Turkish troops and 250 marines, under Lieutenant-Colonel Walker, with the protection of the Pique and *Stromboli*.

The results of the capture of Acre were very important. Ibrahim Pasha evacuated Syria, and Mehemet Ali gave up the whole Turkish fleet, which sailed for Marmorice under Admiral Walker. Soon after, the Sultan sent a *firman*, according to the Pasha the hereditary possession of Egypt, without any interference on the part of the Porte, while a yearly tribute of 2,000,000 pounds was to be paid to the Sultan, besides about 2,000,000 pounds more of arrears.

Thus terminated the part taken by the British at that time in the affairs of Turkey and Egypt.

CHAPTER 3

# Warfare in Chinese Waters
## 1840-1842

The war in China was undertaken to punish the Government for the numerous injuries and insults they had offered to the English, and, by teaching them to respect our power, to induce them to trade with us on fair and equal terms, and to treat us in future as one civilised people should treat another; also to demand reparation of grievances, and payment for the property of British subjects destroyed at Canton; to obtain a guarantee against similar occurrences in future; and, what was of the greatest importance, to open up the trade at the different ports along the coast.*

With these objects to be accomplished, a large squadron and a number of transports, containing a considerable body of troops, were despatched in 1840 by the Governor-General of India to the Chinese seas.

Soon after this a large fleet arrived from England, under the command of Admiral the Honourable G. Elliot, while Sir Gordon Bremer had his broad pennant flying on board the *Wellesley*. Captain Elliot, RN, it must be understood, was acting on shore as Chief-Superintendent of Trade.

The Chinese are a very clever people, but though their civilisation is very ancient it has been stationary for ages, and all change and advance of Western ideas has been violently opposed both by the governing classes and the people. In the matter, however, of armament they have in recent years made great ad-

---

This 1900 view ignores the 'opium' issue. Ed.

vance, but at this time this advance had hardly yet commenced, and they had nothing to oppose to the British fleet.

Not having the real thing, with great ingenuity they proceeded to extemporise an imitation, the appearance of which they hoped would be sufficient to frighten off the foreigner. They purchased an English trading vessel, the *Cambridge*, intending to turn her into, at least in appearance, a man-of-war, and built some strange-looking little schooners upon a European model, for the purpose of employing them against the English. Commissioner Lin also got up some sham fights at the Bogue, dressing those who were to act as assailants in red coats, in order to accustom the defenders to the sight of the red uniform,—the redcoats, of course, being always driven back with tremendous slaughter. They also ran up formidable-looking forts along the banks of many of their rivers, which on examination, however, turned out to be merely thin planks painted. The object of these was to alarm the barbarians, and to prevent them from entering their harbours. But the crowning and most ingenious device was the construction of some vessels, with large paddle-wheels like those of steamers, which were worked inside by men; though, that they might appear to be real steamers, they had, it is said, funnels and fires under them to create a smoke.

Although from these accounts it would appear that the Chinese were not very formidable enemies, it must be understood that they also possessed some forts which were really very strong; and that though the true Chinese are not very fond of fighting, and, from their peculiar temperament, (looking upon discretion as the better part of valour), prefer running away to stopping with the certainty of being shot or bayoneted, yet that, as they fully understand division of labour, they employ a large number of Tartars to do their fighting for them. These Tartars are very brave fellows, and so are their officers; and in numberless instances they preferred death to defeat. They invariably fought to the last; and often, when they could fight no longer, cut the throats of their wives and children, and then their own, rather than yield. This horrible practice arose undoubtedly from ignorance, they believing that their conquerors would ill-treat and enslave them if they captured them alive. Besides these Tartar troops, who were far from contemptible enemies, our gallant redcoats and bluejackets had to contend with the pernicious climate of the south of China, by which, more than by the *jingall*-balls of the enemy, numbers were cut off. The Tartars we have been speaking of are powerful men, armed with long spears, and often they crossed them with the British bayonet, for which the long spear was sometimes more than a match. Hand-to-hand encounters with the Tartar troops were not uncommon, and our men learned to their cost that they had held the Chinese too cheap. Instances occurred in which the powerful Tartar soldier rushed within the bayonet guard of his opponent, and grappled with him for life or death.

A full description of the numerous actions which took place from the commencement to the termination of the war, extending over so many months, would at the present day be far from interesting. We shall, therefore, but briefly allude to some of them.

### Capture of Chusan

The crisis had come. The Chinese had determined to drive away the "foreign devils" from their coasts, and the "foreign devils" had equally determined to show that they were a match for the Celestials.

On 5th July 1840, Chusan, a small island in the Chinese sea, fell into the hands of the British. The previous day, HMS *Conway*, *Alligator*, and *Wellesley*, with a troopship and two transports, arrived in Chusan harbour. The ships took up position opposite a large Joss House or Temple. Sir Gordon Bremer was in command of our force. In the evening a deputation was sent on shore, calling upon the governor to surrender the town of Chusan and avoid unnecessary bloodshed. The Chinese admiral and two mandarins themselves came to refuse this offer. During that night the people were seen strengthening their fortifications, while the inhabitants were flying up the river in their merchant junks, which were allowed to pass without impediment, although their cargoes, probably containing much that was valuable, would have made the fortunes of many a British officer. However, they were allowed through untouched, for our bluejackets had not come to war against civilians and women and children. Indeed, to their credit, in no instance throughout the war did the helpless suffer injury at the hands of either British soldiers or sailors.

On the 5th, vast crowds could be seen along the hills and shores, and the walls of the city were lined with troops. Twenty-four guns were placed on the landing-place, which, with the appearance of several war-junks, showed that resistance was going to be offered.

The troops were landed in two divisions, under Major-General Burrell's supervision. The fire from the batteries and from the shores was soon silenced by the British "men of war." Not far distant from the city was a hill surrounded on three sides by a deep canal and very boggy land, and our troops took up position on this hill; and though fire was opened on them till nearly midnight, the effects of it were scarcely felt. On the morning of the 6th the guns were directed towards the city, but as no sound could be heard or troops seen, it was thought that the city had probably been evacuated, and a party was sent forward to find out if this was the case. The walls of the city were scaled, and then it was found that, with the exception of one or two unarmed Chinese, the place was empty. Over the principal gate was a placard on which was inscribed, "Save us for the sake of our wives and children." The British flag was, without loss of time, hoisted upon that gate.

On 19th August 1840, Captain Smith, in the *Druid*, and a few smaller ships of war and some troops, attacked and defeated the Chinese in a very spirited manner, stationed in some fortifications known as the Macao Barrier. The guns were spiked, and the whole of the troops fled; nor did they ever again occupy the barrier. Two junks were sunk, and the rest allowed to escape round the opposite point, while the barracks and the other buildings were burned. The British, having four men only wounded, re-embarked, and the ships returned the same evening to their former anchorage in Macao roads. This well-timed and important piece of service of Captain Smith's was the last hostile movement of the British during the year 1840. On the 6th November a truce was announced by Admiral Elliot, and on the 29th he resigned his command from extreme ill-health, and returned to England, leaving Sir Gordon Bremer as commander-in-chief.

After this, nothing very remarkable was done till the Bogue forts were captured, on the 7th January 1841. The Chinese Emperor had only opened negotiations for the purpose of gaining time it was resolved, therefore, to attack Canton itself. Several fleets of war-junks were destroyed, some of the junks being blown up with all on board. On the 26th of February the Boca Tigris forts were taken by Sir Gordon Bremer; and, on the 5th of March, the squadron having advanced up the river, Howqua's Fort was captured. Other forts in succession fell into the hands of the British force; and on the 28th of March, the passage up to Whampoa being forced, the forts of Canton and a large Chinese flotilla were captured. After this, the Chinese came to terms; trade was again opened, and went on for some time with great activity. All this time, however, the treacherous Chinese were plotting how they might exterminate the English; and, on the night of the 21st of May, a bold attempt was made by them to destroy the British fleet by means of fire-rafts. The attempt, however, was happily defeated, and warlike operations were once more commenced.

During these operations, Mr Hall performed a gallant act, which probably saved the lives of Captains Elliot and Herbert and all standing near. A Congreve rocket had been placed in a tube and ignited, when it hung within it instead of flying out. In another moment it would have burst, scattering destruction around, had not Mr Hall thrust his arm into the tube and forced it out from behind. The rush of fire, however, severely burnt his hand, and caused him much suffering; it was long, indeed, before he recovered the use of it.

Canton was now attacked both by sea and land; and after some severe fighting, which lasted from the 23rd up to the 30th of May, that important city was taken possession of by the British.

Amoy was captured on the 26th of August in a dashing manner, and Chinghae on the 10th of October 1841, and Ningpo was occupied on the 12th of the same month. Early in the year, Captain Hall and the officers and crew of the *Nemesis* had a spirited brush with the Chinese, to the north of Chusan. After this, the enemy kept at a distance from that place.

Several attempts were made by the Chinese to destroy the ships of the squadron, each time defeated by the vigilance of the officers and crews. On the 13th of May 1843, Chapoo, a large town near the sea, was attacked and captured; and Woosung and Shanghai shared the same fate on the 16th and 19th of June, the greater part of the fighting on both occasions being performed by the seamen and marines of the fleet.

### Capture of Chin-Keang-Foo and Nankin —21st July 1842

We now come to the crowning victory of the British in China in this war.

Considerable reinforcements having arrived, it was resolved to advance on Nankin itself, the ancient capital of the empire, as the most certain way of bringing the Chinese to terms. To reach that city, the admiral had determined to conduct his fleet, consisting of nearly eighty sail, including two line-of-battle ships, up the great river Yang-Tze, into the very heart of the empire, 200 miles from the sea.

On the 6th July, this imposing fleet passed up the river without any opposition, the Chinese having even withdrawn their guns from most of the towns on its banks, to escape the injury they expected would be inflicted had they made any hostile demonstration. At Seshan, however, about fifteen miles below Chin-Keang-Foo, some batteries at the foot of a hill, mounting about twenty guns, opened their fire on the *Pluto* and *Nemesis*, as those vessels were surveying in advance. On the following day, the batteries having fired on the *Modeste*, she very speedily drove out their garrisons, and destroyed them completely.

On the 16th, the naval and military commanders-in-chief went up the river in the *Vixen*, followed by the *Medusa*, to reconnoitre the approaches to Chin-Keang-Foo. They approached the entrance of the Imperial Canal, which passes close to the city walls, and is one of the greatest works in China for facilitating the internal water communication through the country. As no soldiers were seen on the walls, and no other preparations for defence were visible, it was hoped that resistance would not be offered, and that thus all effusion of blood would be spared. When, however, some of the officers landed on Golden Island, which is opposite the mouth of the Great Canal, and climbed to the top of the pagoda in the centre of the island, they discovered three large encampments on the slope of the hills to the southwest of the city. This showed that the Chinese had a large army ready to defend the place, though it was doubted if the troops would fight. The British land force consisted of about 7000 men of all arms. It had been determined that none of the ships-of-war should be engaged in the attack. The *Auckland* was therefore the only vessel which fired into the city, when employed in covering the landing of the troops.

On the evening of the 20th all preparations were completed for the attack, which was to take place at daylight the next day. A body of seamen and marines, however, under Captain Peter Richards, took an active part in the engagement, accompanied by Sir William Parker, who forced his way with the general through the gates of the city. Lord Saltoun's brigade was the first on shore, and, gallantly attacking the Chinese encamped outside the walls, soon drove them over the hills. General Schoedde's brigade, however, was received by a hot fire of guns, *jingalls*, and matchlocks, and in consequence he gave orders for immediately escalading the walls. The Tartars fought with the most determined bravery, often in hand-to-hand combats, and several of the British officers and men were wounded. The walls were soon scaled; and, as the troops scoured them to the right and left, they fell in with Sir Hugh and Sir William, who had forced their way in at the gate, while Captains Peter Richards and Watson, with the seamen and marines, had scaled the walls in another direction. Still, in the interior of the city, the Tartars held every house and street where they could hope to make a stand, determined to sell their lives dearly; and often, when driven back by superior force, they with perfect deliberation put an end to their own lives, and frequently those of their wives and children.

While these events were taking place, another of a more naval character was enacting elsewhere. The *Blonde* was anchored off the mouth of the Grand Canal, and her boats had been employed in the morning in landing the artillery brigade. At ten o'clock they were ordered away to carry some of the artillery, with two howitzers, up the canal, to create a diversion in favour of the troops. They were under the command of Lieutenant Crouch, of the *Blonde*, who had with him Messrs. Lambert, Jenkins, and Lyons, midshipmen. The barge, cutter, and a flat were a little in advance, when, coming suddenly in sight of the west gate of the city, they were assailed by a heavy fire of *jingalls* and matchlocks from the whole line of the city wall, running parallel with the canal. As the wall was nearly forty feet high, the gun in the barge could not be elevated sufficiently to do service, and the fire of the musketry was ineffectual. Lieutenant Crouch and Mr Lyons, midshipman, two artillery officers, sixteen seamen, and eight artillerymen were wounded. As it would have been madness to have remained longer than necessary exposed to such a fire, the men leaped from the boats, which they abandoned, and took shelter under cover of some houses in the suburbs. The crews of the launch and pinnace, however, which were some way astern, remained under cover of some buildings, and escaped without loss. Lieutenant Crouch's party now saw that their only chance of escape was to join the latter, though to do so they would have to pass across a wide space, exposed to the fire from the walls. They succeeded, however, in doing this without loss, and in getting on board the two boats. The whole party returned down the canal to the *Cornwallis*, where they reported what had happened to Captain Richards. They were compelled to leave some of the wounded behind, who, it is satisfactory to report, were kindly treated by the Chinese,—a strong proof of the advantage of the example set by the British.

As soon as Captain Richards was informed of the circumstances which had occurred, he landed with 200 marines at the entrance of the canal, where he was joined by 300 men of the 6th Madras Native Infantry, under Captain McLean.

This body then made their way through the suburbs, to escalade the city walls. At the same time the boats of the *Cornwallis*, under Lieutenant Stoddart, with those of the *Blonde*, pulled up the canal, with orders to bring off the boats and guns which had been left behind, and to endeavour to check the fire of the Chinese, while Captain Richards' party were engaged in escalading the walls. As soon as Captain Richards landed, he was joined by Captain Watson and Mr Forster, master of the *Modeste*, with a boat's crew and a small body of seamen from that ship.

A quantity of rubbish was found near the walls, on which the ladders were planted by Captains Peter Richards and Watson, when, in face of a strong body of Tartars, who opened a tremendous fire on them, they began the hazardous ascent. Captain Richards escaped unhurt; but Captain Watson was wounded, as was Lieutenant Baker, of the Madras Artillery; and a marine, who with them was one of the first on the walls, was killed.

At this juncture, Lieutenant Fitzjames brought up some rockets and lodged one in a guard-house, which, catching fire, threw the enemy into such consternation that they gave way, followed by Captain Richards, who, at the head of his men, had jumped down into an open space between two gateways. At the same moment the gate was blown open by powder bags; and Sir William Parker, with the third brigade under General Bartley, accompanied by Sir Hugh Gough, dashed over its ruins. Several officers and a large number of men suffered from the effects of the hot sun. The Naval Brigade having in consequence rested for some time in a guard-house, on hearing some firing, again sallied out, when they were met by a sudden fire from a body of Tartars, drawn up across a street behind a small gateway. Here Lieutenant Fitzjames was wounded, as were several of the men.

The British, however, uttering a loud cheer, attacked the Tartars with such fury that they were soon driven back and put to flight, when numbers fell by their own hands. The city was speedily in entire possession of the British, when every means was taken to spare life, to prevent plunder, and to restore order. We must not omit to speak of the gallantry of several naval officers mentioned by Sir Hugh Gough. Having heard that the canal was fordable, he had sent Major Gough to ascertain the fact, accompanied by Captain Loch, RN, who acted as an amateur throughout the campaign, as the general's extra aide-de-camp, and Lieutenant Hodgson, of the *Cornwallis*, as also by Lieutenant Heatley. Instantly rushing down the bank, the four officers plunged into the canal and swam across, thus proving the impracticability of fording it.

The city was now completely in the power of the British; but, in consequence of the bad drainage and the number of dead bodies left in the houses, the cholera broke out, and raged with fearful violence among the troops, even though they were removed to an encampment outside the walls. The number of Tartars who destroyed themselves and families was very great; while much damage was committed by the Chinese plunderers, who flocked in from the country, and pillaged in every direction; yet, although the place had been taken by assault, none of the British troops were allowed to plunder or to commit violence of any description.

These triumphant successes of the British had at length brought the Emperor to reason.

The true state of affairs was represented to him; and, on the 20th of August, his commissioner came on board the *Cornwallis*, with authority to treat for peace. On the 24th, the visit was returned by Sir Henry Pottinger, Sir Hugh Gough, Sir William Parker, and upwards of a hundred officers.

On the 29th, a treaty of peace, for which the British had

been so long contending, was happily signed on board the *Cornwallis* by Sir Henry Pottinger on the part of Great Britain, and by Ke-Ying, Elepoo, and New-Kien, on the part of the Emperor of China.

While the British fleet remained in the China seas, several gallant acts, well worthy of record also, were performed by some of the officers of the ships.

Although a very imperfect account has been given of the operations in the China seas, enough has been said to show that the Tartar troops were no despicable enemies, while the bluejackets of Old England had ample opportunities of exhibiting their daring courage, as well as that perseverance, discipline, endurance, and humanity, for which they have ever been conspicuous.

### A Timely Rescue—Callao, 20th August 1844

Her Majesty's ship *Collingwood*, Captain R. Smart, was lying off the port of Callao, in China, on the 20th of August 1844. There were at the time two mates on board, Mr Roderick Dew and the Hon. Frederick William Walpole. The latter officer had, it appears, in the afternoon gone on board a cutter-yacht, belonging to a gentleman at Callao. As night came on there was a fresh breeze blowing, which knocked up a short chopping sea. It was also very dark, so that objects at any distance from the ship could scarcely be discerned. The officer of the first watch on that night was Lieutenant Richard R. Quin, and the mate of the watch was Mr R. Dew. In those seas the currents run with great rapidity, and where the ship lay there was a very strong tide. Just as the quartermasters had gone below to call the officers of the middle watch, it being then close upon twelve o'clock, the look-out man forward reported a boat ahead under sail. The lieutenant of the watch, on going to the gangway, observed a small cutter on the starboard bow, which, as well as he could make out through the obscurity, appeared to be hove to. He judged from the position of the cutter that she wished to communicate with the ship, but it was impossible to see what was taking place on board of her. Shortly afterwards a dark object was observed on the water on the starboard bow approaching the ship, but it did not look like a boat. When it was at the distance of seventy or eighty yards, it was hailed by the sentry. An answer was returned, but too indistinctly for the officers aft to understand what was said. The sentry, however, on the forecastle seems to have made out the answer, for he instantly sung out the startling cry of "A man overboard!" No boats were down at the time; and in that hot tideway in another minute the drowning man would have been swept past the ship, and carried in all probability out to sea, where he must have perished. Mr Dew was forward. Whether or not he knew the person who was in peril of his life, I cannot say; probably any human being would equally have claimed his aid; but without a moment's hesitation he jumped fearlessly overboard, and swam to the assistance of the man he supposed was drowning. He struck out bravely, but could not at first succeed in the object for which he was aiming. Meantime the order for lowering a boat was given; but long before she was got into the water the figure of a human being was discerned close to the ship. The sentry again hailed, when a voice, which was recognised as that of Mr Walpole's, answered with a cry for help. Mr Dew cheered him up by letting him know that he was coming to his assistance; and very soon after he got up to him, and found him clinging to a small boat full of water, and, as he was encumbered with a heavy pea-coat, holding on with the greatest difficulty. Mr Dew, who was lightly clad and fresh, enabled him to guide the swamped boat up to the ship, near which the current was of itself carrying her. As they passed near the gangway, a coil of rope was hove to them, which they getting hold of, the boat was hauled alongside, and Mr Walpole and his gallant preserver Mr Dew were brought safely upon deck. Mr Walpole then gave an account of the accident which had befallen him. He had shoved off from the cutter in her dinghy, which was very soon swamped; and as the tide would not allow him to regain the vessel, he was being carried rapidly to destruction, and would, he gratefully asserted, have inevitably perished, had it not been for the heroic conduct of Mr Dew, who, under Providence, was thus the means of preserving his life.

CHAPTER 4

# Capture of a Venezuelan Squadron
*February 1841*

Among the numerous states which have arisen from the fragments of the Spanish empire in South America is that of Venezuela, of which Carthagena on the northern coast, and on the eastern shore at the entrance of the Gulf of Darien, is one of the chief towns. Although the inhabitants have proved themselves on many occasions to be a brave and gallant people, they too frequently, after they drove out the Spaniards, quarrelled among themselves, and at the time of which we write had allowed their navy to fall into a very disorganised condition. It appears that the British merchant brig *Jane and Sarah*, in company with a sloop called *Little William*, were lying at Sapote, a harbour near Carthagena, when, on the 6th of February 1841, some Venezuelan ships-of-war, under the orders of General Carmona, attacked the two vessels and plundered them of a large amount of goods and specie. A Colonel Gregg and other passengers, together with their crews, were taken on shore and imprisoned. We are not aware of what crime Colonel Gregg and the other persons were accused. They found means, however, to communicate their condition to the British consul resident at Carthagena, who immediately interested himself on their behalf, and applied to the Government for their release.

His intercession was perfectly unsuccessful. As soon, therefore, as he was able, he sent off a despatch to Lieutenant De Courcy, commanding HM brig *Charybdis*, stationed on the coast to protect British interests, and which was fortunately then in the neighbourhood. Immediately on receiving the communication, Lieutenant De Courcy came off the port of Carthagena, and despatched a boat with an officer bearing a letter to the commodore of the squadron, then at anchor inside, demanding the release of Colonel Gregg and the other British subjects.

The Venezuelan squadron consisted of a corvette, a brig, and three schooners of war. When the officer got on board the corvette, he found the commodore, who treated him with great insolence, observing that, as the letter was not written in Spanish, he could not understand it, and therefore could not receive it, treating the threatened interference with the greatest contempt. The unfortunate Colonel Gregg, it appears, was shot, immediately after the application for his release had been made; so that probably the commodore was acting under the orders of the Government, who were little aware of the punishment they were about to draw down on the head of the commander of their ships.

As soon as the British officer had returned on board the *Charybdis*, and reported these circumstances, Lieutenant de Courcy determined to compel attention to his communications. The *Charybdis* was rated as a six-gun brig, but she carried only one long gun amidships and two carronades, and her full complement of officers and men was but fifty-five. Nothing daunted, however, he boldly entered the port, and was passing up to an anchorage, when, without any provocation, he was fired into by the corvette,—the commodore's vessel,—and the forestay of the *Charybdis* was shot away.

This was an insult not for an instant to be borne, and, in spite of the small size of his vessel and the apparently overwhelming force opposed to him, he immediately took up a position, and opened his fire on the corvette. His officers and crew enthusiastically supported him, and, working their guns with a will, so rapidly was their fire delivered, and so well was it directed, that in a short time the corvette hauled down her colours and surrendered, when, on taking possession of her, it was found that the commodore and twenty-five of his men had been killed.

In the meantime, a brig-of-war had been coming down to the assistance of the corvette, followed by three schooners; and scarcely had the first been disposed of when she came into action. Unexhausted by their exertions, the gallant crew of the *Charybdis* fought their guns as before, and in five minutes after they had been brought to bear on the brig, she sank; and in a short time the schooners, after exchanging a few shots, also surrendered.

Thus, in the course of less than an hour, the whole of the squadron was captured or destroyed,—the victor remaining at anchor in their port with his prizes, to await the decision of the admiral on the station as to their disposal. In consequence of Lieutenant De Courcy's capture of the Venezuelan squadron, he at once received his promotion to the rank of commander.

CHAPTER 5

# Suppression of Piracy in Borneo

### Rajah Brooke

Sir James Brooke, Rajah of Sarawak, went out as a cadet to India, where he distinguished himself in the Burmese war, but, being wounded there, he returned home. A warm admirer of Sir Stamford Raffles, by whose enlightened efforts the flourishing city of Singapore was established, and British commerce much increased in the Eastern Archipelago, he took a voyage there to form a personal acquaintance with those interesting islands. He found the people groaning under oppression, piracy unchecked, and commerce undeveloped. He here secretly resolved to devote his life to remedying these evils. On his return home he purchased a yacht, the *Royalist*, of 142 tons, and with care and kindness, for three years, he trained a crew zealously ready to follow his fortunes.

Having been appointed Governor of Sarawak, 24th September 1841, he set himself actively to work to reform abuses, to improve the cultivation of the country, and to secure peace and happiness to the people. Having arranged the internal affairs of his government, he went back to Singapore for the purpose of asking the aid of some ship-of-war to put down piracy. The *Dido*, the Honourable Captain Keppel, was accordingly sent to assist him in carrying out his object. Among the many gallant acts performed by that officer and ship's company, we have space to recount only one.

## Attack on Sarebus Pirates

The *Dido*, after leaving Sarawak, proceeded to the island of Burong, which was appointed as the place of rendezvous. The force selected for the expedition consisted of the *Dido's* pinnace, two cutters, and a gig, with Rajah Brooke's boat, the *Jolly Bachelor*, carrying a long six-pounder brass gun and thirty of the *Dido's* men. Several chiefs sent their fleets, so that the native force was considerable, and it caused no little trouble to keep them in order.

On the 11th, as they passed rapidly up the stream, the beating of gongs and the loud yelling warned them that they were approaching their enemies. A sudden turn in the river brought them in front of a steep hill, which rose from the bank. As they hove in sight, several hundred savages rose up, and gave one of their war-yells. "It was the first," says Captain Keppel, "I ever heard. No report from musketry or ordnance could ever make a man's heart feel so *small* as mine did at that horrid yell. I had no time to think, but took a shot at them with my double-barrel as they rushed down the steep, while we hurried past." As the large boat came up, she gave them a dose from her heavy gun. A barrier of stakes was now encountered, but the gig pushed through, and found herself in the presence of three formidable-looking forts, which immediately opened a heavy fire on her. Luckily the enemy's guns were elevated for the range of the barrier, a few grape-shot only splashing the water round the gig. The boat was drifting fast towards the enemy. The banks of the river were covered with warriors, who yelled and rushed down to secure her. With some difficulty the long gig was got round, and, Rajah Brooke steering, she was paddled up against the stream. During this time Captain Keppel and his coxswain kept up a fire on the embrasures, to prevent the enemy reloading before the pinnace could bring her twelve-pounder carronade to bear. Unfortunately she fell athwart the barrier, and had three men wounded while thus placed. With the aid, however, of some of the native auxiliaries, the rattan lashings which secured the heads of the stakes were cut, and the first cutter got through. The other boats then followed, and kept up a destructive fire on the fort. Mr D'Aeth, who was the first to land, jumped on shore with his crew at the foot of the hill on the top of which the nearest fort stood, and at once rushed for the summit.

This mode of warfare—this dashing at once in the very face of their fort—was so novel and incomprehensible to the enemy, that they fled panic-struck into the jungle, and the leading men of the British could scarcely get a snap-shot at them. That evening the country was illuminated for miles by the burning of the capital, Paddi, and the adjacent villages. The guns in the forts were also taken and the stockades burnt. The banks of the river were here so narrow that it was necessary to keep vigilantly on the alert, as a spear even could easily be thrown across, though for the greater part of the night the burning houses made it light as day. In the evening, Doctors Simpson and Treacher amputated the arm of the captain of the forecastle on board the *Dido*. In the morning, a fleet of *prahus* came sweeping towards them, and were only discovered to be friends just in time to save them from a deadly discharge from the six-pounder.

In the evening, a party under Lieutenant Horton, who was accompanied by Rajah Brooke, was sent up the left stream. Captain Keppel was at supper on board the *Jolly Bachelor*, when the sound of the pinnace's twelve-pounder carronade broke through the stillness of the night. This was responded to by one of those simultaneous war-yells, apparently from every part of the country. Captain Keppel, on this, jumping into his gig, pulled off to the aid of his friends. From the winding of the stream, the yells appeared to come from every direction—sometimes ahead, sometimes astern. Proceeding thus for nearly two hours, a sudden and quick discharge of musketry warned him that he was approaching the scene of action.

He kept his rifle ready for use on his knee; and to give an idea that he was bringing up a strong reinforcement, he ordered the bugler he had with him to strike up *Rory O'More*. This was immediately responded to by three British cheers, followed, however, by a deathlike silence, which made him suppose that the enemy were between him and his friends.

Seeing some human forms before him, he hailed, and, receiving no answer, fired, supposing them to be Dyaks, when, to his horror, Lieutenant Horton exclaimed, "We are here, sir." Providentially no one was hurt. The sound of the current had prevented his hail being heard. The party had taken up a very clever position on the top of a bank from which the jungle had been cleared for about thirty yards, and which rose perpendicularly from a little bay just big enough to hold the boats. Here Lieutenant Gunnel was posted, with seven royal marines as a rear-guard. This was an important position, and one of danger, as the jungle itself was alive with the enemy; and although spears were hurled from it continually during the night, no shot was thrown away unless the figure of a pirate could be distinctly seen. The rain fell heavily, the men wore their greatcoats to keep their pieces dry. Often during the long night a musket was raised to the shoulder, and lowered, as the enemy flitted by. Those in the boats below stood facing the opposite bank of the river, with their arms in their hands.

It appears that the enemy had come down in great force to attack the boats from that side; and as the river was there very shallow, and the bottom hard, they could, by wading not more than knee-deep, have approached to within five or six yards of them. But in the first attack they had lost a good many men, and it is supposed that their repeated advances during the night were more to recover their dead and wounded, than to make any attack on the compact little force of British, whose deadly aim and rapid firing had told with such effect, and who certainly were, one and all, prepared to sell their lives as dearly as possible. For some object, the enemy had begun felling some large trees, and their torches showing their position, Mr Partridge kept up a hot fire on them from the pinnace, till a signal rocket fired among them made them take to flight. Two natives and one marine of the British party were wounded; and the latter poor fellow, a gallant young officer named Jenkins, already distinguished in the Chinese war, volunteered to convey in the second gig, with four boys only, down to the *Jolly Bachelor*. He performed his duty, and was again up with the party before daylight.

At dawn the pirates began assembling in some force; but as the boats advanced up the river towards a spot where they had left their wives and children, they sent in a flag of truce. Several chiefs soon appeared, and the result of the conference was, that they undertook to abandon piracy if their lives were spared. This was agreed to, and they have strictly adhered to their promises.

CHAPTER 6

# Warfare on the Rivers La Plata and Parana

### BATTLE OF THE PARANA—30TH NOVEMBER 1845

Juan da Rosas, having made himself master of La Plata, and taken possession of Buenos Ayres, closed the Rio de La Plata against all strangers. This was contrary to a treaty with the English and French; and accordingly an English and French squadron was despatched to open up the channel of commerce, the lighter vessels forming an expedition to force the Parana.

Rear-Admiral Inglefield was commander-in-chief, with his flag on board the *Vernon*. The French squadron was commanded by Admiral Laine. The command of the English force was given to Captain Charles Hotham, of HM steam-frigate *Gorgon*; and he had under him, *Firebrand*, steam-frigate, Captain J Hope; *Philomel*, surveying brig, Commander BJ Sulivan; *Comus*, eighteen guns, Acting Commander EA Inglefield; *Dolphin*, brigantine, Lieutenant R Levinge; *Fanny*, tender, Lieutenant AC Key.

On the 18th, the expedition arrived within three miles of the very strong defences General Rosas had caused to be thrown up on the right bank of the Parana, on Punta Obligada, to oppose their progress. This spot was about thirty miles below the river San Nicholas, and a hundred from the mouth of the river.

At daylight the following morning the two captains reconnoitred the position of the enemy, and soon discovered that great military skill had been evinced, both in the ground chosen and the plan of defence pursued.

The morning of the 20th broke dark and foggy, but about eight a.m. the weather cleared, and a southerly breeze sprang up. At a quarter to nine, the southern division weighed, and with a light wind stood towards the batteries, followed shortly afterwards by the *San Martin* and *Comus*. The *Dolphin* and *Pandour* had previously anchored on the north shore. Two of the *Dolphin*'s crew—R Rowe, gunner's mate, and W Ross, caulker's mate—though severely wounded, refused to leave their quarters till the day was won.

At about ten minutes before ten the batteries commenced the action by opening a heavy fire on the *Philomel* and the southern division, which Commander Sulivan speedily returned with interest. On this occasion the gallant Lieutenant Doyle, of the *Philomel*, had his arm shot away, and for some time his life was despaired of; but, notwithstanding the agony of his wound, he still showed his interest in the progress of the action. On this the *Dolphin* weighed, to support the ships in action; but as some of her sails were shot away before she could reach her appointed station, the current drove her astern, and compelled her to anchor. Lieutenant Levinge, however, contrived to place her in a position where her guns did good execution; she, however, was unavoidably exposed all the time to a tremendous shower of shot, shell, grape, and rockets, which came flying over her. During it several of her people were wounded; and Mr G Andrews, clerk in charge, was unhappily killed while assisting the surgeon in his duties to the wounded.

The remaining ships of the north division were gallantly led into action by the brave Captain Trehouart, whose brig succeeded in reaching her appointed station.

A terrific cannonade was now taking place, increasing as the ships, one after the other, got into action. It had, however, unfortunately the effect of making the wind fall light; and, in consequence, the ships of the northern division, having to contend with a current running three miles an hour, were compelled to anchor two cables short of the stations assigned to them. About this time the Spaniards cast loose the fire-vessels, chained two and two together; and as they came drifting down rapidly towards the squadron, the steamers kept moving about to tow them clear, should they drift against any of the ships. Fortunately they did no harm; but, till they had drifted past, the steamers could neither anchor nor open their fire.

At about ten minutes to eleven the action became general; and the effect of the admirable gunnery practice, both of the English and French crews, was soon evident by the unsteadiness with which the enemy continued their fire. No men could, however, have fought more bravely than they did. No sooner had the fire from the British ships swept one set of men from their guns, than they were replaced by others, compelled, if not determined of their own accord, to fight to the last. At length the fire from the batteries began to slacken, some of the guns being dismounted, and the gunners driven from the others; and at four p.m., an occasional shot only being fired, Captain Hotham made the signal for the boats of the squadron, manned and armed, to rendezvous alongside the *Gorgon* and *Firebrand*, sending at the same time to the French commander, to propose that the remaining part of their plan, which was that they should land and storm the batteries, should be carried into immediate execution. Captain Hotham landed with 180 bluejackets and 145 marines, when, giving three hearty British cheers, they formed on the beach preparatory to making a rush up the hill. Commander Sulivan, who had under him the skirmishing party and light company of seamen, led the way up the hill; the rest quickly followed, and, as they reached the crest, they were received by a smart fire of musketry. The enemy were, however, quickly driven back before the bayonets of the marines, under the command of Captain F Hurdle, RM; while, at the same time, the light company of seamen, under Lieutenant AC Key, made a dash at the wood, which it was most important to hold. In a few minutes it was carried and taken possession of. Shortly after this the French brigade landed; and, the enemy taking to flight in all directions, little more remained to be done, beyond spiking the guns and destroying the batteries. Captain Hope, after cutting the chain across the river, landed with Captain Hotham, and acted as his *aide-de-camp* throughout the day.

In consequence of this action, Captain C Hotham was made a Commander of the Order of the Bath; Commander BJ Sulivan was posted; and Lieutenants Inglefield, Levinge, Doyle, and Key were made commanders; R Rowe, gunner's mate, was made a gunner, and W Ross, caulker's mate, was made a warrant officer, both of whom, though severely wounded, had refused to quit their quarters till the battle was over.

Two ships of war being left to prevent the enemy offering any obstruction to the navigation of the Parana, the squadron proceeded to convoy a fleet of merchantmen up the river.

Captain Hope, in a very gallant way, pursued and destroyed the schooner *Chacabuco*, belonging to the enemy.

### Engagements With the Batteries of San Lorenzo

After the squadron and convoy had passed up, which they did without the loss of a single vessel or man, Rosas set to work to fortify the cliffs of San Lorenzo. This he did in the most effectual way in his power, by throwing up large works of earth, and in collecting guns from every direction, and also in training his men to the use of them. He had plenty of time to effect these objects, as the squadron was detained some time at Corrientes, while the merchantmen were disposing of their cargoes, and collecting fresh ones to take back in return. May 1846, indeed, had arrived before the different vessels of the convoy had settled all their affairs, and to the number of 110 were ready to descend the river.

In the meantime, a constant communication had been kept up with the admiral at Monte Video by the men-of-war, which had on each occasion to run the gauntlet of the batteries, and in some instances with severe loss, their commanders at the same time affording a noble display of gallantry, in obeying the orders they had received. Commander Sulivan, among others, made himself very conspicuous by the accurate knowledge he possessed of the river, which enabled him to pilot the ships up without risk.

The *Philomel* having been despatched from Corrientes to Monte Video, as she approached the batteries of San Lorenzo, Commander Sulivan made preparations to pass them. Knowing that he could pass under the cliffs, he judged it best to hug them as closely as possible, lest any guns should already be mounted. Having made a barricade of hammocks and bags for the helmsman, he sent all hands below to be out of harm's way,—he himself only, and his first lieutenant, remaining on deck to con the brig. Slowly and silently the little vessel drew near the point of danger. A light and favourable air filled her sails, and, almost grazing the perpendicular cliff, she glided slowly by. When the brig was close under the first battery, the enemy opened their fire at her; but so near was she to the cliffs, that they could not sufficiently depress their guns to touch her decks, their lowest shot going through the boom-mainsail, four or five feet above the hammock-netting. They continued their ineffectual fire till the gallant little *Philomel* was quite clear and out of range.

HM steamer *Lizard*, HM Tylden, lieutenant in command, which was sent up the Parana on the 21st of April, was not so fortunate in escaping without damage. When about six miles from San Lorenzo, Lieutenant Tylden observed that large batteries had been erected on a commanding point, and that the adjacent coast was lined with artillery and field-pieces. As the *Lizard* approached the batteries, Lieutenant Tylden ordered three ensigns to be hoisted, as a signal to the enemy that he intended to fight as long as the ship floated. At half-past eleven a.m., the northern batteries opened a heavy fire; and on approaching nearer, the other batteries and artillery commenced a quick and well-directed fire also, which was returned by the *Lizard* with rockets and her forecastle gun, until the rocket-stand was shot away, and the gun could no longer be elevated sufficiently to bear on the enemy.

When the gallant commander found that the heavy shot, grape, and musketry were riddling his vessel from stem to stern, he ordered the officers and men to go below, with the exception of those absolutely required on deck, in the hopes that they might thus escape injury. Scarcely, however, had they gone below, when two shots entered the gun-room, one of which killed Mr Barnes, clerk in charge, and the other Mr Webb, master's assistant. Two seamen also were killed; and Mr Miller, assistant surgeon, and three men were wounded. As the wind and current were against her, and there was a great deal of water in the hold, she made but slow progress, and it was not till twenty-five minutes past one p.m. that she got out of fire. She received 7 shot between wind and water, besides 9 cannon, 14 grape, and 41 musket-balls in the hull and bulwarks, and 7 cannon and grape in the funnel and steam-pipe; while her boats, mainmast, and rigging were pierced through and through by round shot.

HM steam-sloop *Alecto*, Commander FW Austen, had previously, early in April, gone up, towing three heavily-laden schooners against a current of three knots and a head wind. On approaching a place called Tonelero, a number of workmen were seen throwing up batteries, clearly for the purpose of annoying the convoy on their way down. Opening her fire on them, she soon put the men to flight. She came up to the batteries on the morning of the 6th, with a strong wind and current against her, and the heavy schooners in tow. She had been accompanied all the way by a squadron of cavalry, who kept pace with her in an easy walk, halting every now and then. At two her crew went to quarters; and at forty minutes past two, having before fired a few shot, her three guns and rockets were got into full play. This was answered by the lower guns on the batteries with round shot until she reached the narrowest part, when the enemy opened with round shot and grape together. Their guns were raking her at this time from head to stern in such a way that none of her guns could be brought effectually to bear on them. In this state she remained for twenty minutes, scarcely going ahead, and receiving the fire of seven eighteen-pounders, several of which were pointed down on her decks. During this time she fired away in return at the enemy, who appeared abreast of her, every charge of grape and canister on board, and was then reduced to round shot. For a few minutes, also, she exchanged with them a sharp fire of musketry. She then went gradually ahead, and as the river widened, and the current decreased in strength, she drew out of shot, having been an hour and fifteen minutes under fire.

Captain Austen, her commander, was the only person hurt, a spent grape-shot having struck him a severe blow on the thigh. Commander Mackinnon, then a lieutenant, who has written a most amusing account of the affair, says "that in going into action the men appeared to take it as a matter of course; but as the plot thickened and they warmed at the work, they tossed the long guns about like playthings, and indeed managed them in an admirable manner." This he attributes to the system taught on board the *Excellent*.

The crews of the Monte Videan schooners were in a dreadful fright all the time, expecting to be sent to the bottom. On sounding the well on board the *Alecto*, a considerable quantity of water was found in the hold. When search was made, a shot-hole was discovered forward, between wind and water. This was speedily plugged. Just as she came in sight of the convoy, after her long and tedious voyage, she got on shore, and there remained for some days before she was again floated off.

### Gallant Exploit of a Rocket-Battery

Santa Fe is situated on the east bank of the river. It is a place of some size. Built partly at the foot and partly on the side of a lofty hill, surrounded by *corrales* where thousands of cattle are slaughtered, their hides and their tallow being shipped from the port, while vast flocks of vultures, carrion crows, and other birds of prey hover over them to consume the refuse beef, which there are not human mouths sufficient to eat. As may be supposed, it is far from an agreeable place. The greater part of the English and French men-of-war were lying at Baxadar de Santa Fe, which was the appointed rendezvous of the merchantmen. Here the larger number, having effected their object, collected towards the middle of May. The difficulty was now to get the convoy safely back past the batteries of San Lorenzo. Sir Charles Hotham had got up to settle some diplomatic affairs with the Government of Corrientes, and on the 16th of May he returned in the *Alecto*.

A plan had occurred to Lieutenant Mackinnon of that ship, by which the passage of the convoy might be facilitated; and, having proposed it to Sir Charles Hotham, he, after a short consideration of its possibility, expressed his willingness to have it carried out, should everything be as supposed.

Lieutenant Mackinnon stated that opposite to the heavy part of the batteries of San Lorenzo he had observed an island covered with long reeds, grass, and small trees, but completely commanded by the guns of the battery. He proposed, the night before the convoy was to fight their way down, to take on shore a certain number of Congreve rockets, to land them at the back of the island, and to place them in readiness for use when the time of action should arrive; this could be effected in a few minutes,—then to dig by the side of each rocket a hole large enough to contain the men working them, and to throw the earth up as a kind of barricade before it; at the signal given by the commander-in-chief, when all the enemy's batteries were fully manned, waiting for the convoy, to commence a tremendous fire of rockets, which, being totally unexpected by the enemy, would be proportionally effective and destructive. The chances were that they would return this fire, which the prepared holes would render harmless; and if the rocket-stands or tubes were hit,—very difficult objects,—poles and instruments would be at hand to repair them immediately. Besides, when the vessels were passing, the chances were that, from the height of the cliffs, the rockets would strike the enemy over the mast-heads of the ships, thus causing a double-banked fire of great force.

Sir Charles Hotham having consulted Captain Hope and Captain Trehouart, who highly approved of the plan, provided the ground when reconnoitred was found as suitable as expected, the execution of it was entrusted to Lieutenant Mackinnon, of the *Alecto*, with Lieutenant Barnard, of the *Firebrand*, as his second. For several days the preparations were going on; and on the 25th of May, all being ready, the convoy and men-of-war dropped down the river, and anchored about five miles above the batteries of San Lorenzo, while the *Alecto*, continuing her course, brought up still nearer to them.

At length, on the night of the 1st of June, Sir Charles Hotham and the French captain, with some other officers, reconnoitred the locality. Besides the island we have spoken of, there were several others of nearly the same size, and at the same distance from the western shore; to the eastward of them, again, was an immense archipelago of low swampy islands, covered with brushwood, extending in that direction six or eight miles between them and the main shore of Entre Rios.

There was just sufficient light for the reconnoitring party to see their way as they steered through the intricate passages to the east of the large islands. With muffled oars and in dead silence they pulled on till they reached the island they wished to examine; and as they shoved the boat's bow into the mud, a loud rustling was heard in the brushwood, and a wild beast of some sort, which they took for a tiger, rushed towards them. They dared not fire, of course, and without allowing a moment's hesitation to interfere with the service they were upon, proceeded to land according to seniority. As the first officers leaped on shore, sword in hand, the supposed tiger, with a loud snort, jumped into the river, proving to be a harmless capybara, or water-hog, peculiar to the large rivers of South America.

They now advanced cautiously, among the reeds and brushwood, across the island, when, to their great satisfaction, they found that the river itself had performed the very work required, by throwing up, when swelled by the rains, an embankment many feet high along the entire length of the island, so as completely to screen them from the enemy's batteries,—a work, indeed, which many hundred men could not so well have executed in a week. Behind this the land rising, there was consequently a large natural trench; here the rockets might be placed in comparative safety. The only difficulty would be to get the men into the trench and to retire safely after the ammunition was expended, and also to avoid any suspicion on the enemy's part of the proximity of such a foe. The party then returned to the ship, and completed the necessary preparations.

The next night the rocket-party, in the *Alecto*'s paddle-box boat, took their departure under the command of Lieutenant Mackinnon. He was accompanied by his second in command, Lieutenant Barnard, of the Marine Artillery, by Mr Hamm, the boatswain of the *Alecto*, and Mr Baker, the pilot, with twelve artillerymen and eleven seamen. Silent as the grave, they pulled behind the islands, and without accident reached the appointed spot. They first set to work to get the rocket-stands and rockets up to the embankment; and very fatiguing work it was to the men, for they had to carry them through a swamp, into which they sank up to their knees, and then a considerable distance over rough and uneven ground, among thick reeds and brushwood. A glass of grog, with some pork and biscuits, set them to rights again; and without delay they planted the rocket-stands, pointing them so that the rockets might just clear the top of the batteries. Fortunately, a few yards beyond the little bay where the boat had been lying all night, a large willow tree had fallen into the river, of her exact length, and beyond that was a point of land running out likewise; between these she was hauled in. Branches of willow were stuck in all round and inside the boat, which most effectually concealed her,—so much so, that when Lieutenant Baker arrived the next night at the spot, he was observed standing up in the stern-sheets of the gig, looking wistfully towards the sandy beach, without seeing anything of the boat, though the starboard bow-oar of his gig splashed the water in Lieutenant Mackinnon's face. The latter officer whistled; upon which Lieutenant Baker pulled in, and began conversing.

All this time Lieutenant Mackinnon was standing with one leg on the gunwale of the boat and the other on land, the boat's gunwale being flush with it; it appeared, therefore, as if he was partly standing on a tree in the water, and so completely deceived Lieutenant Baker that he exclaimed, "But where on earth have you put the boat to?" The low laugh from the men, who were hid under a tarpaulin, revealed where she was. When they were moving about in daylight, they were obliged to crouch down like a herd of kangaroos, creeping behind the bushes and among the long grass, so as not to be seen by the enemy, to whom the whole island was then exposed to view. Had the Spaniards found out that they were there, of course they would have sent boats across to attack them, and would have fired on them from the forts; and though no doubt the bluejackets would have made a good fight of it with their rockets, the plan for preserving the fleet must have failed entirely.

The first day all hands were roused from their sleep in the boat and mustered at two p.m.; their arms being examined, they were ordered to remain at the boat in readiness for any emergency, while the officers and two artillerymen relieved the lookout at the battery. Twenty-eight embrasures, with heavy guns in them, were counted in the enemy's forts; and so close were the party, that with pocket-telescopes they could clearly distinguish the faces of the people, and observed General Moncellia, the brother-in-law of Rosas, drive up in his carriage with four horses, and, dismounting, inspect the troops and guns. Little did he suspect the foe he had near him. Having remained some time, the officers crawled back to the boats to take some rest, but they were far too anxious to sleep long; and the next night was passed, as before, in paying constant visits to the rocket-battery. Once they were nearly discovered, by one of the men incautiously exposing himself. As Lieutenant Mackinnon was watching the battery, he observed the sentry suddenly stop, and eye the spot narrowly. "Hold fast," he whispered to the man; "don't move, as you value your life." The man obeyed, and, to the lieutenant's infinite relief, he at last saw the sentry move on.

Daybreak of the 4th came at length; the wind blew fairly down the stream, and everyone was on the tiptoe of expectation, listening for the report of two guns, the preconcerted signal of the fleet being about to sail. It was a time of the greatest anxiety, for any moment, if discovered, the twenty-eight pieces of ordnance might have commenced playing on them, and blown them all to atoms; but fortunately the eyes of the enemy were turned up the stream, towards the point from whence the fleet was expected to appear. Slowly the hours seemed to pass, till at length, at nine a.m., the welcome sound of the two guns came booming along the water; and immediately the men proceeded from the boat to the rocket-stands, creeping along like a band of North American Indians on a war expedition to surprise a sleeping foe.

A long pole, with the British flag made fast to it, had been prepared, on the elevation of which the first discharge of rockets was to take place. The squadron of men-of-war and merchantmen now approached, the *Gorgon*, *Fulton*, and *Alecto* leading. Majestically they glided on till they came within range of the batteries, at which they commenced firing their shells with admirable precision. The long and anxious moment at length arrived for the discharge of the rockets. Lieutenant Mackinnon waved his cap aloft; at this signal Lieutenant Barnard planted the British flag under the nose of the enemy, and, taking off his cap, made them a low bow.

Up went a flight of rockets; two of them flew into the very centre of the most crowded part of the batteries, completely clearing them of their defenders, two went over their heads, and two stuck in the cliffs beneath them. The elevation of the four stands which were wrongly pointed being rectified, they were once more charged; and as soon as the enemy had returned to their guns, and were looking along the sights to take aim at the steamers, Lieutenant Mackinnon, jumping up on the embankment, thoughtless of how he was exposing himself, sang out, "Pepper, lads! pepper, lads! pepper, pepper, pepper!" and pepper away the men did with a vengeance. The crash was tremendous.

The enemy, with dismay, deserted their guns; and terrific must have been the slaughter among them, for in one minute, forty rockets, admirably directed, were poured in among them. To add to their confusion, a rocket had penetrated an ammunition cart, which, blowing up with a prodigious sound, filled the air with smoke. At the same time the dry grass about the seamen catching fire, they were surrounded by so dense an atmosphere that it was impossible for some moments to see what was going forward. The wind, however, soon blowing aside the murky veil, the fleet of merchantmen were seen passing quickly down, while the steamers took up their position directly under the batteries.

On this up went another shower of rockets, which continued without cessation, filling the air with long delicate threads of smoke, under which the vessels passed in safety, the effect being most beautiful. These events occupied some time; and as soon as the sternmost ships of the squadron were well out of range of shot, the *Gorgon* hoisted the signal for their return. The enemy's guns, as soon as they had no floating opponents directly in front, directed their fire at the island, but, misled by the flagstaff, peppered away at that, to the great delight of the rocket-party, who were safe behind the bank; however, the enemy discovered their mistake, and turned their guns in the proper direction of the rocket-battery. The shot fell harmless, as they either stuck in the bank or passed over the men's heads like cricket balls.

Now and then a single rocket was sent into some of the enemy's embrasures, which accelerated a return of shot. When the little *Dolphin* came down, leading the convoy, at the order, "Cover the *Dolphin*," another volley and running fire burst forth, accompanied with loud cheers for the gallant little vessel, which passed down with slight damage.

Preparations were made for decamping, and, as a last salute, the flagstaff was waved in the face of the enemy, which appeared to annoy them much, as a heavy fire was drawn towards the retreating party; but, as they spread out wide apart, the shot passed through without touching a single man or article belonging to them. The boat was soon reached, the willows cast off, and all hands got on board, when "Out oars!" was the word, and away they pulled down the stream to join the fleet.

After these events, the British and French squadron relieved Monte Video from an attack made on it by some of the allies of Rosas, and for some time their marines and seamen occupied it, and assisted in placing it in a better position of defence.

Chapter 7

# Expedition to San Juan De Nicaragua

### Capture of Fort Serapaqui—21st February 1848

The state of Nicaragua will be found towards the southern portion of that narrow neck of land which joins the two continents of North and South America. A variety of outrages and insults having been offered to British subjects,—two individuals especially having been carried off from San Juan by Colonel Salas, of the Nicaraguan army,—Mr Walker, Her Majesty's Consul-General and Agent stationed at Bluefields, requested Admiral Austen, the Commander-in-chief on the West India station, to send some ships-of-war to support and protect British interests in that part of the world.

In consequence of this request, the admiral despatched HMS *Alarm*, Captain Granville G. Loch, and HMS *Vixen*, Commander Ryder, to Bluefields. They reached the mouth of the river the following day, where the ships came to an anchor. The nearest Nicaraguan settlement was at Serapaqui, about thirty miles up the river, but this, owing to the strength of the current and various rapids, was generally a four days' journey by boats. It was understood that Colonel Salas was stationed at this fort with a considerable body of troops. Nothing daunted by this, by the known strength of the fort, or by the difficulty of approaching it on account of the rapidity of the current of the river which there flows by the place, Captain Loch resolved to insist on Colonel Salas making all the reparation in his power, or, in the event of his refusal, to compel him to do so by force.

The fort of Serapaqui was situated on a point projecting into the river very abruptly, and rising to the height of fifty feet. It was protected in the rear by a dense forest, and in the front by an abattis formed of large trees felled, with their heads and branches reaching into the river. The defences of the fort consisted of six angular stockaded entrenchments, formed of very tough timber, eight feet high and four feet thick, one side of each stockade looking across the river, and the other down the reach. The principal stockade commanded the only landing-place, on which also a gun was at the time mounted. The fort was only to be approached by heading a rapid current of nearly five knots an hour, in order to pass the fort and descend towards the landing-place, which was above the stockaded batteries, and excessively steep and narrow. The fort is situated at the head of a straight reach about a mile and a half long, the woods on either side affording an almost impenetrable shelter to a concealed foe.

As soon as the ships anchored, the expedition, consisting of 260 officers and men, left their sides in twelve boats.

The representations as to the strength of the current were found to be in no way exaggerated; but, with a gallantry, zeal, and perseverance never surpassed, Captain Loch and his brave followers pulled on hour after hour against the stream. Often they had to pass over downfalls and rapids, when it was only by the greatest exertions that the heavy boats could in any way be forced along. In this service, Lieutenant Scott, first of the *Vixen*, showed the most praiseworthy zeal and gallantry.

At night they rested, but at an early hour again each morning they recommenced their exertions, and at length, after a most fatiguing pull of seventy-two hours, they anchored a short distance below the fort. Early on the morning of the 12th of February the expedition got under weigh, and proceeded up towards the fort. Captain Loch and Commander Ryder went on ahead in their gigs, in order to communicate with Colonel Salas, and to state the object of Her Majesty's forces being in the river.

No sooner, however, were they seen from the fort than they were fired at by two guns, and directly afterwards by musketry from both sides of the river. As this act effectually prevented any

Pepper, lads! Pepper!

peaceable arrangements, Captain Loch immediately ordered up the boats for the purpose of storming the fort. The two gigs then took the lead, followed pretty closely by some of the lighter-pulling boats. On they went, pulling against the rapid current, which, as they advanced, grew still stronger, and exposed all the time to a hot fire of musketry from men concealed behind both banks of the river, so that there was little use even in attempting to return it. From this severe fire several men were wounded, and one officer very severely,—Mr R. Turner, midshipman,—and two killed. The boats were also almost riddled with shot, and nearly half the oars were broken; it seems, indeed, surprising, considering also their crowded state, with the mill-stream rate of the current, that a greater number of casualties did not occur. In this exposed position, often appearing to be quite stationary, they had to pull one hour and forty minutes before they were enabled to pass the batteries sufficiently high to drop down to the landing-place previously mentioned.

By this time nearly all the boats were up, and Captain Loch gave the order to land, he himself leading the way. The boats' crews, with a British cheer, leaped on shore, and gallantly charged the enemy. The Nicaraguans withstood them for some time, but the cutlass and pistol soon did their work; and in ten minutes they had taken to flight, and the British flag was hoisted on the fort. One of the first on shore was a seaman of the *Vixen* (Denis Burke, stoker), who quickly fought his way up to the enemy's colours, and captured them. As the enemy fled, the British pursued them into the thick woods; but after they had been chased for about thirty minutes, Captain Loch, considering that they had been sufficiently punished, ordered the recall to be sounded. The English then destroyed the stockades, spiked the guns, broke the trunnions, and threw them, together with all the muskets and ammunition left behind, into the river. The force was next embarked, when the whole of the defences were set on fire.

From the dangers to which the party were exposed, and the difficulties they overcame, this affair may well be considered as one of the most gallant among those we have to record.

CHAPTER 8

# The Destruction of Lagos
## 26th December 1851

The town of Lagos, built at the mouth of the River Ogun, which debouches in the Bight of Benin, is a healthy place, and well situated for trade. It is the seaport also of Abbeokuta, a town of considerable dimensions, sixty miles inland from it, and which it is hoped will become a very important place, now that Lagos is open for legal commerce.

The more immediate cause of the attack on Lagos was in consequence of an application made for assistance by Akitoye, the lawful chief of Lagos, to Mr Beecroft, the British consul for the Bight of Benin, residing at Fernando Po.

Akitoye, the younger of two brothers, had, by his father's will, succeeded as king of Lagos. The elder, Kosoko, had been, for misbehaviour, banished. After the death of the old king, Akitoye recalled Kosoko, and took him into favour; but Kosoko, bribing the army, usurped the government, and drove Akitoye to take refuge at Badagry. On this, Kosoko prepared to attack Badagry, and, had he been successful, would doubtlessly, as he intended, have attacked Abbeokuta also, and given a severe blow to the advancement of Christianity and civilisation in Africa. On this account Mr Beecroft felt it his duty to apply to the senior officer on the coast for a force to destroy Lagos, his movements being hurried by hearing that the king of Dahomey had sent 1000 picked troops for its support.

The commodore, however, sent only the *Bloodhound* and a few boats; and Lagos being really a strong place, they were compelled to retire with the loss of several men.

The first expedition against Lagos having failed solely from want of sufficient force to keep possession of the town, Commodore Bruce sent one of ample strength, and thoroughly organised, to drive the slave-dealing chief Kosoko from his stronghold.

The squadron appeared off Lagos by the 24th December. The boats of the *Sampson* and *Bloodhound* were for some time employed in ascertaining the position of the enemy's fortifications. The *Bloodhound* and *Teazer* at this time got on shore, and while they were being hove off, their people were exposed to a very hot fire from the negroes, who soon proved that they were no contemptible antagonists.

As the fire from *jingalls*, petrals, and muskets continued from the ditch and embankment abreast of the ship, and as the enemy were observed trying to bring their guns into position, at half-past two, Lieutenant Thomas Saumarez, with the boats of the *Sampson*, accompanied by Lieutenant E. McArthur, R.M.A., in command of the Marine Artillery, was despatched to attempt a landing and to spike the guns. They did all that men could do; but it was found impossible to make their way through the showers of musketry opened against them. Mr Richards, a gallant young midshipman, was mortally wounded, and ten men were severely wounded; while so hot was the fire, that there seemed every prospect of the whole party being cut off. Still they bravely persevered. While undaunted efforts were being made to get on shore, Mr William J. Stivey, carpenter of the *Sampson*, setting a noble example, which others followed, leaped on shore, and, axe in hand, hewed manfully away at the stakes to make a passage for the boats to go through them.

All, however, was in vain; their numbers were thinning rapidly; and at length Lieutenant Saumarez himself, being hit in three places, reluctantly, but very properly, gave the signal for return. The remainder of the day was spent in throwing shot and shell, as circumstances required, so as to prevent any guns being moved against the steamer. The nearest shot passed about ten yards astern of her.

The *Teazer* still continuing on shore, it became evident that before the tide rose the enemy would destroy her, unless the guns which were annoying her were captured. It was resolved, therefore, at once to effect this.

All being ready, the boats pulled in towards the stockade, where the best place for landing appeared to exist, keeping up all the time a continued fire of spherical, grape, and canister shot. As the boats touched the shore, they received a discharge directly in their faces of some 1500 muskets; but, notwithstanding this, the men undauntedly landed, and, forming on the beach, after some severe fighting forced their way into the stockade, driving out the enemy, who fled into the thick bush close to the rear of it. Among those who landed and charged with Captain Lyster were Mr Walling and Mr Sproule, surgeons of the *Penelope*, and who afterwards exposed themselves equally in their attendance on the wounded under fire. Scarcely had the blacks retreated than Lieutenant Corbett rushed ahead and spiked all the guns in the fort.

This object being accomplished, Captain Lyster issued orders for the re-embarkation of the party; but scarcely had he done so, when it was discovered that the enemy, having made a desperate rush at the first lifeboat, had succeeded in getting hold of her, and were tracking her along the beach towards the spot where the guns were posted which had first opened on the *Teazer*. On seeing this, the British, headed by their gallant leader, Captain Lyster, hurried down to the shore for the purpose of retaking her; but some delay occurred in consequence of having to divide her crew of sixty men among the other boats, which somewhat crowded them. The enemy, on seeing this, rushed back from their concealment in the woods by swarms, and poured in a destructive, crushing fire on the boats at pistol range.

On this occasion a gallant young officer, Mr F.R. Fletcher, midshipman in command of the second cutter, and who had charge of the boats while on shore, was shot through the head and killed. Several officers and men had before been wounded on shore, among whom was Lieutenant Williams, of the Marine Artillery, who, though hit in three places, had continued at the head of his men till they returned to the boats. Commander Hillyar was also wounded, and very many of the men were killed. Among the latter was James Webb, gunner's mate, belonging to the first lifeboat. When he saw that she was likely to fall into the hands of the blacks, he made a desperate attempt to spike her gun; but, while thus engaged, he was cut down by the enemy, and mortally wounded.

While Commander Hillyar was arranging the boats so that they might keep up their fire as they retreated to the *Teazer*, some of the *kroomen* on board Mr Beecroft's *Victoria* let go her anchor, and there she lay exposed entirely to the fire of the blacks. On seeing this, Captain Lyster pulled back to her to learn what was the matter. "What has occurred now?" he asked of Mr Blight, the boatswain. "The *kroomen* let go the anchor without orders," he replied. "Then slip your cable, and get out of this," exclaimed Captain Lyster. "It's a chain cable, clenched to the bottom, and we can't unshackle it," replied Mr Blight. On hearing this disheartening intelligence, Captain Lyster jumped on board to see what assistance he could render. Just then Lieutenant Corbett staggered up towards the stern, exclaiming, "I have done it, and am alive!" In truth, he had cut the chain cable with a cold chisel, and in so doing, while leaning over the bows of the boat, had received five different wounds, which, with the addition of a severe one received on shore, rendered him almost helpless. His right arm was hanging to his side, but he still with his left worked away, and assisted in getting the *Victoria* off to the *Teazer*.

While Captain Lyster was leaving the *Victoria* to get into his own boat, he was shot in the back with a musket-ball. On account of the hot fire to which they were still exposed, and the number of men already killed and wounded, he judged that he should not be justified in attempting to recover the lifeboat on that occasion. Leaving her, therefore, on the beach, the party returned to the *Teazer*. The people who had at first got possession of the lifeboat had afterwards abandoned her; but they now returned, and some forty or fifty got into her, intending to carry her off. Seeing this, Mr Balfour, acting mate, assisted by Mr Dewar, gunner, pulling back to the shore in the first cutter, threw a rocket towards her, and so well-directed was it that it entered her magazine and blew it up. As soon as the party got back to the *Teazer* (having now pretty well silenced the fire of the enemy), they set to work to get all the provisions out of her, and then, having thrown overboard all her coals with the exception of ten tons, they contrived to shore her up, to await the rising of the tide. At length their exertions were crowned with success, and at sunset they succeeded in heaving her off. Then, getting up the steam, they anchored out of gunshot for the night.

On this unfortunate occasion there were no less than thirteen men killed belonging to HMS *Penelope*, besides Mr Fletcher and Mr H.M. Gillham, master's assistant, who afterwards died of his wounds; while Captain Lyster, Commander Hillyar, Lieutenant Corbett, and First Lieutenant of Marines J.W.C. Williams were wounded severely, together with fifty-seven men of the *Penelope* and two of the *Teazer*, most of them also very severely wounded. Crowded together in so small a vessel during the night, the poor fellows suffered greatly, though the medical officers of the expedition, Mr R. Carpenter, senior surgeon, Mr Walling, assistant surgeon of the *Penelope*, Dr Barclay, acting surgeon, and Dr Sproule, assistant surgeon, exerted themselves to their very utmost in the performance of their duty to the wounded. During the day they had never flinched from exposing their own lives, as, in the midst of the fire, they stepped from boat to boat to alleviate the sufferings of the wounded and dying.

Soon after seven o'clock in the morning the *Teazer* was got under weigh, and, finding the right channel, steamed up towards the *Bloodhound*, with the squadron of boats in her company. As soon as she was seen from the *Bloodhound*, Captain Jones ordered that the guns of the *Bloodhound*'s gunboats should open a deliberate flanking fire on the west part of the enemy's defences; and he then sent a boat under Mr Bullen, his clerk, who was acting as his aide-de-camp, to point out to Captain Lyster the position in which he wished the *Teazer* to be anchored. At ten minutes past eight, the *Teazer* having anchored, Captain Jones pulled on board her, to consult further with Captain Lyster on the plan of proceeding. The rocket-boats were then ordered to take up a position to the northward of the *Bloodhound*. This was quickly done, and Lieutenant Marshall threw some rockets with beautiful effect, setting fire to several houses, among which, to the satisfaction of all, was that of the Prime Minister Tappis. When this was seen, a hearty and spontaneous cheer ran through the whole squadron for the crew of the rocket-boat, who had thus punished the chief instigator of the former attack on the British boats.

After this, the rocket-boat shifted her position ahead of the *Teazer*, and a general but deliberate fire was opened from the whole force. At forty-five minutes past ten, Lieutenant Marshall threw a rocket, which struck the battery below Tappis' house, and at the same time a shot from the *Teazer* capsized the gun. The firing became still more rapid; an awful explosion ensued; a magazine of the enemy's had blown up. And from this moment the fate of Lagos was decided; house after house caught fire, and the whole town was shortly in a general blaze. More ships-of-war now came in, and Kosoko, finding his case hopeless, took to flight, and Akitoye was reinstated.

The only portion of the British forces landed was a small body under Commander Coote, who went on shore to spike guns.

The next morning he and Commander Gardner, with the boats' crews of the *Sampson* and *Penelope*, were employed in a similar way. They returned in the afternoon, having by extraordinary exertions embarked or destroyed fifty-two pieces of ordnance.

Lagos has now become a British province.

CHAPTER 9

# The Burmese War
## 1851-1852

By the treaty of Yandaboo in 1824 the Burmese granted security to English merchants and English commerce. It seemed then as if the first Burmese war had really had some good results, and as if civilisation had taken an immense stride in the country.

But, twenty-six years after this treaty had been signed, numerous complaints reached the supreme government of Calcutta of the oppressive tyranny of the governor of Rangoon, which, it appeared, was directed chiefly against traders in Rangoon.

One of the immediate causes of British interference was the conduct of the governor towards certain captains of British trading vessels; one of whom, on the false representations of a Burmese pilot, was placed in the stocks and fined nine hundred *rupees*. A representative at Ava was placed on an island on the Irrawaddy without provisions, and left there till the river rose and nearly swamped him. Sooner than irritate the court, the representative was withdrawn. Insult after insult was heaped upon the British, and though every means was taken to ensure peace and conciliate the Burmese, it was soon seen that sterner measures must be taken with them.

On 7th January the governor of Rangoon ordered a merchant, Mr Birrell, to take down a flagstaff he had erected, and to remove a gun placed on his landing-stage. Mr Birrell refused to comply with this order, as the flagstaff had been placed there by consent of the commodore, as a means of communication between the Europeans on shore and the men-of-war.

The governor, enraged at this refusal, ordered all communication with the shipping to be stopped. Commodore Lambert, sooner than give the Burmese any cause of offence, directed the flagstaff to be removed, and for the time trade was resumed.

Not long after this a deputation from the British to the governor was treated with the utmost incivility and contempt, and was even refused admission to his presence.

The commodore now resolved to take action. He ordered the King of Burmah's ship, which was lying in the harbour, to be seized, and sent a message to all the British residents in Rangoon to come on board the frigate, and at the same time informed the governor that as the British flag and Government had been grossly insulted, he intended to place the town under blockade.

By the same evening all the British subjects had embarked, and the men-of-war moved down the river.

Some of the Burmese officers now came to the flagship to offer apologies for their rudeness; but as the viceroy himself refused to apologise, none of these were accepted. The Burmese, seeing that the British were in earnest, tried to avert the war for a time; and the commodore, also anxious to avoid hostilities, allowed twenty-four hours' grace to give the viceroy time to change his mind. Instead of an apology, however, came a message, to the effect that if the British ships attempted to pass the stockades on the banks of the river, they would be fired on.

Information was received that nearly 5000 troops were assembled near the stockades, and during the night and the following day numerous war-boats, each containing from fifty to eighty men, were discovered coming down the river. At the same time several vessels full of armed men arrived at the general rendezvous from the Pegu River. The war had begun.

On the next morning active hostilities commenced. The *Hermes* steamer, Captain Fishbourne, first towed the *Fox* frigate to within 400 yards of the stockade, where she anchored to protect the merchantmen as they passed by to be out of fire. In the meantime the *Hermes* went in search of a large Burmese war-vessel, with which she soon returned as her prize in tow.

The English vessels, having dispersed or sunk a fleet of war-boats which came out to meet them, steamed along the shore, pouring in an iron shower, which tore the stockades to pieces and quickly silenced the enemy's batteries.

The squadron now took up a position at the mouth of the Rangoon River, the commodore declaring the rivers of Rangoon, the Bassein, and the Salween above Maulmain, to be in a state of blockade.

Meanwhile the steamer *Proserpine*, after landing the hostages from Rangoon at Maulmain, was ordered to proceed to Calcutta with despatches from the commodore.

On her arrival on the 17th of January, the Governor-general being absent, the Supreme Council resolved to equip a force to carry on hostilities against Burmah; while reinforcements were despatched with unusual promptitude, to strengthen the forts guarding the passes leading from the Burmese territory.

General Godwin, the commander-in-chief, arrived on the 13th of April; and the Burmese Emperor having offered no apology, the steamers ran close in with Martaban, rapidly firing broadside after broadside. The enemy for some time returned their fire with spirit; but their guns being silenced, the troops were thrown on shore, and they fled in every direction. The walls and defences exhibited the terrific effects of the broadsides poured in on them. Of the English, only eight were wounded.

The squadron was now augmented by twelve East India Company's steamers, which had, besides marines, 5767 troops on board.

With this formidable force Rangoon was attacked on the 12th of April. The steamers fired for many hours shot and shell without intermission, which destroyed and set on fire the enemy's stockades and other defences. A small naval brigade, commanded by Lieutenant Darville, HMS *Rattler*, did good service on shore. For three days the Burmese garrison held out; stockade after stockade was stormed and taken in a most gallant way by the troops. On the 14th the grand attack was made, and the great pagoda was stormed, when, after some more severe fighting, Rangoon fell into the hands of the British. Captain Armstrong and several other officers and men of the land forces were killed, and many wounded.

Bassein was captured in the same spirited way on the 19th of May. At the pagoda here, the Burmese defended themselves with much determination; but it was stormed by some troops and some of the naval brigade, when Lieutenant Rice, RN, was wounded severely, three men killed, and seven officers and twenty-four men wounded.

While these operations were going on, Martaban, in which only a small garrison had been left, was attacked by the Burmese, but they were driven back in a very gallant manner by Major Hall and his men.

### Capture of Pegu—14th June 1852

An attack on Pegu, seventy-five miles north of Rangoon, being next resolved on, an expedition, consisting of 230 troops, who were embarked on board the *Phlegethon*, and the boats of that vessel and HMS *Fox*, under the command of Captain Tarleton, left Rangoon on the 3rd of June, and proceeded up the river.

As the boats advanced, a sharp fire of musketry was opened on them from the Pegu side. On this, Captain Tarleton, seeing the disadvantage under which they laboured from being beneath the enemy's fire, with no effectual means of returning it, landed with the boats' crews of HMS *Fox*, and was shortly after joined by Captain Neblett and the boats' crews of the *Phlegethon*,—in all about fifty men. Meantime Mr McMurdo, mate, was left in charge of the boats.

As Captain Tarleton and his party advanced, the Burmese fired on them, but were driven from point to point, until completely broken,—one party retreating by the riverside to the northward, and the other within the old wall of the city. The object of the British being attained, they were retiring in close order to the boats, when a fire of *jingalls* and musketry was opened on them from the walls. Deeming it unwise to allow the Burmese to suppose they were retreating, Captain Tarleton led his party to the attack, having found a native guide to show them the causeway through the ditch. Having halted a few seconds to gain breath, they rushed in over the causeway, and through a breach to the right of the gateway. On the storming-party getting over the wall, after a stout defence the enemy fled, and ultimately retired within the great pagoda.

Meantime the boats had been attacked, but were bravely defended by Mr McMurdo, who succeeded in getting them to the other side of the river, Major Cotton having sent a detachment to their support. After the troops and seamen had rested for some time, the Burmese were observed issuing from the pagoda in considerable strength, with the evident intention of attacking them. The troops lost not a moment in getting under arms, and the seamen forthwith came on shore. The British instantly advanced; and before the Burmese could recover from their surprise at a movement so little expected, the place was carried without another casualty. HMS *Fox* had three men wounded, and the *Phlegethon* one seaman killed.

The force, after destroying the fortifications, returned to Rangoon on the 5th.

## Expedition Up the Irrawaddy

It being important to ascertain the number and position of the enemy posted on the banks of the Irrawaddy, Commodore Lambert directed Captain Tarleton to take under his orders HMS *Medusa* and three Company's steamers, and to proceed up the river for the purpose of obtaining that information. Accordingly, on the 6th of July, the vessels proceeded up the Irrawaddy.

At a place called Konnoughee, twenty-five miles below Prome, a large body of armed men were observed collected on the banks; and on a shell being fired among them, they opened a vigorous fire from six guns and from a large number of musketry. At a short distance from Prome the river divides into two streams,—the left, or western, being the deepest, and the only navigable branch at any season but the rainy one. At sunset the expedition anchored off Meaoung. At daylight on the 8th it again weighed, and proceeded till within sight of an extensive fortification, crowning the end of a ridge of hills 300 feet high, terminating abruptly at the town of Akouktoung, which completely commands the river. Here, the position being strongly fortified, a Burmese army of about 10,000 men had been assembled, under General Bundoola, to guard the passage to Prome and the capital. Captain Tarleton having been warned of the resistance he would meet, and hearing from the native pilots that at that season the eastern stream was navigable, determined to try it. Instead, therefore, of keeping on, to the disappointment of the enemy, who had begun to fire on him, he turned off through the eastern channel, and was quickly beyond their reach, having had not less than two fathoms water in the channel. By steaming through the night, the rest of the squadron came off Prome by daylight on the morning of the 9th. At the south end of the town, near the water's edge, four heavy guns were seen, but no troops were observed in the place.

Captain Tarleton accordingly anchored the *Medusa* abreast of the spot, and soon hove them off. The iron guns were disabled and sunk in deep water, and the brass ones were taken on board. When the other vessels joined their crews with the boats' crews of the *Fox*, heartily entering on the work, every gun in Prome, twenty-three in number, was brought off. In the afternoon the *Medusa* ascended the river ten miles higher; but Captain Tarleton felt himself bound by his orders to return. His feelings may be supposed when he thus found himself at Prome, within four days' steaming of Ava, with a certain knowledge that there was nothing to oppose him, and with a broad, deep river, easy of navigation, before him. Had he had with him one regiment and half a battery of guns, there is every reason to believe he might have taken the capital, so totally unprepared were the Burmese for any advance in the rains.

However, he was of course compelled to obey the orders he had received. After remaining there for twenty-four hours, the place was evacuated, and the flotilla returned. On reaching the main stream, the army of Bundoola was observed in motion, crossing the river, evidently with the intention of following the steamers. They in consequence opened with shot and shell upon the confused masses on shore and on the boats, spreading havoc and dismay among them. Between forty and fifty boats were captured and destroyed. The general's state-barge, several large war-canoes, a standard, two gold umbrellas, and other spoil fell into the hands of the British. The whole trip occupied only nine days. In its progress the expedition received the most convincing proofs that the population of Burmah were adverse to the war, and anxious to come under the British rule. Looking at the expedition by itself, it was as gallant and dashing an undertaking as any which took place during the war.

When Captain Tarleton returned and reported what had occurred, a large body of troops were sent up the river on board the steamers to Prome, which was captured on the 9th of October, after a slight loss, only four men being wounded on the side of the British.

The inhabitants of Pegu were friendly to the English; but soon after the troops had been withdrawn, a strong Burmese army re-entered the town, and commenced fortifying the city. A force was accordingly sent to drive out the enemy and reoccupy it. This was done in a spirited manner on the 21st November. The morning being foggy, the Burmese, who did not see the English approaching, were taken by surprise. They retreated as usual to the pagoda, from whence, by a rush of the troops, they were driven out. The fighting was severe, as no less than six men were killed and thirty-one wounded of the troops. The navy, as usual, did their part well.

The principal towns of the province being in the hands of the British, it became important to clear the intermediate country of the enemy, especially the banks of the rivers, where they were of much annoyance to the provision-boats. In this service the naval force were constantly and very actively employed. Several of the expeditions were under the command of the lamented Captain Granville Loch, who displayed in them the same zeal and daring courage for which he had already made himself conspicuous.

## Attacks on Mya Toon, the Robber Chieftain

The rapidity and success of the first movements of the British in Burmah paralysed the Burmese authorities; but their subsequent inactivity again gave heart to the Government at Ava, and encouraged the idea that it was possible to drive them back to the sea.

In consequence of the absence of all local government, robbers sprang up in every direction, and, being allowed to organise themselves, devastated and almost ruined the country. Among the most noted of these robber chieftains was Mya Toon. He burned down Donabew, Zaloon, and many other villages. His stronghold was about twenty-five miles inland from Rangoon. In consequence of the depredations he was committing, Brigadier Dickenson, the commandant at Rangoon, and Commodore Lambert resolved to send a combined naval and military force to dislodge him. The military force consisted of 300 men of the 67th Regiment Bengal Native Infantry, who, together with a body of marines and bluejackets from HM ships *Fox*, *Winchester*, and *Sphinx*, were placed under the command of Captain Granville Loch. There were 185 seamen, 62 marines, and 25 officers; but of these, 42 seamen and 5 officers were left in charge of the boats. This force was conveyed from Rangoon to Donabew on the 2nd July, in the *Phlegethon* and ships' boats. They landed at Donabew without opposition, and, having procured some natives to act as guides and to aid in drawing the two three-pound field-guns belonging to the *Phlegethon*, they proceeded to march on the following day towards the position the enemy was supposed to occupy.

The whole of the 3rd of February they marched along a pathway which lay through a jungle of forest trees and brushwood. Encamping in a deserted valley, about fifteen miles from Donabew, they were disturbed occasionally by the distant shots and noises of the marauders. Early on the following morning, the column moved on about five miles farther along the same path, until it abruptly terminated on the side of a broad *nullah* or creek, the opposite side of which was high enough to command the approach, and the whole well entrenched and armed, after the manner of the native fortifications of Burmah. The road at this point had been narrowed by an abattis of sharp-pointed bamboos, which rendered it impossible to deploy the whole strength of the column; indeed, the advance-guard, consisting of seamen and marines, marched with difficulty two or three abreast, and the field-guns were in the rear. At this moment a heavy and murderous fire was opened by the enemy upon the British troops, the Burmese being wholly concealed by the breastworks, and the British, on the contrary, entirely exposed.

Almost every man who approached the edge of that fatal creek was mowed down. Lieutenant Kennedy, of the *Fox*, and Captain Price, of the 67th Bengal Infantry, were killed on the spot. Captain Loch, with the daring which had always distinguished him, led on his gallant followers to the attack. For ten minutes he seemed, to use the expression of one of his companions, "to bear a charmed life," for he stood unhurt in the midst of that terrible fire. Twice he made an unsuccessful attempt to lead his men across the *nullah*, to storm the fort hand to hand, but each time he was driven back. As he again rallied the seamen and marines for a third attack, a ball fired by a man in a tree struck him on the left side, on his watch, and with such force that it drove the watch itself into his body. He instantly felt that he was mortally wounded, but had still strength and self-possession to fall back about fifteen paces to the rear.

The command of the naval force, which had hitherto sustained the brunt of the action, devolved by the death and wounds of the senior officers on Commander Lambert, the son of the commodore. Twice with his brave companions he made determined but vain attempts to get across to the enemy, when many more lives were lost. He himself received four balls through his clothes, though he fortunately escaped unhurt; but a large proportion of officers and men were already wounded. It therefore became absolutely necessary to provide without delay for the retreat of the party by the only road left open to them, the one by which they had advanced, the jungle being impervious in every other direction. The fire of the enemy was still very severe, and each instant more of the British were falling.

Most of the native *dooly*-bearers and guides had in a cowardly and treacherous manner decamped; and it was therefore necessary to employ every man in carrying the wounded. As, under these circumstances, it was impossible to carry off the guns, they were spiked, and the carriages destroyed. The party were compelled even to leave their dead on the field. The enemy kept up a distant fire, but never ventured to approach within fighting distance of the rear, which was manfully covered by the grenadier company of the 67th.

For twelve hours of a most fatiguing march did the dejected and mourning party retreat towards Donabew, displaying in adversity the same courage, discipline, and goodwill they had so often exhibited in success. Lieutenants Glover and Bushnell, and also Messrs. Hinde and Wilson, mates, though themselves suffering from their own wounds, successfully exerted themselves in keeping up the spirits of their men, who, under a burning sun, without water, had to carry the heavy burden of their wounded leader for nearly twenty-four miles. At Donabew, the seamen and marines embarked in their boats, and the troops were conveyed in the *Phlegethon* to Rangoon. The gallant Captain Loch was removed to the *Phlegethon*, where he expired on the morning of the 6th February, about forty hours after he had received his wound. He was buried near the great pagoda at Rangoon, amid the general grief of all who served under him or knew him.

It was not till some time after this that Mya Toon was dislodged from his stronghold, by a strong force under Sir John Cheape, when several officers and men were killed and wounded.

The war itself was soon afterwards brought to a successful conclusion.

CHAPTER 10

# The Crimean War

Towards the end of 1853 difficulties had arisen between Turkey and her ancient enemy Russia. The matters in dispute were of no real importance. Russia was persuaded that the Turkish Empire was breaking up, and that the time for its partition was at hand, and that therefore any pretext was good enough upon which to found a quarrel. France and England, however, were not willing to see Constantinople in the hands of Russia, and accordingly formed forces to assist Turkey. On the 30th of November a Russian fleet leaving Sebastopol under cover of a dense fog made a dash upon the Turkish harbour of Sinope. Here they surprised a Turkish squadron of eight frigates, two schooners, and three transports utterly unprepared for battle. Without warning, the Russian Admiral Nachenioff opened fire upon them, and though the Turks fought bravely, in the course of a few hours all their ships but two were destroyed. This action cannot be described as a battle, but as an inhuman, unnecessary massacre, 5000 men, including the wounded, being destroyed by the fire of the Russians, who offered no terms and gave no quarter.

This barbarity aroused the utmost indignation in Europe, and the prospect of war with Russia was greeted with enthusiasm by the British. The allied fleets of Great Britain and France, the former consisting of forty-nine ships mounting an aggregate of 1701 guns, and the latter of thirty-six ships with 1742 guns, entered the Black Sea in January following, and on the 28th of March war was formally declared.

On 11th March Queen Victoria reviewed at Spithead the

most powerful fleet that up to that time had ever been collected. This was under the command of Sir Charles Napier, with his flag on board the *Duke of Wellington*, of 131 guns,—which ship alone would almost have been capable of contending with the largest fleet Howe, Jervis, or Nelson ever led to victory. That superb fleet was intended chiefly for the Baltic, where it was hoped that not only would it humble the pride of the Czar, by capturing Sveaborg, Helsingfors, and Cronstadt, but might lay Saint Petersburg itself under contribution. Some of the ships went to the Black Sea and in other directions; but Sir Charles Napier found himself in command of a fleet in the Baltic, consisting altogether of thirty steamers and thirteen sailing ships, mounting 2052 guns. The French also had a fleet of twenty-three ships carrying 1250 guns.

### Bombardment of Odessa

The naval operations were opened with two very regrettable incidents. The steamer *Furious* was sent to Odessa early in April, to bring off the British consul. Having anchored in the bay with a flag of truce at her mast-head, she sent off a boat, also with a flag of truce flying, to the shore, when, against all the laws of civilised warfare, the batteries opened fire on them. No one was hit, and the *Furious* steamed back to the fleet.

The allied admirals, indignant at the outrage, addressed a note to the Russian governor, General Osten-Sacken, pointing out the outrage which had been committed, and demanding "that all the British, French, and Russian vessels now at anchor near the citadel or the batteries of Odessa be forthwith delivered up to the combined squadron; and that if at sunset no answer or a negative be received, they will be compelled by force to avenge the insult offered, though, for humanity's sake, they adopt the alternative with regret, and cast the responsibility of the act upon those to whom it belongs."

No satisfactory answer having been received, the combined fleet opened fire on the fortifications of Odessa on the 22nd of April. The bombardment lasted for ten hours, during which the Russian batteries were considerably injured, two batteries blown up, vast quantities of military stores were destroyed, and several ships-of-war were sunk.

On the 12th of May, during a thick fog, the steam-sloop *Tiger*, sixteen guns, Commander Gifford, went on shore on the rocks near Odessa. While she was thus utterly helpless, the Russians, as soon as she was observed, opened fire on her, and Captain Gifford, being desperately wounded (mortally, as it proved), was at length compelled to strike his flag. The Russians, having removed her guns and stores, set fire to the vessel, and forwarded the flag as a trophy to Saint Petersburg. It was one of the very few, either from redcoats or bluejackets, they got during the war.

### Operations in the Baltic

Sir Charles Napier's squadron reached Wingo Sound on the 15th March, and on the 25th it entered the Great Belt, and anchored in Kiel Bay. Soon afterwards, Sir Charles was reinforced by Admiral Corry, with the second division of the fleet. On the 12th of April Sir Charles sailed for the Gulf of Finland, where he established a rigorous blockade. As, even at this season of the year, there is a considerable amount of ice in the Baltic, the navigation of the ships demanded all the vigilance of the officer in charge. Sir Charles, hearing that a Russian squadron, consisting of seven line-of-battle ships and one frigate, was shut up at Helsingfors, made sail in that direction for the purpose of preventing a junction between the two portions of the Russian fleet. In this very important object, in which the enemy's plan of naval operations was completely defeated, he was entirely successful.

Admiral Plumridge meantime was scouring the Gulf of Bothnia, and in a short period captured or destroyed forty-six merchantmen and a quantity of naval stores, without losing a man.

### A Spirited Action

On the 19th May the *Arrogant* and the *Hecla*, two steamers—the first a screw, commanded by Captain Yelverton, and the second by Captain Hall—had been detached from the fleet, and employed for a considerable time in reconnoitring the forts of the enemy about Hango Bay. Propulsion by means of a screw was at this time a novelty, the steamships of war being generally large paddle boats and sailing ships combined, a state of transition between the frigate of Nelson's day and the modern steamship.

The two captains, hearing that some ships lay off the town of Eckness, some way up a narrow river, determined to cut them out. They boldly entered the river, and on the evening of the 19th came to an anchor.

A boat from one of the men-of-war was sent on ahead, but before she had got 800 yards from the ship, a hot fire was opened on her from behind a sandbank in a thickly-wooded place. At the same time some round shot struck the *Hecla*. Both ships instantly beat to quarters, and, casting loose their guns, poured showers of shot and shell into the wood, from whence they speedily dislodged the enemy. They then shifted their berth, and were not further molested during the night. A bright look-out was kept, however, to prevent surprise.

At two a.m. both ships weighed, the *Hecla* leading, and the crews being at their quarters. They slowly and carefully felt their way along the intricate navigation of the river, till they suddenly found themselves within range of the guns of a battery posted on a promontory before them, which was crowded with Russian soldiers—stout-looking fellows, habited in long grey coats and spiked helmets of steel, which glittered brightly in the sun; and the bluejackets now for the first time saw the enemy.

The *Hecla* immediately opened fire, which the battery returned with spirit; and the *Arrogant* now coming up, let fly a whole broadside among the soldiers, just as some horse artillery had made their appearance, and were unlimbering preparatory to engaging. As the smoke cleared off, the troop of artillery were seen scampering away at full speed. A heavy fire of musketry now burst forth from a wood on one side, and continued for some time without intermission, the bullets falling thick on board both ships.

While this work was going forward, the *Arrogant* ran aground within twenty yards of the battery, but most fortunately in a position which allowed her guns full play on it. At this close range the ship's guns were more than a match for those in the fort, and so smartly were they worked that in a short time they dismounted all the guns of the enemy and drove the gunners from the fort.

The crew were now able to turn their attention to the position their ship was in, and turning to with a will, unmolested by the enemy, they succeeded in getting afloat again. As they passed close to the fort, they witnessed the state of complete ruin which they had so speedily caused,—guns dismounted, carriages blown to fragments, and accoutrements and helmets scattered around.

As they proceeded up the river the town of Eckness now opened ahead of the two steamers, and before the town lay the vessels which they wished to carry off. The water now shoaled, and the *Arrogant* could proceed no higher. Just then artillery opened on them. The *Arrogant* accordingly anchored, swung broadside to the shore, and engaged the batteries; while the *Hecla*, throwing shells at the enemy, steamed up to Eckness, and running alongside a barque, the only one of the vessels afloat, to the astonishment and dismay of the inhabitants took her in tow, and carried her off in triumph. The two ships then returned down the river with their prize.

## An Unsuccessful Venture

On the 1st of June a gallant adventure similar to the last narrated was not so successful. The *Odin* and *Vulture*, two steamers belonging to Admiral Plumridge's division in the Gulf of Bothnia, employed in destroying the shipping and marine stores in various places along the coast, had arrived in the neighbourhood of Old Carleby.

At seven p.m., two paddle-box boats, two pinnaces, four cutters, and one gig,—nine boats in all,—containing 180 officers and men, carrying six twenty-four-pounder howitzers and two twelve-pounders, were sent away under the command of Lieutenant Wise, of the *Vulture*, who was accompanied by Lieutenants Madden and Burton, Marine Artillery, and by Dr Duncan.

After a long pull, the boats anchored near some store-houses at the mouth of a narrow creek, when, with a flag of truce, Lieutenant Wise went on shore and communicated with the authorities.

On his return, the flag of truce was withdrawn, and some of the boats went ahead to sound, the others following closely. A narrow creek appearing, leading to the town, Lieutenant Carrington, in one of the boats, was ordered up it to explore. On passing some buildings some soldiers were seen, and the boat was on the point of returning to report the circumstance, when a wall was thrown down, and a volley of musketry was poured on her, which killed Lieutenant Carrington, Mr Montague, mate, and Mr Athorpe, midshipman, and wounded Lieutenant Lewis, R.M., and Mr McGrath, midshipman, and fourteen men. The boat, which was much injured, was taken in tow, and carried out to the *Odin*. The other boats immediately opened fire, the gunner of the *Vulture* firing no less than twenty-seven times before he fell, badly wounded.

One of the *Vulture*'s boats, with Mr Morphy, mate, and twenty-five seamen, was disabled, and, drifting on shore, was captured by the enemy. In another of her boats one marine was killed and six were wounded. By this time the enemy had brought five field-pieces into action; the remaining boats, therefore, pulled off out of range, having lost altogether fifty-two killed, wounded, and missing, in this most unfortunate though gallant affair.

No fault was found with the way in which the expedition was commanded, while both officers and men behaved with the most perfect intrepidity and coolness.

Most of the crew of the missing boat escaped with their lives, and were made prisoners.

### Bomarsund—21st June

A small squadron, consisting of the *Hecla*, *Valorous*, and *Odin*, under Captain Hall, was sent in to engage the batteries of Bomarsund on the 21st of June. This they did in the most spirited manner, receiving a hot fire in return both from the forts and from riflemen posted in the neighbourhood, rifle bullets and shot and shell falling thickly on board. The British bluejackets were, however, far better pleased to have a few shot sent among them, than to be doomed to play at long bowls, with all the firing on their side, as was sometimes the case during the war.

The casualties were very slight. After engaging for three hours, and setting some buildings on fire, the ships drew out of action.

It was clearly perceived that the fleet alone could not take the place. Bomarsund, indeed, might well be considered the Sebastopol of the Baltic, its evident object being to overawe the neighbouring kingdoms of Sweden and Denmark. Its destruction, therefore, was of the greatest importance. The allied fleet lay at anchor at Ledsund, about eighteen miles from Bomarsund, anxiously waiting for the arrival of the French troops promised for the service.

It was not, however, till the end of July that the first division reached Ledsund, brought in British ships-of-war. They were under the command of General Baraguay D'Hilliers. On the 5th of August the siege artillery arrived, and on the 8th more troops and marines were landed. The fortifications of Bomarsund lie on the eastern point of the largest of the Aland Islands. The principal fortress commands a semicircular bay on the south, with intricate passages leading to it. At the northern side of the fort the land rises considerably; and the defence on that part consisted of three round towers, one on the highest ground to the west, a second in the centre, and a third to the east. On the 8th of August, 11,000 men were landed on the north side of the island, in the short space of three hours, after the *Amphion*, *Phlegethon*, and *Edinburgh* had blown a fort to atoms, and cleared the ground with their fire. The army then marched across the island, and encamped against the western fort. The English and French marines, with some seamen, were landed.

Batteries were immediately thrown up round the fortress, while thirteen ships of the allied fleet attacked from the sea. The towers were taken in succession; and the large circular fort, mounting nearly 100 guns, surrendered, with a garrison of 2000 men, soon after the effect of the fire from the ships had been felt. The effect of the shot on the fort is thus described by an eye-witness:

Three or four shots set the big stones visibly clattering, as I could mark by a pocket-telescope. One block then fell out, then another, then a third, fourth, *etcetera*; and these were followed by an avalanche of loose rubbish, just as you see a load of gravel pour out from the end of a cart when the back-board is removed.

From this it was argued that the fortifications of Sebastopol would be as easily knocked to pieces; but experience showed that there was a vast difference in the two works. Bomarsund was somewhat of contract work. The sea towers of Sebastopol were as strong as hewn stone scientifically put together could make them.

The navy lost only one man killed and one wounded. A number of brave and dashing acts were performed by naval men during the operations of the fleet in the Baltic, to which it is impossible to refer in detail. Amongst the many gallant acts performed by seamen on this occasion one may specially be mentioned. During the first attack upon the batteries at Bomarsund, a live shell fell on the deck of the *Hecla* with its fuse still burning. Had it remained there and been permitted to explode, great damage to the ship and loss of life must have occurred. Lieutenant Charles D. Lucas seeing this, with the greatest presence of mind and coolness, and regardless of the risk he incurred of being blown to pieces, took up the shell, carried it to the side and dropped it overboard.

## A Capture of Despatches

While Captain Yelverton's squadron was off the island of Wardo, information was received that an *aide-de-camp* of the Emperor of Russia was about to land in charge of a mail and despatches for the Russian general. As there could be little doubt that these despatches would contain valuable information for the guidance of the Allies, it was important to secure them.

It occurred to Commander Bythesea that he could render this service to his country. He accordingly offered his services, and obtained permission for himself and William Johnstone, a brave fellow, a stoker, to proceed on shore for the purpose of intercepting them. Being well armed, they put on disguises, and went on shore, leaving the boat at some distance; they then, ascertaining the spot where the mail-bags would be landed, concealed themselves in some bushes in the neighbourhood.

At length, after it was dark, on the night of the 12th of August, their anxiety was relieved by the arrival of the Russian officer and the mails, but they were accompanied by an escort of soldiers. It would have been madness to attack so large a body, and there appeared no prospect of carrying out their bold attempt. Great was their satisfaction, however, to see the soldiers, believing that the coast was clear, take their departure. The officer and four men, however, still remained. The odds against them would have been great, had the men not been loaded with the bags.

As soon as the soldiers were out of hearing, the gallant commander and his companion sprang from their concealment, attacked the five men; two of them fled; the other three they succeeded in making prisoners and dragged them off to the boat with the mail-bags, which they also secured, and then rowed off in triumph to the *Arrogant*. The despatches were carried to General Baraguay D'Hilliers, who expressed high admiration at the bravery and dash of the exploit. Both Commander Bythesea and William Johnstone obtained the Victoria Cross.

### Attack on Viborg—13th July 1855

The *Arrogant*, Captain Yelverton, having been joined by the *Magicienne*, Captain Vansittart, proceeded with the *Ruby* gunboat along the coast to Kounda Bay, where a large body of Cossack troops were encamped. The *Ruby* and the boats of the two ships stood in, and dislodged the enemy with shells and rockets. In spite of a fire kept up on them from behind hedges, they landed; but as it was found that the place contained only private property, it was not injured.

Next morning Captain Yelverton, having driven some soldiers from a station at the mouth of the Portsoiki River, and destroyed some barracks and stores, proceeded off Viborg. Here the ships anchored as close as they could get to the island of Stralsund. An expedition was at once formed to look into Viborg. It consisted of the *Ruby*, commanded by Mr Hale, mate, and the boats of the *Arrogant*, commanded by Lieutenants Haggard and Woolcombe, and those of the *Magicienne*, under the command of Lieutenants King and Loady; Captains Yelverton and Vansittart, with Captain Lowdes, R.M., in command of a strong detachment of marines, going on board the *Ruby*, which steamer towed the boats. The expedition having opened the bay of Trangsund, a Russian man-of-war steamer, with two large gunboats in tow, was seen not far off.

This novel and unexpected sight of a Russian man-of-war for once clear of a stone wall, and to all appearance prepared for a fair and honest fight, created the greatest enthusiasm among men and officers. The *Ruby* at once opened fire on her, and compelled her to retire out of range, with some damage. The entrance of the Sound being reached, Viborg was now in sight, and there was a fair prospect of attacking three large gunboats lying with another steamer under an island about a mile off, when suddenly an impenetrable barrier was found to have been thrown across the passage. At the same moment, at about 350 yards off, a masked battery on the left opened on the *Ruby* and boats, which they, however, kept in check by an ably-directed return fire.

The enemy's steamer and gunboats now approached from under the island, and opened fire on the expedition. As it was impossible to get the *Ruby* through the barrier, Captain Yelverton ordered her other boats to return towards Stralsund,—the enemy's riflemen, who followed along the banks, being kept off by their fire. Unhappily, an explosion took place on board the *Arrogant*'s second cutter, by which the midshipman commanding her, Mr Storey, was killed, and the boat was swamped. In this condition the boat drifted under the enemy's battery, when a hot fire was poured into her.

All probably would have been killed or taken prisoners, had not George Ingouville, one of the *Arrogant*'s crew, though already wounded, of his own accord jumped overboard, and, taking the painter in hand, towed her off the shore. Probably his gallant conduct might not have availed to save the lives of his shipmates, many of whom were by this time wounded, had not the condition of the cutter been perceived from the *Ruby*.

On this, Lieutenant George Dare Dowell, R.M.A., of the *Magicienne*, calling out for a volunteer crew, jumped into the *Ruby*'s gig, where he was joined by Lieutenant Haggard of the *Arrogant*, and together they pulled off, under a fire which grew hotter and hotter, to the rescue of the boat and men. Lieutenant Dowell was waiting at the moment on board the *Ruby* while his own boat was receiving a supply of rockets. Taking the stroke oar, he and his three companions pulled on, in spite of the shower of grape and musketry which the Russians poured on them to prevent them from accomplishing their object. They succeeded, in spite of this, in taking in three of the cutter's crew, and were mainly instrumental in keeping the boat afloat and bringing her off to the *Ruby*. Two were killed and ten wounded during the whole affair. Captain Yelverton speaks highly of the conduct of all the officers engaged, where their cool and determined courage enabled them to handle most severely, and to keep in check for upwards of an hour, a far superior force of the enemy. These were perhaps the most creditable acts of individual gallantry performed at this time in the Baltic. Both Lieutenant Dowell and George Ingouville received the Victoria Cross.

It would be scarcely interesting or useful to describe the numberless performances of the boats of the fleets in destroying barracks, stores, and shipping.

It was a stern though painful necessity which demanded this mode of proceeding. The object was to show the enemy the power of the Allies to injure them, and to make them earnestly desire peace, at every cost. In no instance was private property on shore intentionally injured.

The shipping, however, did not escape; and in the two nights of the 23rd and 24th of July, the boats of the *Harrier*, Captain Storey, destroyed in the harbour of Nystad forty-seven vessels, amounting to nearly 20,000 tons.

On the 6th July the first shot was fired at Cronstadt, from a gun slung on board a timber barge, by Captain Boyd.

The Russians, in return, endeavoured to injure the vessels of the Allies, and to protect their shores by the employment of infernal machines, as they were then called. We call their much more certain and more dangerous successors submarine mines, and regard them as a regular means of defence. These were intended to explode under water, and some were fired by voltaic batteries, but invariably failed of going off at the proper time; others exploded on being struck; but though the *Merlin* ran on to one, which went off under her bottom, comparatively slight damage was done her. The articles in her store-room, directly over the spot where the machine struck her, were thrown about in every direction, showing the force of the concussion. Admiral Dundas and several officers with him had, however, a narrow escape, one of the machines exploding while they stood around it examining its structure.

### Bombardment of Sveaborg

Among the more important performances of the allied fleet in the Baltic was the severe injury inflicted on the fortress of Sveaborg, one of the strongest belonging to Russia to keep her neighbours in awe in that part of the world.

The fortress of Sveaborg is built on a granite island about a mile in advance of Helsingfors, the Russian capital of Finland. There are eight island rocks connected by strong fortifications, and in the centre is situated the fort in which the Russian flotilla was congregated. It was looked upon as the Gibraltar of the North, and had been considerably strengthened since the commencement of the war. The citadel of this water-surrounded fortress is called Wargon. The allied fleet, consisting of seventeen British men-of-war, fifteen gunboats, and sixteen mortar-vessels, with two French men-of-war, six gunboats, and five mortar-vessels, left Nargen on the 6th of August, and anchored the same night among the islands about five miles from Sveaborg. During the night and next day, some batteries were thrown up on the neighbouring islands; and early on the morning of the 9th, the squadron having taken up their positions,—several behind the islands, where the enemy's guns could not reach them,—the bombardment commenced. The showers of shot and shell told with terrific effect on the devoted fortress; powder magazines and stores of projectiles one after the other blew up, and fires broke out in various directions, which all the efforts of the garrison could not extinguish, and in a short time the whole of the arsenal was reduced to ashes. Still the mortars continued to play, to prevent the fires which were blazing up around from being extinguished. Very few men were wounded, and none were killed during the whole of the operations. Although the naval and military stores were destroyed, the fortress still remained intact. The Russians, however, had been taught the lesson that it would be better for them in future not to make aggressions on their neighbours, or to venture hastily into war.

Captains Yelverton and Vansittart had already shown them how little they could rely on their boasted fortifications, by destroying all between Viborg and Helsingfors, Fredericksham, Kotka, and Swartholme.

## THE WHITE SEA SQUADRON

A small squadron, consisting of the *Eurydice*, twenty-six guns, *Miranda*, fifteen, and *Brisk*, fourteen, had been sent in July 1854 into the White Sea, to destroy the Russian shipping and forts on the coasts of Russian Lapland.

On the 23rd of July the town of Novitska was attacked and burned by the *Miranda* and *Brisk*.

On the 23rd of August the *Miranda* anchored off Kola, the capital of Russian Lapland. A flag of truce was sent on shore, demanding the surrender of the fort, garrison, and government property. All night the crew remained at their quarters, and no answer being returned in the morning, the flag of truce was hauled down, and the ship, getting within 250 yards of the battery, opened a fire of grape and canister. A party was then landed under command of Lieutenant J. Mackenzie and Mr Manthorpe, mate, who, at the head of a party of bluejackets and marines, rushed up, sword in hand, to dislodge the enemy from the batteries and to capture the guns. A hot fire was opened on them from the towers of a monastery; but they soon drove out the garrison, who took to flight, and it, with all the government stores and buildings, was immediately set on fire and completely consumed.

Kola lies thirty miles up a river of most difficult navigation, with a strong current, and often so narrow that there was scarcely room for the ship to swing. Captain Lyons also had a very uncertain knowledge of the strength of the enemy; but nothing could check his determination, and it was, as we have seen, rewarded with complete success. Taking into consideration the difficulties to be encountered, this was one of the most daring naval exploits performed in the north. The *Miranda*, at the approach of autumn, returned to England, and from thence went out to join the fleet in the Black Sea.

### ACTION ON THE DANUBE—JUNE AND JULY 1854

The blockade of Sebastopol having been established, some of the lighter cruisers were sent along the coast on various detached enterprises, for the purpose of annoying and misleading the Russians, and effecting the destruction of government property.

Two of the cruisers, the *Firebrand*, Captain Hyde Parker, and the *Vesuvius*, Captain Powell, were despatched to destroy the guard-houses and signal-stations on the banks of the Danube, which kept up the communication with the Russian forts. On the morning of the 22nd of June the boats of the two steamers, manned and armed, with a Turkish gunboat, all under the command of Lieutenant Jones, of the *Firebrand*, pulled off towards a guard-house and signal-station about twenty miles north of Sulineh. As they approached, the signal was made from station to station, summoning aid. Behind some banks, close to the beach, were posted bodies of Cossack cavalry, while others were scattered about wherever they could find shelter from the shells and shot fired from the boats' and ships' guns. They, however, could not stand this long, and fled in confusion.

On the boats reaching the shore, the seamen and marines landed, and, forming on the beach, advanced in skirmishing order towards the Cossacks, who, mounting their horses, fled in all directions. The guard-houses were immediately burnt, the signal-staff destroyed, and the men returned to their ships in admirable order. Several other stations were destroyed on that and the following days; and on one occasion, on the night of the 27th of June, Captain Parker surprised the garrison of Sulineh, whom he put to flight, after capturing the officer in command and others. The officer was forwarded to Lord Raglan, who obtained some important information from him.

The *Firebrand* and *Vesuvius* now kept up a strict blockade of the Danube, and the crews were allowed to land without opposition; but at length Captain Parker suspected that the gabion battery attached to the quarantine ground was occupied, and, for the purpose of examining it, entered the river on the 6th with the boats of the two ships. Nothing was discovered until Captain Parker's galley arrived opposite the gabion battery, when a single rifle-shot was fired, which passed through the boat, and this was followed by a volley, piercing the boat, grazing the captain's elbow, and severely wounding one man. Captain Parker on this ordered the boat to pull round, and, as she retreated, with the greatest coolness he discharged his rifle at the enemy, who were now pouring in a galling and heavy fire on all the boats. The pinnace, being in advance, was especially exposed, and unhappily grounded within fifty yards of the battery.

On seeing this, Captain Parker leaped on shore from his galley, exclaiming, "We must storm—follow me, my men!" and gallantly rushed forward, followed by all who had then come up. Parallel with the river, and at about fifteen yards from it, ran a line of high canes growing in a marsh. He advanced along this, and having fired and knocked down a Cossack, he was reloading, when a volley of bullets came flying round him, one of which pierced his heart, and he fell dead into the arms of his coxswain, Mr Everard, a naval cadet, being at the moment by his side.

Commander Powell, who succeeded to the command, ordered a heavy fire of shell and Congreve rockets to be opened on the battery, under cover of which the marines and seamen stormed the place, and drove out the Russians, who took shelter in the marsh, where they could not be followed.

Captain Parker was a most gallant officer, and his loss caused deep regret among all his brother officers.

On the 13th, the *Spitfire*, Lieutenant Johnstone, towing the boats of the *Vesuvius*, crossed the bar at the Sulineh mouth of the Danube, and, having driven off the enemy, the marines and bluejackets landed and totally destroyed the town of Sulineh, by setting it on fire in every direction.

### BOMBARDMENT OF SEBASTOPOL—17TH OCTOBER 1854

We have now to give an account of the chief naval exploits of the war, when the wooden walls of Old England were to try their strength with the stone ramparts of Russia. While the heavy artillery of the Allies opened fire on the city from the newly-erected batteries on the neighbouring heights, it was arranged that the fleets should attack from the sea. The fleet was to form a semicircle before the harbour's mouth; the French to engage the forts on the south, the English the forts Constantine and Alexander and the Stone and Wasp forts on the north. The morning was actively spent by the crews in preparing for action.

At fifty minutes past ten the signal for weighing was made; and the fleet, the fine old *Agamemnon* leading, stood towards the batteries. She was followed in order by the *Sanspareil*, screw, the sailing—ships being moved by steamers lashed alongside,—*Albion*, by *Firebrand*; *Queen*, by *Vesuvius*; *Britannia*, by *Furious*; *Trafalgar*, by *Retribution*; *London*, by *Niger*; *Vengeance*, by *Highflyer*; *Rodney*, by *Spiteful*; *Bellerophon*, by *Cyclops*; *Arethusa*, by *Triton*; while *Samson*, *Tribune*, *Terrible*, *Sphinx*, *Lynx*, and *Spitfire* acted as look-out ships, and were allowed to take up independent positions. Besides the stone fortifications, the enemy had thrown up numerous earthworks, and placed guns along the cliff to the north. To one of these forts the seamen gave the name of the Wasp; to another, the Telegraph battery.

The French weighed first, a little before ten, and proceeded to their position, on the south of the line, when the enemy opened fire on them. The Turks took up a position in the centre; and now the magnificent *Agamemnon* steamed on, with the gallant little *Circassian*, commanded by the brave Mr Ball, piloting the way, sounding as he went, and marking the position the larger ships were to take up. At half-past one the *Agamemnon* began to draw in close with the land, when, to try range, she opened fire from her large pivot-gun on the Wasp battery, which instantly returned it; and in a short time Fort Constantine commenced firing with terrible effect, the *Agamemnon* suffering fearfully.

At two p.m. she anchored, head and stern, in a quarter less five fathoms, 750 yards off Fort Constantine, on which she immediately opened her fresh broadside. At five minutes past two, the *Sanspareil* and *London* anchored astern, and ably seconded the gallant Sir Edmund by the fire which they poured into the Star Fort and the smaller forts on the cliff. At twenty minutes past two, the *Albion* anchored, and engaged the Wasp, to take off the fire from the *Agamemnon*, which, from her position, exposed to a cross fire, was suffering more than the other ships. The *Britannia*, now in fifteen fathoms water, and some two thousand yards off, opened fire, and the action became general.

The commander of the detached steamers determined that they also should play their part. The *Terrible* and *Samson* dashed on inside the other ships, and engaged the northern forts in the most gallant manner. Nothing could exceed the steady way in which the *Vesuvius* carried her huge consort into action, nor the spirited manner in which the *Albion* engaged Fort Constantine. The *Arethusa*,—a name long known to fame,—urged on by the little *Triton*, well preserved the renown her name has gained, by boldly engaging the huge stone fort, at which, in rapid succession, broadside after broadside was discharged, the crew of the *Triton* coming on board to assist in manning her guns. At length, with her rigging cut to pieces, and numerous shot-holes in her hull, and eighteen killed and wounded, and five wounded belonging to the *Triton*, she was towed out of action.

The *Albion*, though farther out than the *Agamemnon*, was in reality suffering far more than that ship, and she at length was compelled to haul off, with one lieutenant and nine men killed, and three other officers and sixty-eight men wounded. The *London*, also, with four killed and eighteen wounded, was at the same time taken out of action. All this time the gallant Sir Edmund Lyons refused to move; indeed, his ship was suffering more aloft than in her hull, and, notwithstanding the tremendous fire to which she had been exposed, she had only four killed and twenty-five wounded. This was owing to the vice-admiral's bravery in going so close to the shore; the majority of the shot, flying high, struck her rigging instead of her hull. Still she was struck 240 times, and became almost a wreck,—her hull showing gaping wounds, her main-yard cut in two places, every spar more or less damaged, two shot-holes in the head of the mainmast, and her rigging hanging in shreds; the ship also having twice caught fire,—once when a shell fell in her maintop and set fire to the mainsail, and another having burst in the port side and set fire to the hammock-nettings. The *Rodney*, however, suffered still more in masts and rigging, she having tailed on the reef, whence she was got off by the gallant exertions of Commander Kynaston, of the *Spiteful*. The *Albion* and *Arethusa* suffered greatly in their hulls.

At length one ship after another had drawn off; and the fire of the forts being concentrated on the *Agamemnon*, Sir Edmund despatched one of his lieutenants in a boat, to summon the *Bellerophon* to his aid. The appeal was nobly and immediately answered, and she contributed greatly to take off the fire which the Wasp and Telegraph batteries were showering on her. As the *Agamemnon* was the first to go into battle, so she was one of the last to haul out of the engagement, which she did soon after six p.m., but not till darkness had compelled the combatants on shore to cease from firing. The action lasted altogether from half-past one to half-past six,—the loss being 44 killed and 266 wounded.

A naval brigade had at this time been formed, and a considerable number of officers and men belonging to the different ships were consequently serving on shore. Owing to this circumstance, probably, the casualties were lessened. The admiral had also left all the spare top-masts and spars on board the *Vulcan*, with the sick and prisoners, at the anchorage off the Katscha; so that the ships were soon able to repair the damages they had received aloft. No sooner had the fleet once more anchored in safety, than the captains went on board the *Agamemnon*, to pay their respects to Sir Edmund Lyons, as did the French on the following day, all declaring that his ship had held the post of honour. Still, many other ships were not behind his in the gallant way in which they were fought.

The French ships were also fought with great courage and judgment, and suffered even more than the English. The Turks, from being much farther out, escaped with slight damage.

The result of the action, bravely as it had been fought, was not satisfactory. It was a trial of strength between stone and wood, and the stone was undoubtedly the victor. Probably a considerable number of Russians were killed and wounded, and it served as a diversion to the land attack; but next day not a gun the less frowned from the batteries of Fort Constantine, and but a trifling damage had been done to the stonework.

However, the diversions caused by these attacks from the sea were of much consequence; and on other occasions the smaller steamers, gun and rocket-boats, were sent off the mouth of the harbour during the night to distract the attention of the Russians.

## Crimean Naval Brigade

Soon after the army reached Balaclava, portions of the crews of most of the larger ships had been sent on shore, at first simply to assist in garrisoning the heights above Balaclava, and placed under the command of Captain Lushington. The brigade was soon afterwards increased by a party under Lord John Hay, of the Wasp. Both officers and men, however, very soon volunteered for other services, and in every post of danger there was some portion of the naval brigade to be found. It was here that Captain William Peel first showed the gallantry and judgment for which he became so conspicuous. He took command of one of the advanced batteries before Sebastopol, which did good service. During the first six days of the bombardment, ending October 22nd, the naval brigade lost twelve killed and sixty-six wounded.

From the first, the conduct of all the men, though placed in a novel situation, was excellent, and the gallantry of officers and men conspicuous. From being near Balaclava, and from being supplied with tents and clothing and food from their ships, they had not the same dreadful hardships to endure as the soldiers; they yet sought out danger, and as readily exposed their lives on shore as they are accustomed to do at sea.

Among all the acts exhibiting gallantry, coolness, and judgment, one performed by Mr N.W. Hewett, then acting mate of HMS *Beagle*, stands conspicuous.

On the 26th of October 1854, the day after the battle of Balaclava, he was in charge of the right Lancaster battery before Sebastopol, with a party of bluejackets under him, when the Russians made a desperate sortie from the walls against Sir De Lacy Evans' division. The advance of the Russians placed the gun in great jeopardy; and their assault was so vigorous that their skirmishers had got within 300 yards of the battery, and were pouring in a sharp fire from their Minie rifles. By some misapprehension the word was passed to spike the gun and retreat; but Mr Hewett, taking upon himself to disregard what he heard, answered, "That order did not come from Captain Lushington, and till he directs us to desert the gun, we'll not move." This proceeding was hazardous, for at the time the gun was in an ineffectual position, in consequence of the enemy advancing on its flank. With the assistance, however, of the seamen with him, and of some soldiers who came to his aid, he got round the gun into position; then, blowing away the parapet of the battery, he opened on the advancing column of the Russians so effective a fire, that they were completely staggered, and their progress was stopped. Seconded by his companions, whom his spirit animated, again and again he discharged his death-dealing gun, till the enemy gave way and retreated.

A story is current that he actually did receive an order to abandon the gun, and that afterwards, while he was reflecting what might be the consequences of having disobeyed it, his commanding officer inquired, "Mr Hewett, were you not ordered to spike that gun and retreat?"

"I was, sir."

"And you chose to disregard the order, and fight the gun?"

"I did, sir; but I am sorry if—"

"Well, then, you are promoted." Sir Stephen Lushington brought Mr Hewett's conduct before the commander-in-chief, and he received from the Admiralty, as a reward, his lieutenancy, which he so well merited. At the battle of Inkermann his bravery was again conspicuous, and he was soon afterwards appointed to the command of the *Beagle* gunboat in the Sea of Azov.

A LIVE SHELL AMONG THE POWDER

Captain Peel of the *Leander* repeated the exploit of Mr Lucas, already related, under even more exciting circumstances.

He was in command of a battery outside Sebastopol on the 18th of October, when a live shell with fuse burning fell among the powder cases outside the magazine. Had it exploded, it would in any case have created great havoc, but there was the additional risk that it might explode the magazine, in which case everyone near would have been killed. The moment it fell, Captain Peel seized it and threw it over the parapet, which was not quite the same as throwing it overboard at sea, for it exploded as it fell, but happily, being outside the battery, caused no mischief.

Captain Peel distinguished himself on many occasions during the war. At the battle of Inkermann he joined the officers of the Grenadier Guards, and assisted them in defending and saving the colours of the regiment when hard-pressed in the Sandbag Battery. At the assault of the Redan he volunteered to lead the ladder-party, and carried the first ladder until disabled by a severe wound.

### Edward Saint John Daniels

This young officer, a midshipman of Captain Peel's ship, took example from the conduct of his noble chief, and vied with him in feats of daring. In Captain Peel's battery there was a call for volunteers to bring in powder to the battery from a wagon in a very exposed situation, a shot having disabled the horses. Instantly Mr Daniels sprang forward, and, followed by others, performed the dangerous service. At the battle of Inkermann he followed his captain as his *aide-de-camp* through the terrific fire of that eventful day. Again, on the 18th of June, he accompanied Captain Peel when he led the ladder-party in the assault on the Redan. Together they approached the deadly breach, when Captain Peel was struck in the arm, and might have bled to death, had not young Daniels remained by him on the glacis under a terrific fire, and with admirable devotion and perfect coolness applied a tourniquet to his arm, not leaving him till he was able to gain a less exposed position.

### Bravery of Five Seamen at Inkermann

During the battle of Inkermann, while the right Lancaster battery was fiercely attacked by the Russians, five gallant blue-jackets, picking up the muskets of the disabled soldiers, mounted the banquette, and, under a fierce fire, kept rapidly discharging them, while their comrades below loaded and handed them up others as fast as they could, contributing much to keep the enemy at bay. Two were killed, or died from their wounds; but the three survivors, Thomas Reeve, James Gorman, and Mark Scholefield, obtained the Victoria Cross.

### Commander Roby

John Taylor, captain of the forecastle, and Henry Curtis, boatswain's mate, were in the advance sap opposite the Redan on 18th June 1855, immediately after the assault on Sebastopol, when they observed a soldier of the 57th Regiment, who had been shot through both legs, sitting up, and calling for help. Lieutenant D'Aeth, of HMS *Sidou*, was also of the party, but died of cholera soon after. The brave seamen could not bear to see their poor countryman thus perishing, and, though the Redan was still keeping up a tremendous fire, climbing over the breastwork of the sap, Captain Roby and the two seamen proceeded upwards of seventy yards across the open space towards the salient angle of the Redan, and, at the great risk of their own lives, lifted up the wounded soldier and bore him to a place of safety.

John Sullivan, boatswain's mate, while serving in an advanced battery, on the 10th of April 1855, showed the most perfect coolness and bravery, by going forward and placing a flag on a mound in an exposed situation, under a heavy fire, to enable another battery, Number 5, to open fire on a concealed Russian battery, which was doing great execution on the British advanced works. Commander Kennedy, commanding the battery, spoke in the highest terms of Sullivan's bravery on that and on other occasions, and recommended him for promotion.

### Dashing Service of John Shepherd, a Boatswain

While he was boatswain's mate of the *Saint Jean d'Acre*, and serving in the naval brigade, he volunteered to proceed in a punt, during a dark night, into the harbour of Sebastopol, and to endeavour, with an apparatus he carried, to blow up one of the Russian line-of-battle ships. He reached the harbour, and had got past the enemy's steamboat at the entrance of Careening Bay, when he was prevented from proceeding farther by a long line of boats, which were carrying troops from the south to the north side of Sebastopol. On the 16th of August, he again made the attempt from the side of Careening Bay, then in possession of the French.

The above are only some few of the gallant deeds done by the officers and men of the naval brigade before Sebastopol. All, from Sir Stephen Lushington downwards to the youngest midshipman or ship-boy, did their duty right nobly; and though the bluejackets of England have no cause, as a rule, to complain that their gallantry is not sufficiently appreciated, perhaps on this occasion the service they rendered to their country is scarcely understood as it should be. On the disastrous assault on the Redan, 18th of June 1855, the naval brigade consisted of four parties of sixty men each, one for each column; but two only went out, the other two being kept in reserve. They were told off to carry scaling-ladders and wool-bags, and to place them for the storming-parties. They were led by Captain Peel. Severely they suffered. Out of the two small parties, fourteen were killed and forty-seven were wounded.

When the soldiers, overwhelmed by the terrific fire of the batteries, retreated towards the trenches, several officers and men were left behind wounded, and endured fearful agonies for hours, without a drop of water or a cheering voice to comfort them. Among others, Lieutenant Ermiston lay for five hours under the abattis of the Redan, and was reported dead; but he had only a contusion of the knee, and, watching his opportunity, he got safely away.

Mr Kennedy, mate of the *London*, was also left behind, close to the abattis, and, after several hours of painful suspense, concealed among the dead, he rolled himself over and over down the declivity, and managed to get into the trench.

Lieutenant Kidd came in all safe, and was receiving the congratulations of a brother officer, when he saw a wounded soldier lying out in the open. He at once exclaimed, "We must go and save him!" and leaped over the parapet in order to do so. He had scarcely proceeded one yard on his errand of mercy, when he was shot through the breast, and died an hour afterwards.

Lieutenant Dalyell, of the *Leander*, had his left arm shattered by a grape-shot, and underwent amputation. Lieutenant Cave, and Mr Wood, midshipman, were also wounded; as was Captain Peel, as has been described. Indeed, of the whole detachment, only three officers came out of action untouched.

Not only were the subordinate officers of the navy thus conspicuously brave and active, but a sailor was from the first one of the ruling spirits of the campaign. To Sir Edmund Lyons did England owe, in an incalculable degree, the success which attended our arms on the shores of the Euxine.

He it was who organised and conducted the expedition to the Crimea, prepared the means of landing, and superintended all so closely, that "in his eagerness he left but six inches between the keel of his noble ship and the ground below it." Not only in matters connected with the transport of the troops, but also in every subsequent stage of the expedition, Sir Edmund Lyons gave the most valuable assistance to Lord Raglan and his successors. How, at the battle of the Alma, he supported the French army by bringing the guns of his ship to bear on the left flank of the Russians, and what a conspicuous part he took with the *Agamemnon* on the first bombardment of Sebastopol, are incidents well-known at the time. But he had more to do in the way of advice and of encouragement than the public ever heard of. Day after day he might have been seen on his grey pony, hovering about the English lines on the heights of Sebastopol; he was present at Balaclava, and he was present at Inkermann. It was thus that, having conveyed our soldiers to the Crimea, he saved them from being compelled to leave it, baffled, if not vanquished. A day or two after the battle of Balaclava, Sir Edmund Lyons, on landing, learnt to his astonishment that orders had been issued to the naval brigade to embark as many guns as possible during the day, for Balaclava was to be evacuated at night,—of course, surrendering to the enemy the greater portion of the guns. On his own responsibility, the admiral at once put a stop to the execution of this order, and went in search of Lord Raglan, who, it appears, had come to the resolution of abandoning Balaclava, in consequence of the opinion expressed by the engineers, that, after the loss of these redoubts in our rear lately held by the Turks, we ought to concentrate our strength on the plateau. Taking Lord Raglan aside, Sir Edmund Lyons strongly opposed these views. He pointed out that the advanced position in the valley in front of which these redoubts were situated had been originally occupied in accordance with the advice of those very officers, and in opposition to that of Sir Edmund, who had suggested at the time that they were covering too much ground. He argued that, as the engineers had been mistaken once, they might be wrong again; and he clinched his argument by saying that, whatever might be the value of his opinion in such a case, he was at all events entitled to pronounce an opinion as to the insufficiency of Kamiesch as a harbour for the allied armies; that this harbour was utterly inadequate; and that the abandonment of Balaclava meant the evacuation of the Crimea in a week. After some conversation, Lord Raglan said, "Well, you were right before, and this time I will act upon your advice." Sir Edmund obtained leave to countermand the orders which had been issued; Balaclava was maintained as our base of operations, and the army was saved from what might have proved an inglorious defeat, if not a terrible disaster. This, as we have said, was perhaps the most important of all the services rendered by the admiral, and he well deserved the peerage which it earned for him.

Sir Stephen Lushington, having attained his rank as admiral in July 1855, was succeeded in the command of the naval brigade by Captain the Honourable Henry Keppel, whose gallantry on various occasions had been especially conspicuous. At length, on the 19th September, Sebastopol having fallen, the gallant naval brigade was disbanded,—the jovial bluejackets leaving Balaclava to return to their ships, amid the enthusiastic cheers of their red-coated comrades, among whom but one feeling was universal, that of regret at losing the company of so merry a band. Not a soldier but admired their bravery, their invariable good-humour, and marvellous aptitude in adapting themselves to whatever circumstances they might fall in with.

### EXPEDITION TO KERTCH

The importance of securing the outlet to the Sea of Azov had long been seen; and on the 22nd of May an expedition sailed from Balaclava, under the joint command of Sir George Brown and General D'Autemarre, for the purpose of capturing the fortresses of Kertch and Yenikale, which command its entrance. They had under them 15,000 troops and five batteries of artillery. Admirals Lyons and Bruat accompanied the expedition. While the troops were landed some miles to the south of

Kertch, the squadron proceeded on to attack it in front; but, before they arrived, the Russians, believing that they could not defend the place, evacuated it, as did most of the inhabitants. Yenikale was deserted in the same manner, and the armies and fleets achieved a bloodless victory, while the smaller steamers of the squadron were sent off up the Sea of Azov in chase of the Russian men-of-war.

A light squadron of English and French vessels was placed under the command of Captain Lyons of the *Miranda*, with directions to capture and destroy all the ships, magazines, and stores of provisions belonging to the enemy. The larger quantity of provisions for the Russian army in the Crimea had hitherto been conveyed across the Sea of Azov. In a few days the *Miranda* and her consorts destroyed four months' rations for 100,000 men, and not less than 300 Russian vessels.

This work was ably done, and individuals often even thus had opportunities of exhibiting their gallantry. Arriving off Genitchi on 29th May 1855, with his little squadron, Captain Lyons sent Commander Craufurd with a flag of truce, to demand the surrender of a number of vessels which were seen, as well as government stores. This demand being refused, the squadron opened fire on the town, while the boats under the command of Lieutenant Mackenzie pulled in, and set fire to seventy-three vessels and some corn-stores on shore. The wind shifting, there seemed a probability that the more distant vessels and stores might escape.

As the enemy had had time to make preparations, another expedition would be, it was evident, more dangerous than the first. As, however, the vessels were in a favourable position for supplying the Russian armies in the Crimea, and their destruction was of the greatest importance, Captain Lyons despatched the boats, commanded and officered as before.

Seeing that there would be great risk in landing a party in presence of a superior force out of gunshot of the ships, Lieutenant Cecil Buckley, *Miranda*, Lieutenant Hugh Burgoyne, *Swallow*, and Mr J. Roberts, gunner of the *Ardent*, volunteered to land alone and fire the stores. While these three gallant officers proceeded on their dangerous undertaking, Lieutenant Mackenzie pushed on under a fire of four field-guns and musketry, and destroyed the remaining vessels, the ships resuming their fire on the town. The shore party succeeded in reaching the stores, to which they effectually set fire. On their retreat to their boat, they were, however, very nearly cut off by a body of Cossacks who charged down on them, but they got safe on board. Though several shots struck the boats, only one man was slightly wounded.

### Proceedings at Taganrog—3rd June

Captain Lyons arrived off this place with a large mosquito fleet of steamers, gunboats, and boats from the English and French men-of-war. Taganrog was summoned to surrender, but the governor refused, and a brisk fire was opened on the place. In vain the enemy endeavoured to get down to the store-houses on the beach to protect them. Lieutenant Mackenzie, first of the *Miranda*, had charge of a separate division of light boats, with rockets and one gun, to cover the approach of Lieutenant Cecil Buckley, *Miranda*, who, in a four-oared gig, manned by volunteers, accompanied by Mr Henry Cooper, boatswain, repeatedly landed and fired the different stores and public buildings. This dangerous, not to say desperate, service, when carried out in a town containing upwards of 3000 troops, constantly endeavouring to prevent it, and only checked by the fire of the boats' guns, was most effectually performed.

### Gallantry of S. Trewavas, Seaman

The *Beagle*, to the command of which ship Lieutenant Hewett had been appointed on the 3rd July, was off the town of Genitchi, where there was a floating bridge which it was most important to destroy, as it communicated with the town and the Arabat spit. Mr Hewett accordingly despatched his gig, under command of Mr Hayles, gunner of the *Beagle*, and paddle-box boats under Mr Martin Tracy, midshipman of the *Vesuvius*. The undertaking was one of considerable danger, for troops lined the beach not eighty yards off, and the adjacent houses were filled with riflemen, all of whom opened a hot fire on the boats. The *Beagle* fired on them in return, as did Mr Tracy from the paddle-box boats, causing great confusion and dismay in their ranks. However, Mr Hayles pulled in, ably seconded by a seaman lent from the *Agamemnon*, Stephen Trewavas, who, though already wounded from the fire of the enemy, cut the hawsers and cast the boats adrift. Mr Hayles was also wounded. Trewavas obtained the Victoria Cross for his coolness and determination on this occasion.

The squadron continued its course round the coast, destroying fisheries, guard-houses, barracks, stores of forage and provisions, and vessels, wherever they could be found.

### Brave Devotion of F. Kellaway, Boatswain

The *Wrangler*, Commander Burgoyne, came off Marioupol, Sea of Azov, where some boats, fishing-stations, and haystacks were discovered across a small lake. On this, Commander Burgoyne despatched Mr Odevaine, mate, and Mr Kellaway, boatswain, to destroy them. They had nearly reached the spot, when they were fired on by a party of Russians, who suddenly rushed out from their ambush, and endeavoured to cut off their retreat. One seaman fell into the enemy's hands, but the rest of the party were making good their escape, when Mr Odevaine tripped up and fell. Mr Kellaway, believing that his commanding officer was wounded, though at the risk of his life, ran back to his rescue. While lifting him up they were surrounded by the Russians, and though the gallant boatswain made a stout resistance, they were both made prisoners and carried off. Commander Burgoyne and the other officers of the ship were witnesses of the devoted conduct of Mr Kellaway, but were unable to render them assistance.

### LIEUTENANT G.F. DAY AT GENITCHI

While Lieutenant Day was in command of the *Recruit* he performed several very gallant acts, but none surpassed the following:

It was important to ascertain the practicability of reaching the enemy's gun-vessels which lay within the Straits of Genitchi, close to the town. With this object in view, Mr Day, having provided himself with a pocket-compass, went on shore one dark but fine night, and proceeded through the enemy's lines, traversing a distance of four or five miles, occasionally up to his knees in water, till he got within 200 yards of the vessels. From the perfect silence which reigned on board them, he was persuaded that they were without crews; and when he returned, it was with the conviction that the expedition was a feasible one. The correctness of this opinion he was induced to doubt on the following day, in consequence of the increased activity apparent in the direction of the vessels. Notwithstanding the danger he must have been aware he was running,—for it was in attempting a reconnaissance on the same ground that Captain L'Allenand, of the French steam-vessel *Monette*, lost his life,—he resolved to pay another visit to the spot. The night was squally, and he thought it wiser to take a larger circuit than before. He persevered, and gained the spot, when he ascertained that the vessels were manned, and that their crews were apparently on the alert. He decided, consequently, that it would be out of the question to make any attempt to surprise them.

### CLOSELY PURSUED

Captain Commerell, having ascertained that large quantities of corn-forage were collected on the Crimean shore of the Sivash, considered that it was of importance to destroy them, and determined himself to undertake the dangerous task, accompanied by Mr Lillingston, mate, William Rickard, quartermaster, and George Milestone, A.B., and another man. Having left the ship at nightfall, they hauled their small boat across the spit of Arabat, and traversed the Sivash to the Crimean shore of the Putrid Sea. Here Mr Lillingston and one man remained in charge of the boat. They had now a distance of two miles to proceed, to reach the magazine of corn and forage, amounting to 400 tons, which they had devoted to destruction. They had also two rivers to ford,—the Kara-su and Salghir,—the magazine being on the banks of the latter stream. Near the magazine was a guard-house, and close to it a village, in which twenty or thirty mounted Cossacks were posted. Nothing daunted, they pushed on, and, having crossed the two rivers without being discovered, they set light to the stacks. With unexpected rapidity the whole blazed up, and soon gave notice to the enemy of what had occurred. They beat a rapid retreat, and, having recrossed the Salghir, ran for their lives, pursued by the Cossacks, who soon opened on them a hot fire. On they ran, fortunately taking the right road, the Cossacks increasing in numbers. Milestone at length gave signs of being exhausted. The boat was yet some way off. The Cossacks were scarcely fifty yards behind, when Milestone fell in some deep mud, from which, in his tired condition, he had no power of drawing himself out. On this, Rickard, discovering his condition, entreated his captain to make good his escape, while he attempted to help Milestone. This he succeeded in doing, though the Cossacks were now not forty yards from them, Mr Lillingston and a man who remained in the boat covering them with their rifles; and there fortunately being some 200 yards of mud for the horsemen to traverse, all the party reached the boat in safety. Both Captain Commerell and his brave boatswain Rickard most deservedly received the Victoria Cross.

### Capture of Kinburn—17th October 1855

The allied fleet left Kamiesch on the 7th of October, with about 5000 British troops on board, and a still larger number of French. Appearing off Odessa to alarm that place, and to mislead the Russians, they proceeded directly for Kinburn.

The troops landed about three miles south of Kinburn early on the 15th, and the bombardment soon afterwards commenced; but it was not till the 17th that the grand attack took place, thus described by an eye-witness:

Continually on the move, the steamers and gunboats, firing as they went, swept down the defences of the Russians, silencing their guns, killing the men, or forcing them to take refuge underground. Then a grand movement of the fleet took place. The admirals and their three-deckers were observed at noon entering into action in splendid order, French and English advancing in line under steam, and approaching close into the land. The fleet in the lagoon closed in at the same moment, and simultaneously heavy broadsides were poured in from all quarters. The central fort was the only one which replied, and then only with a solitary gun at long intervals. Nothing of a grander or more imposing effect could be witnessed than the three-deckers veering round to deliver their fire, their jibs set to bring their guns to bear. Three times the *Montebello*, commanded by the French admiral, delivered a broadside from every gun in her sides. As she did so, she became lost in wreaths of white smoke. The iron shower swept over the fort with a din that surpassed all other sounds, and the air reverberated with the roar of ordnance. All round the enemy the fire was delivered in continuous discharges, and there was no pause. It was then that the Russians gave signs of surrender. A struggling form was seen on the ramparts, waving a white flag as a token. As by magic, the firing ceased.

The old Russian general shortly afterwards came out of the castle, and delivered his sword to Admiral Sir Houston Stewart and General Bazaine. Only two seamen were hit; but the Russians lost 43 men killed, 114 wounded, and upwards of 1200 prisoners.

CHAPTER 11

# The Indian Mutiny

### The "*Shannon's*" Brigade in India

From the Journal of Lieutenant E. Hope Verney, RN, published by Saunders and Otley.

HM screw steam-frigate *Shannon*, of fifty-one guns, 600 horsepower, and 2667 tons, at that time the largest frigate afloat, was commissioned at Portsmouth by Captain William Peel on the 13th of September 1856, and destined for the China Seas. On her arrival at Hong-Kong, Lord Elgin, hearing of the outbreak of the mutiny in India, embarked in her with a body of troops for Calcutta. She arrived on the 6th of August in the mouth of the Ganges, when Captain Peel offered the services of his crew, with the ship's guns, to the Governor-General to form a naval brigade. On the 14th, Captain Peel, with a number of officers and 450 seamen, embarked in a flat, towed by a river steamer, and proceeded up the Hooghly, to join the force advancing to the relief of Lucknow. On the 18th, they were followed by another party of five officers and 120 men, under the command of Lieutenant Vaughan,—the frigate being left with 140 men, under the command of Mr Waters, the master.

The steamers were of light draught, and could proceed but slowly with the heavily-laden flats in tow against the strong current. The vessels anchored at night, and proceeded on their voyage during the day, when the men underwent a course of drilling, to fit them for the service they had undertaken. At length, towards the end of October, they reached Allahabad, at the junction of the Jumna and Ganges; and while one division was left to garrison that place, the remainder proceeded on towards Cawnpore by land. While at Futtehpore, near the Ganges, information was received that a party of rebels were in the neighbourhood; and 100 men of the naval brigade, commanded by Captain Peel, with Lieutenant Hay, Mr Garvey, Lieutenant Stirling, RM, and Mr Bone, and 430 men of different regiments, under command of Colonel Powell, started in pursuit.

> After marching about twenty-four miles, at three p.m. they came in sight of the enemy, found entrenched in a strong position behind some hillocks of sand; and, driving their skirmishers out of a field of corn, engaged and defeated them, capturing two guns and an ammunition wagon. The whole force of the enemy exceeded 4000 men, of whom about 2000 were Sepoys, who fought in uniform. The enemy's artillery was well served, and did great execution. The gallant Colonel Powell, pressing on to the attack, had just secured two guns, when he fell dead with a bullet through his forehead.
>
> Captain Peel then took the command. It was not till half-past four that the enemy fired their last shot and retreated, leaving 300 killed behind them, while the British loss was 95 killed and wounded. Of the naval brigade, Lieutenant Hay, RN, was wounded in the hand, and Lieutenant Stirling, RM, severely in the leg.
>
> On the 12th of November, the naval brigade arrived before Lucknow. On the 14th, an attack was made on the city, when the Martiniere College and another large building were captured. While the brigade's guns were in action, one of them exploding, killed Francis Cassidey, captain of the maintop and severely wounded several other men.
>
> Again, on the 16th, the naval brigade guns were engaged in the attack on Secundra Bagh, when Lieutenant Salmon, RN, was severely wounded, and Martin Abbot Daniel, midshipman, was killed by a round shot in the head.
>
> In writing to his father, Captain Peel says:

It was in front of the Shah Najeef, and in command of an eight-inch howitzer, that your noble son was killed. The enemy's fire was very heavy, and I had just asked your son if his gun was ready; he replied, 'All ready, sir'; when I said, 'Fire the howitzer'; and he was answering, 'Ay, ay,' when a round shot in less than a moment deprived him of life. We buried him where he fell, our chaplain reading the service; and, in laying him in his resting-place, we felt, captain, officers, and men, that we had lost one the best and noblest of the *Shannon's*.

Twelve or thirteen of the naval brigade were wounded on this occasion, and three or four were killed. On the following day, that masterly movement took place by which the women and children, and sick and wounded, were safely brought out of Lucknow; and on the 24th, one of England's noblest heroes—Sir Henry Havelock—died.

On the 28th of November, the brigade marched on Cawnpore, when, meeting the enemy, a party of thirty-six bluejackets, with two twenty-four pounders, under Lieutenant Hay, with Mr Garvey, mate, and Mr H.A. Lascelles, did good service. Mr Lascelles, naval cadet, aide-de-camp to Captain Peel, greatly distinguished himself, seizing a rifle from a wounded man of the 88th, and charging with that regiment. About this time the brigade was joined by Captain Oliver Jones, RN, on half-pay, as a volunteer, who did good service on various occasions.

> Our army on the march is a sight affording much interest and amusement,—such a menagerie of men and beasts, footmen and cavalry, soldiers and sailors, camels and elephants, white men and black men, horses and oxen, marines and artillery, Sikhs and Highlanders.
> 
> When we leave the encampment, all is shrouded in darkness, and everyone naturally feels a little grumpy; but when the first streaks of dawn appear, and we have been an hour on the road, the welcome note is heard in the distance of the bugles sounding the 'halt.' With great rapidity it passes from regiment to regiment, and dies

away in the rear. Cavalry dismount, infantry pile arms in the middle of the road, and for a few minutes the whole army disperses on each side of it. The favourite refreshment of officers is bread, cold tongue, and 'brandy *pawnee*,' which find their way out of innocent-looking holsters. And now we take off overcoats and monkey-jackets, which were needed when we started in the cold and damp night; the bluejackets fasten theirs over their shoulders, and the officers strap theirs to their saddles. The brief halt is too quickly at an end, and after a ten minutes' rest the advance again sounds down the line from bugler to bugler. All at once fall in, arms are unpiled, and, enlivened by our band, we again step out; now feet begin to ache, and boots to chafe; but the cheery music of the bands, bugles, or drums and fifes of the regiments marching next to us, generally the Rifles, infuses energy into the most footsore. We make three halts in a march of thirteen or fourteen miles, of which the last is the longest, to allow the quartermaster-general and his staff to ride on and mark out the camp. As the sun rises, the heat rapidly increases, and the camels and elephants are seen making short cuts across the fields, and keeping always clear of the road. When our bands have blown as much wind as they can spare into their instruments, our men strike up a song; and old windlass tunes, forecastle ditties, and many a well-known old ballad resound through the jungles and across the fertile plains of Bengal, and serve to animate our sailors and astonish the natives.

On the 2nd of January 1858, the naval brigade were engaged at the battle of Kallee-Nuddee. A party of seamen, under Lieutenant Vaughan, had been repairing the bridge across that river, when the Sepoys opened fire on him from a small gun in the opposite village. He returned it, and, crossing the bridge with three guns, held in check a body of the enemy's cavalry visible beyond the village. Brigadier Greathed's division and other troops were engaged all the time. Lieutenant Vaughan now pointed and fired one of his guns at a small gun of the enemy, which was concealed behind the corner of a house. His first shot struck the roof of the house; his second struck the angle of the wall about half-way down; and a third dismounted the gun, and destroyed the carriage. Captain Peel, who was standing by, said, "Thank you, Mr Vaughan; perhaps you will now be so good as to blow up the tumbrel." Lieutenant Vaughan fired a fourth shot, which passed near it, and a fifth, which blew it up, and killed several of the enemy. "Thank you," said Captain Peel, in his blandest and most courteous tones; "I will now go and report to Sir Colin."

The village was stormed and the enemy driven out by the 53rd Regiment, when the cavalry pursued and cut up the rebels terribly, capturing all their guns.

Soon after this, as Captain Peel and Captain Oliver Jones with three men of the 53rd were passing through the battery, five Sepoys jumped out of a ditch, and attacked them frantically. All were killed, Captain Jones shooting the last with his revolver,—one man of the 53rd, however, being dangerously wounded.

Eighteen or twenty bluejackets were attached to each gun, and with drag-ropes ran them about with the greatest rapidity. On the march they were dragged by bullocks; but if a gun stuck, the animals were taken out, and the wheels and drag-ropes manned by bluejackets; and having an elephant to push behind with his forehead, they never failed to extricate a gun from the worst position. This was carrying out to perfection the principle of a "steady pull and pull together."

On the 3rd of March the brigade were before Lucknow, and engaged in the taking of the Dilkoosah, when two were mortally wounded.

Captain Oliver Jones was at this time serving as a volunteer with HM 53rd Regiment. He was the second to mount a breach at the capture of one of the forts, when he received a wound on the knuckles, but cut down the fellow who gave it him.

The naval brigade guns were now posted to the right of the Dilkoosah, and near the river Goomtee. Mr Verney had a narrow escape. The enemy brought two guns down to the corner of the

Martiniere, and opened on them. A shot struck the ground close to where he was standing, and so completely surrounded him with dust that his comrades supposed he had been killed, and were surprised to see him standing in the same place when the dust cleared off.

Lieutenant Vaughan was now made a commander, but resumed his former duties.

On the 9th of March, the brigade's six eight-inch guns and two twenty-four pounders went down in front of the Dilkoosah, with four rocket-*hackeries*, the whole under command of Captain Vaughan, accompanied by Lieutenants Young, Salmon, Wratislaw, Mr Daniel, and Lords Walter Kerr and Arthur Clinton, midshipmen. Captain Peel was also there, with his two aides-de-camp, Watson and Lascelles. Unhappily, while looking out for a suitable spot in which to post some guns for breaching the Martiniere, he was severely wounded in the thigh by a musket-ball. The brave captain was carried to the Dilkoosah, where the bullet was extracted by the surgeon of the 93rd Highlanders. The brigade's guns were most actively engaged in battering the Begum's palace; and it was here, on the 12th, that Mr Garvey, mate, as he was riding fast on in front of a row of *cohorns* to deliver a message, and not perceiving that the quick-matches were alight, was struck dead by one of the shells. He was the second officer of the brigade killed, and a most promising young man.

All the guns of the brigade were on that memorable day very hotly engaged. Several had been posted behind some earthworks thrown up by the enemy. As the men could not see over the bank to point their guns, Captain Oliver Jones placed himself at the top, and, though thus becoming a clear mark for the enemy, with the greatest coolness directed their fire.

On the 13th the naval guns were placed in a more advanced battery. While warmly engaged with the enemy, some sandbags forming the front of the battery caught fire. A coloured man of the name of Hall, a Canadian, under a heavy fire of bullets from loopholes not forty yards distant, gallantly jumped out and extinguished some, and threw away others that were burning. In the performance of this service he was severely wounded. He was a man of athletic frame, and always remarkable for his steady good conduct. He afterwards received the Victoria Cross.

The next day, after Sir James Outram had, by his admirable manoeuvre, driven the rebels from their lines, Captain Vaughan being in front, Sir Colin Campbell met him, and desired him to bring up a gun's crew of bluejackets to man an abandoned gun, which was to be turned against the retreating enemy. Lord Walter Kerr was sent back for the gun's crew, and Captain Vaughan and Mr Verney proceeded to the gun itself, which was at the gate of an outer court of the Kaiser Bagh. They found that a body of Sepoys were defending themselves in an adjoining court, and that it was necessary to blow away the gate of it, that the troops might storm. It was for this object that Sir Colin ordered the guns to be turned against them. In the meanwhile, however, they kept a continual fire on the little band of British, from the walls and over and round the gate, whenever they approached the gun. Captain Vaughan then fired a few rounds at the gate, Mr Verney loading and sponging, three of the *Shannon's* bandsmen bringing up the powder and shot, and some of the men of the 38th, under command of Lieutenant Elles, running the gun up after every round. Near them, all the time, was a house full of loose gunpowder, while close to it was another in flames. A sentry, however, was posted to give warning in time, should the flames approach the loose powder. Captain Vaughan now went back to meet the gun's crew that had been sent for, and to show them the way, leaving orders with Mr Verney to keep up the fire. He discovered that the Sepoy charges were so heavy that the shot went clean through the solid gate every time he fired. By reducing the charges, the firing at last began to tell; and when the bluejackets came up, under command of Lieutenant Hay, the gate was blown open, and the court captured by the company of the 38th.

On the 16th of March, the guns of the naval brigade were

advanced to the Residency, whence they occasionally fired a shot over the town. On the 22nd, the last of the rebels evacuated Lucknow; and, on the 29th, the brigade handed over to the artillery, to go into park in the small Imaumbarah, the six eight-inch guns which they had brought from the *Shannon*. The word "*Shannon*" was deeply cut into each carriage, and must last as long as the wood exists. There they will remain, a memorial of what sailors can do on land. Here the active services of the gallant naval brigade ceased. Mr Verney had been sent to the Kaiser Bagh to bring out one of the King of Oude's carriages for the conveyance of Captain Peel to Cawnpore. He selected the best he could find, and the ship's carpenter padded it and lined it with blue cotton, and made a rest for his feet, and painted "HMS *Shannon*" over the royal arms of Lucknow. When, however, he saw it, he declined making use of it, saying that he would prefer travelling in a *doolie*, like one of his bluejackets. Alas! the *doolie* chosen for him had in all probability carried a smallpox patient, for he was shortly afterwards seized with that dire disease, under which, already weakened by his severe wound, he succumbed, and the country lost one of the most gallant captains in the naval service.

The brigade now once more turned their faces towards Calcutta, and on the 12th and following days of August rejoined their ship. On the 15th of September, the *Shannon* sailed for England.

The officers received their promotion as follows:—Commander Vaughan received the Order of C.B., an honour never before accorded to any officer of that rank, and after serving a year he was posted. Lieutenants Young, Wilson, Hay, Salmon, and Wratislaw were promoted to the rank of commanders; Dr Flanagan, assistant surgeon, was promoted to the rank of surgeon; Mr Verney, mate, was promoted to the rank of lieutenant; Mr Comerford, assistant paymaster, was promoted to the rank of paymaster; and each of the engineers and warrant-officers received a step. On passing their examination, all the midshipmen and naval cadets have been promoted.

The Victoria Cross was presented to Lieutenants Young and

Salmon, and to three bluejackets, "for valour" at the relief of Lucknow. The Indian medal with the Lucknow clasp was presented to each officer and man who formed part of the naval brigade. The following officers, who were present at the relief of Lucknow on the 19th of November, received also the "Relief of Lucknow" clasp:—Lieutenants Vaughan, Young, Salmon; Captain Grey, RN; Reverend EL Bowman, Dr Flanagan, Mr Comerford; Messrs. MA Daniel, REJ Daniel, Lord Walter Kerr, Lord Arthur Clinton, and Mr Church, midshipmen; Messrs. Bone and Henri, engineers; and Mr Brice, carpenter. Never was medal more highly prized or clasp more nobly won.

The following letter from Sir Edward Lugard to Captain Vaughan shows the high estimation in which the *Shannon*'s naval brigade was held by the military officers high in command:

> The *Shannon*'s Brigade advanced upon Lucknow with my division, and acted with it during the entire operations, as you well know. The men were daily—I may say hourly—under my sight, and I considered their conduct in every particular an example to the troops. During the whole period I was associated with the *Shannon*'s Brigade, I never once saw an irregularity among the men. They were sober, quiet, and respectful; and often I remarked to my staff the high state of discipline Sir W. Peel had got them into. From the cessation of active operations until I was detached to Azimghur, I commanded all the troops in the city; and all measures for the repression of plundering were carried out through me, and, of course, every irregularity committed was reported to me. During that period, not one irregularity was reported to me. Indeed, in the whole course of my life, I never saw so well-conducted a body of men... All I have written about the good conduct and discipline of the *Shannon*'s men would, I am convinced, be confirmed by the unanimous opinion of the army at Lucknow. Poor Adrian Hope and I often talked together on the subject; and many a time I expressed to Peel the high opinion I had of his men, and my admira-

tion of their cheerfulness, and happy, contented looks, under all circumstances of fatigue and difficulty.
Believe me, my dear Vaughan, sincerely yours—
*Edward Lugard*
Captain Vaughan, C.B.

Another naval brigade was formed from the officers and ship's company of HMS *Pearl*, which did good service, and won the respect of all associated with it.

CHAPTER 12

# The Second Chinese War
## 1856-1860

The Chinese Government, forgetting the lesson they had received in the former war with Great Britain, or believing that they could follow the bent of their inclinations with impunity, committed a series of aggressions on British subjects, which demanded our immediate interference. Sir Michael Seymour, the admiral on the station, commenced vigorous measures, without loss of time, to recall them to their senses, with the squadron and marines under his command. He began by opening fire on Canton in October. On the 5th of November he destroyed several Chinese war-junks; and on the 12th and 13th of that month, the Bogue Forts, mounting 400 guns, were captured. On the 12th of January 1857, the marines, with a detachment of the 59th Regiment, attacked the suburbs of the city of Canton, when a few casualties occurred both among the seamen and troops.

We now come to the month of May, when more active operations were commenced. Near Canton several creeks run into the Canton river, with which the English were but slightly acquainted; up these the war-junks had to take refuge whenever the British ships approached. Commodore Elliot heard that a large number of war-junks were collected some five miles up one of them, called Escape Creek, and accordingly, early on the 25th of May, he went on board the *Hong-Kong* gunboat, and got under weigh, followed by *Bustard*, *Staunch*, *Starling*, and *Forbes*, towing the boats manned from the *Inflexible*, *Hornet*, and *Tribune*.

Steaming into the creek, they before long came upon forty-one Mandarin junks, moored across the stream. Each junk had a long twenty-four or thirty-two pounder gun forward, and carried also four or six nine-pounders. The *Hong-Kong* gallantly led. No sooner had she got within range, than the Chinese, with much spirit, opened fire, the first shot striking her, and others following rattling thick and fast on board. The other gunboats coming up, formed in as wide order as possible, and opened fire. It was wonderful, considering the exposed position of the Chinese guns, that the crews so long stood the return shower of shot sent at them by the gunboats. In time, however, they began to show signs of not liking the treatment they were receiving. First one was seen to cut her cable, get out her oars, or hoist her sails, and, falling out of the line, turn her stern for flight up the creek.

The example set by one was quickly followed by others. The whole Mandarin fleet was soon in full flight, firing away, however, with their stern-chasers; but they were guns of light calibre, and were not well served, thus doing little damage. The junks were fast craft, and the crews pulled for their lives, to aid the sails, so that the steamers had to put on all speed to come up with them. They had not got far before the water shoaled. The gunboats drew upwards of seven feet, the junks less than three. One after the other the gunboats grounded. "On, lads, on!" cried the commodore, leaping into one of the boats towing astern; "never mind the vessels." Imitating his example, officers and men jumped into the boats, each boat having a gun in her bows; and after the junks they pulled with might and main. Away went the junks up the creek, the boats hotly pursuing them. The guns in the bows of the latter kept up a hot fire on the enemy, and told with great effect. The speed of several lessened, and, one after the other, numbers were overtaken. Though all hope of escape was gone, when a boat got alongside, the Chinese fired a broadside of grape into her, and then, leaping overboard on the opposite side, swam towards the shore, and were soon beyond pursuit among the rice-fields which bordered the banks of the stream. In this way sixteen junks were captured in succession, and destroyed in the principal channel. Ten more took refuge in a channel to the left, but a division of the boats was sent after them. No sooner, however, did the English appear, than the crews, setting fire to their vessels, abandoned them, and swam to shore. They burned like touch-paper, and were quickly destroyed. Another turned into an inlet on the right, but some boats were quickly after her; and so frightened were the crew, that they forgot to set her on fire, and she was thus towed out in triumph.

The heat of the sun was terrific, many men suffered from sunstroke, and the casualties from the shot of the enemy were considerable. Thirteen junks escaped by dint of hard pulling, and the commodore determined to have these as well as many more which he suspected were concealed in the various creeks.

Next day he accordingly blockaded the mouths of all the creeks. Captain Forsyth, in the *Hornet*, was stationed at the mouth to prevent escape, the *Inflexible* at that of Second Bar Creek, and the *Tribune* at the Sawshee channel entrance. This done, the commodore, with the gunboats and a large flotilla of the boats of the squadron in tow, proceeded up the Sawshee channel. For twelve miles no enemy was seen. At length, leaving the steamers, he pulled up another twelve miles, when suddenly he found himself in the midst of a large city, with a fleet of war-junks before him, one of large size and richly adorned, while a battery frowned down on the invaders. It was not a moment for hesitation. Every gun and musket was discharged at the enemy ahead, and then, with a cheer, the British seamen dashed alongside the big junk. As they climbed up the side the Chinese sprang on shore, and immediately a hot fire from *jingalls* was opened on the boarders. The marines at the same time were landed from the other boats, and, forming, prepared to charge the enemy. As they were about to do so, flames burst out from the houses near the big junk. "To the boats! to the boats!" was the cry of the officers on board her. It was discovered that a quantity of powder had been left in her, and that a train was laid from her to the shore. Not a moment was to be lost. Her captors sprang into their boats; the crew of the last, a pinnace, were leaping from her sides, when up she went, with a loud explosion. Several of the seamen were singed, if not more seriously hurt. The other twelve junks were immediately set on fire, while the gallant marines charged down the street, and put all the *jingall* firers to flight. No work could have been accomplished more effectually, though at severe loss, for one man in ten at least had been hit. The surgeons having attended to the hurts of the men, the boats' heads were once more turned down the creek. The crews had fitted them, from the captured junks, with an extraordinary variety of sails,—some of matting, others of coloured cloths, or any material which could be stretched on spars to hold wind. In this guise they returned to the steamers. The town thus unexpectedly entered was found to be Tunkoon.

### BATTLE OF FATSHAN

To the south of Canton, one of the numerous creeks of that river runs up to the city of Fatshan. Some considerable distance up this creek, and nearly south of Canton, is the long, low island called Hyacinth Island, making the channels very narrow. On the south shore of the creek is a high hill. On the summit of this hill the Chinese had formed a strong fort of nineteen guns. A six-gun battery was erected opposite it, and seventy junks were moored so as to command the passage. The Chinese fully believed that this position was impregnable. The British squadron had rendezvoused a short distance below this formidable obstruction of the navigation. The admiral was on board the little *Coromandel* steamer, and before dawn on the 1st of June he led the way up the channel, towing a whole flotilla of boats, with 300 soldiers on board them. The other steamers followed, all towing boats with red-and bluejackets on board. The *Coromandel* was steaming up the left-hand channel, when she ran on to a line of junks which had been sunk across the passage. The admiral had wisely chosen the time of dead low water to commence the ascent. Lieutenant Douglas leaped into a dinghy, and sounded on all sides. A passage was found close in shore; but the little steamer could not get off, and a heavy fire was opened on her from the nineteen-gun battery. In vain her crew ran from side to side to start her. Several were struck. The boats had been cast off, and landed the troops. Now Commodore Keppel came up in the *Hong-Kong*, and obtained leave to proceed through the channel Mr Douglas had discovered. The *Haughty*, with boats in tow, *Bustard* and *Forester*, followed. *Plover* stuck on the barrier; but *Opossum*, casting off her boats, dashed up the right-hand channel. Now boats of all descriptions raced up, each eager to be first, many a brave fellow being picked off as they passed through the showers of shot hurled on them from the Chinese batteries. The Chinese were showing themselves to be of sterner stuff than many had supposed. The garrison of the hill battery fought bravely.

Meantime the troops were climbing the heights, the admiral had landed, and so had Commodore Elliot and many other naval officers, leading their bluejackets. As the stormers got within fifty yards of the summit, the garrison fired a volley, and then retreated down the hill; nor could the fire of the marines, who had gained the fort, make them run. The fort gained, the naval officers hurried down to their boats and pulled up towards the junks, which, as the flotilla advanced, opened a heavy fire. As the boats dashed alongside, the Chinamen invariably discharged a round of grape, but generally too high to do damage; and the seamen boarding under it, they leaped overboard and swam on shore. Then junk after junk was set on fire and blown up. It being low tide, they were nearly all on shore, and could not escape. The *Haughty* ran stem on into one, and crumpled her up as if she had been paper. Thus seventy-two were either burnt or captured. Heavy firing was heard in the distance. Commodore Keppel had meantime gone up through the right-hand channel. His own steamer grounded, and so did the *Plover*; and he, therefore, with seven boats of the *Calcutta*, *Bittern*, and *Niger*, pulled on under the fire of the six-gun battery, and boarded a big junk, which, when the boats were scarcely free of her, blew up. On he went, right through the junks, till he came to an island causing two narrow channels. One was thickly staked. Across the other were moored twenty large junks, their guns so placed that they could sweep both channels. In vain the commodore attempted to dash through with his galley. Three boom-boats following took the ground. Grape, canisters, and round shot came tearing among them. Numbers were struck. Major Kearney, a volunteer, was torn to pieces; Barker, a midshipman of the *Tribune*, was mortally wounded; the commodore's coxswain was killed, and every man of his crew was struck. A shot came in right amidships, cut one man in two, and took off the hand of another. Lieutenant Prince Victor of Hohenlohe was leaning forward to bind up with his neck-cloth the arm of the seaman whose hand had been taken off, when a round shot passed between his head and that of the commodore, wounding two more of the crew. Had he been sitting in his place, it would have taken off his head. The boat, almost knocked to pieces, was filling with water. The commodore jumped on one of the seats, to keep his legs out of the water, when a third round shot went through both sides of the boat, not more than an inch below the seat on which he was standing. Many of the boats had now got huddled together, the oars of most being shot away. A boat of the *Calcutta* being nearest, Commodore Keppel and his officers got in, hauling all the wounded men after them. The commodore had a dog with him, "Mike" by name, and the animal having been a favourite of the coxswain, Tolhurst, and always fed by him, refused to leave his dead body, and remained in the wreck of the boat drifting up towards the junks. It became absolutely necessary to retire for reinforcements. As the boats began to pull down the stream towards the *Hong-Kong*, the Chinese in triumph redoubled their fire, setting up loud shouts and strange cries, and beating their gongs with increased vigour. One shot knocked away all the oars on one side of the *Calcutta*'s boat. The commodore had just directed Lieutenant Graham to get his boat, the pinnace, ready for his pennant, as he would lead the next attack in her, when a shot wounded Mr Graham, killing and wounding four others and disabling the boat. Mr Graham appeared to be a mass of blood, but it was that of a marine who stood next to him, and part of whose skull was forced three inches into another man's shoulder. The *Hong-Kong*, supported by the *Starling*, was meantime throwing shot and shell among the Chinamen, to which they responded with considerable vigour.

At length the deck of the *Hong-Kong* was reached. Her deck was covered with the wounded who had been brought on board; but the whole fire of the Chinese was now concentrated on her, and she was hulled twelve times in a few minutes. One shot struck a marine standing near the wounded, and he fell dead among them. The sound of the firing had, however, brought up numerous others boats. The commodore had got a piece of blue bunting ready to represent his broad pennant. "Let us try the row-boats once more, boys," he shouted, as he jumped into the *Raleigh*'s cutter. A true British seaman's shout was the answer to the proposal, and a sign that it was all up with John Chinaman. He might sink twenty boats, but thirty others would be ready to follow. On dashed the British boats. The Chinese did not wait their coming, but, cutting their cables, with oars and sails attempted to escape; still, however, keeping up a hot fire, and retiring in good order. Again three cheers rose from the British boats, and the chase commenced, not to end for seven miles. As the shot and shells from the English guns began to play on the junks, they ran on shore, the terrified crews leaping out and escaping. Junk after junk was captured, but some eight remained. Suddenly entering a fresh reach, the pursuers close astern of the pursued, the British found themselves almost in the middle of a large city, Fatshan itself, with shops and other houses lining the quays, and trading-junks along the banks. Five of the junks were headed, abandoned, and captured; three escaped, and they would have been farther pursued, had not a large body of troops—militia probably—turned out to repel the invaders. The commodore instantly landed his marines, who, firing a volley, made ready to charge. The Chinese braves, not liking their aspect, went about, and marched double-quick time into the town, where they could not be seen. Commodore Keppel proposed landing and fortifying himself in the city, and demanding a ransom; but a message from the admiral recalled him, and he had to give up his daring scheme. Most unwillingly he obeyed the mandate; and, having secured five junks, he towed them out astern of his flotilla, promising the Chinese that he would pay them another visit before long. As he went down the river, a dog was seen on the shore, and, plunging into the stream, the animal swam off to his boat. It was his faithful "Mike," who had escaped the shower of shot and shell and the hungry Chinese, and now recognised the boat of his master.

Of the fleet of war-junks captured, only five were saved from destruction; and for some time during the night they were burning away, sending their shot right and left, and occasionally one of them would explode. The British lost, in killed and wounded in these two engagements, no less than eighty-four men, and found to their cost that the Chinese were no contemptible opponents.

### Capture of Canton—29th December

Although the capture of Canton may be looked upon as a military exploit, the bluejackets took so large a share in it that it must not be passed over.

The British had now been joined by a considerable French force; and the united squadron having proceeded up the river, the troops prepared to land at Kupar Creek, on the north shore, just to the east of Napier's Island, on the 28th of December. The *Actaeon*, *Phlegethon*, and a squadron of English gunboats, followed by the French fleet, had in the meantime gone on, and anchored directly facing the city, opposing a line of forts along the banks of the river.

A naval brigade was formed under the command of Commodore Elliot, consisting of 1501 men, formed in three divisions,— the first under Captain Stuart, second under Captain Key, and third under Captain Sir R. McClure, who landed with the troops. At a signal given, the steamers and gunboats opened fire on the devoted city, and immediately the landing commenced. The fleet gave ample occupation to the Chinese, and drew off their attention from the operations of the troops. These now landed, and, while the fleet continued their slow and steady bombardment, marched to the capture of Lin's Fort, a powerful battery on a hill to the east of the town. The British naval brigade entered a village to the right, and from thence clambered up the height to storm the fort; but, as they rushed in, the Chinese rushed out and down the hill, while the bluejackets in hot haste made chase after them, led by Captains McClure and Osborne. On they went, rifle, cutlass, and bayonet pitted against *jingalls* and rockets. Meantime Lin's Fort blew up. While reconnoitring the walls to discover a suitable spot for placing the ladders, the much-esteemed and excellent Captain Bate, RN, was shot dead. Early on the morning of the 29th the signal for the assault was given. The English and French troops rushed on most gallantly to the attack. Of the bluejackets, Commander Fellowes was the first on the walls, from which, after a stout resistance, the Chinese were driven into the town, which, after a week, was occupied by the Allies.

The fleet, with the army on board, now proceeded to Tientsin, preparatory to an attack on Peking. The naval officers obtained deserved credit for the admirable way in which so large a fleet of eighty ships or more, including men-of-war and transports, was navigated, and for the perfect order and regularity with which the army was landed.

CHAPTER 13

# The Slave Trade

Ever since the settlement of Europeans on the continent of America and the West Indian Islands, a trade in slaves had existed to a very great extent. The slaves were taken from among the many tribes in the interior of Africa in large numbers, and transported across the Atlantic. The evils of such an inhuman custom were manifold, and were a very dark stain on civilisation. In course of time the conscience of England was awakened to the evil, and the nation decided to take some stern steps to put a stop to this trade in human beings, both in the interests of humanity and justice, and for the sake of Africa.

On 25th March 1807 the Royal assent was given to a Bill for the total abolition of the British slave trade on and after 1st January 1808. At first only a penalty of money was exacted from those who were convicted of slave-dealing. This, of course, was soon found to be without much effect, and in consequence, in 1811, slave-dealing was made punishable by transportation for fourteen years. Even this was found to be very inadequate. The slave-dealer knew that the risks of his being caught at his illicit trade were very small, and as the profits were very great he was quite willing to run that risk. Slave-dealing still continued with renewed zeal, and, if possible, greater cruelty than before.

In 1824, therefore, the offence was declared to be piracy, and punishable with death. In 1837, however, the punishment inflicted on British subjects for trading in slaves was changed to transportation for life.

A squadron of small vessels supposed to be suited for the purpose was forthwith equipped and sent to the African coast, to capture slavers wherever they could be found north of the equator, either embarking their cargoes or prepared to receive them, or with full ships, and whether up rivers, on the coast, or out at sea.

These expeditions were full of excitement for the bluejackets, and countless were the chases after slavers by the ships of the squadrons. The danger was great in many cases. The slave-dealers were of the lowest grade of humanity, and cruel to the last degree. The barbarity with which they tore away the poor blacks from their native country, and the cruelty with which they treated them on board, is indescribable.

The slaves were treated worse than animals, and many died during the voyage, but that mattered little to the slave-dealer, who had paid nothing for them, and who could find plenty more where they came from. Often the slave-dealers had on board, or rather in the hold of the ship, something like 900 slaves. When the decks were battened down during storms the tortures they endured were frightful. Often when the hatches were opened after a hurricane more than one-third of the slaves were found to be dead from suffocation or want of food, and often, sooner than have the trouble of hauling up the dead bodies, the hatches were battened down again and the poor slaves left in their misery till the end of the voyage, when perhaps another third were found to have died.

It was to prevent atrocities such as these that our sailors were called upon to perform such gallant deeds on the African Coast, and their gallantry and powers of endurance were never displayed to better purpose than during the chases and captures of slavers. Accounts of some of them are given, to show the sort of work our officers and men are called upon to perform to keep down this horrible evil.

### Capture of Brazilian Slaver *Firme* by the Boats of HMS *Dolphin*—1840

At daylight on the 30th May 1840, the *Dolphin* being under easy sail off Whydah, a brigantine was observed on the lee-bow.

All sail was immediately made in chase; but as the stranger increased her distance, the cutter, a twenty-foot boat, with nine men, including the officer, and the gig with six, were despatched at half-past six o'clock, under command of Mr Murray and Mr Rees, to endeavour to come up with and detain the chase before the setting in of the sea-breeze. Both boats being soddened from constant blockading pulled heavily, and the crews had been employed during a squally, rainy morning in trimming and making sail; but after a harassing pull of two hours and a half under a hot sun, they came up with the chase, the gig being rather ahead. The brigantine bore down upon her, opening a sharp and continued fire of musketry, which was returned, when both boats, after steadily reloading under her fire, cheered and boarded on each quarter. The sweeps of the brigantine were rigged out, which prevented their boarding by the chains, thereby rendering it difficult for more than one or two to get up the side at a time.

Mr Murray was the first on board; and though knocked back into the boat with the butt-end of a musket, which broke his collar-bone, he immediately clambered up the side again, in which act his left hand was nearly severed at the wrist with the blow of a cutlass. Another cut was made at his head, which he parried, cutting the man down. The bowman of the gig was shot through the heart while laying his oar in, and the bowman of the cutter in getting up the side. After a resistance of twenty minutes, the vessel was captured, most of the crew running below, firing their muskets as they retreated.

Mr Rees had previously proved himself a most zealous and active officer, particularly in the destruction of the slave factories at Corisco, by the boats of the *Wolverine*, Captain Tucker.

### Voyage of A Prize from Accra to Sierra Leone
### —12th August 1840 to 5th January 1841

The *Dores*, a schooner of about sixty feet in length and fifteen in breadth, had been taken at Quettah in June, and sent in charge of the *Dolphin*'s gunner to Sierra Leone. Six weeks afterwards she was found about twenty miles below Accra, having performed scarcely thirty miles of her passage, and lost almost all her prize-crew, including the gunner, from fever. Mr Murray, who had but just recovered from wounds received in the action with the *Firme*, was then put in command of her, with a crew of two men, two boys, and a prisoner boy, the only one who had survived the fever.

His orders were to proceed to Sierra Leone; and the indomitable perseverance with which he adhered to them, through formidable dangers and difficulties, together with his care for the men under his command during a voyage of 146 days, are well worthy of being recorded.

The only cabin which was at all habitable was eight feet in length, five in height at the centre, and three at the sides, the breadth decreasing from eleven to two and a half. It was entirely destitute of furniture, swarming with vermin, and, before the end of the voyage, the fumes of the rotting tobacco, with which the vessel was laden, clinging to the beams, formed a coat nearly an inch in thickness. This, with an awning of monkey skins, manufactured by themselves, was the only refuge for the young officer and his men. The fourth night of the voyage was ushered in by the most fearful squalls, which gradually freshened till about two in the morning, when a tremendous storm came on, and obliged them to bear up under bare poles; the seas washing over the little vessel, and the wind blowing in the most terrific manner until about seven, when it moderated and fell calm. The schooner was then observed to float much deeper than before, and on sounding, nearly three feet of water were found in the hold. The pump was immediately set to work, but it had hardly fetched when it broke and became useless. This was repaired by about sunset, and in two hours afterwards the vessel was cleared.

They then made sail and tacked, steering for Sierra Leone, till, on the morning of the 14th of September, they sighted land just below the river Sestos. Finding that they had but three days' provisions left, the commander determined to make them last six, and stood on, in the hope of weathering Cape Palmas. This was baffled by a tide that set down along shore; but, on the 20th of September, they anchored off Cape Coast Castle. They had no provisions remaining, but the governor supplied them with sufficient for forty days; and, having refitted the schooner, they put to sea again on a close, sultry morning, which was succeeded by a violent gale, lasting three days.

About two o'clock one afternoon, a rakish-looking brigantine was perceived standing towards the *Dores*; and judging her to be a slaver, the young officer called his crew together, and having loaded the muskets and got the cutlasses ready, they silently awaited her coming up, determined to defend themselves. To their great joy, when she got within two miles and a half of them, a strong breeze sprang up, which placed the schooner dead to windward, and in the morning the brigantine was out of sight. Their sails were now so worn that they were obliged to lower them, and drift about for a whole day to repair them. Having neither chronometer nor sextant, and only a quadrant of antique date, often ten and even twenty miles out of adjustment, the position of the vessel could only be guessed. The men behaved admirably during this weary time, employing themselves in cleaning their arms, fishing, or mending their clothes. The rain generally fell in torrents till the 4th October, when the day closed in with appearances threatening heavy weather. All preparations were made for the coming gale; the sails were lowered down with the exception of the fore-staysail, and everything lashed and secured. The fore-staysail was kept up in order to put the schooner dead before the wind.

At about five in the evening it became a dead calm, the atmosphere close, and all around dark. After about half an hour, a sound like heavy thunder was heard in the distance, and through the gloom a bank of foam was seen hastening towards the schooner; in a few minutes the staysail was stowed, and the wind caught her, gradually freshening until it burst upon her in all its fury; the rolling sea broke in upon her, and completely filled her upper deck; but the side bulwarks were open, and the sea found vent. Having battened his crew down below, Mr Murray lashed himself to the deck, and steered the vessel through the storm, which continued with heavy thunder and torrents of rain till about two in the morning, when, completely exhausted, he fell asleep, and was aroused by the crew (who, having knocked once or twice without reply, believed him to have been washed overboard) hammering at the skylight to get out. This gale so strained the schooner that the water gained two feet a day, and, to add to their disasters, one of the crew was ill for a fortnight.

From the 10th of October till the 4th of November, when land was again discovered, the *Dores* continued her course for Sierra Leone, experiencing the whole weight of the rainy season. It now became evident that she could not stem the current, for in the course of many days she had not made more than four or five miles. Mr Murray then determined to try again to reach Cape Palmas, by standing along the land; and thus nearly incurred a new danger from the natives, who assembled on the beach, armed with pikes and clubs, and as night drew on prepared to attack the schooner should she run on shore. Happily a slight breeze sprang up, which gave her steerage way, and enabled her to draw off the land. No resource remained but to shape her course again for Cape Coast Castle, to obtain provisions, their stock being exhausted. The governor made every effort to prevail on Mr Murray to relinquish the undertaking, which now appeared so hopeless, but he was resolute in staying by the charge entrusted to him; and, calling his men together, he gave them the choice of going on shore to await a passage down to the *Dolphin*. With one consent they replied that they would never leave him; holding to the old feeling of a true seaman, never to leave his officer at a time of difficulty till death parts them. Their provisioning was just completed when a fatal accident diminished the number of the crew. They had been bathing after their day's work, and one of them, a black, was still in the water, when he was seized by a shark, and so fearfully injured that he died before he could be got on board. The weary voyage recommenced, and, as before, their chief diversion was fishing. The sharks, skipjacks, dolphins, and bonetas which were caught were counted by hundreds, for they literally sailed through a sea of fish. Two parrots had been added to their crew, and were a great amusement, becoming so tame that they would obey their master's call, and follow him afterwards through the streets like a dog.

The 9th of December was marked by a serious disaster. Seeing a huge shark alongside, they had fastened a boneta as a bait to a piece of small line, and made a running bowline in the end of a peak-halliard with the fish towing a little ahead of it; the shark immediately saw it and swam after it; they were already on the bowline to run him up the side with his head a little out of water; gliding silently along, not two feet from them, he came up to the bowline, which was held wide open, while the bait was quietly hauled ahead until he was far enough through it; then, giving a sudden jerk on it, they closed it just behind the two side-fins and tried to catch a turn with the rope; but, quick as lightning, the shark gave a terrific plunge and tore it through their hands, when Mr Murray unfortunately got in the middle of the coil, and as the men had all let go, it had got a half-hitch round his leg, and in an instant he was drawn up and over the gunwale. Catching at the peak-halliards, which were belayed close to him, he held on with his only sound hand as he was flying overboard, the men also seizing him by the arm. Before he could be extricated, the limb was severely injured and torn. The only remedy which could be applied was bathing it in oil.

In the meantime the *Dores* progressed, though very slowly; she had become much more leaky, the cargo was completely rotten, and the stench drove them all on deck; nor could they heave a particle of it overboard, for then the vessel would have capsized, as she had no ballast in. The sails were perfectly rotten—so bad that the vessel was often a whole day without a stitch of canvas set when the wind fell light, that they might be repaired with monkey skins, of which there was a good stock on board.

The fourth month closed, and the schooner had not yet performed a voyage of ten days, from seven to fifteen miles a day being the progress lately made; but now the current seemed to favour her, for a change of forty miles a day was observed in the latitude, and the hearts of officer and men grew lighter, notwithstanding their miserable plight, always wet to the skin, and unable to change their clothes for days together. Two terrific storms were still to be encountered; and, at the commencement of the second, Mr Murray sent the men below, and remained alone on the deck, which he never expected to leave alive. The heat of each flash of lightning was felt as if from a fire; the rain falling in torrents, leaked in every direction through the deck, and the schooner was fast filling with water. At length the rain ceased, and the lightning became fainter, when they made sail again, pumped out, and proceeded till they had made sufficient northing for Sierra Leone. They then bore up east, and, on the 31st December, the colour of the water showed that they were nearing the land. On this day they kept their Christmas, and many were the hearty toasts they drank to those at home. It was not till the 6th January, 146 days from the commencement of their voyage, that they anchored off Sierra Leone, where it was fully believed that they were lost. Here Mr Murray found his promotion awaiting him for the capture of the *Firme*, and was at once invalided home.

## CAPTURE OF AN ARMED SLAVER BY A FOUR-OARED GIG—1844

On the 13th of August 1844, Mr John Francis Tottenham, mate of HMS *Hyacinth*, Commander Scott, performed a gallant and dashing exploit, which obtained for him his promotion to the rank of lieutenant, and the testimony of his commander to the coolness, decision, and gallantry displayed by him on the occasion. When off Fish Bay, on the West Coast of Africa, Mr Tottenham was sent in a four-oared gig, with one spare hand, to communicate with the Portuguese governor. The weather became thick, and he missed his port; but knowing that the *Hyacinth* was working along the coast, he anchored for the night, and pulled to the southward. On the morning of the 13th he discovered a brig at anchor without colours, and saw her slip and make sail, on which he gave chase. Being to windward, and the breeze light, he was enabled to approach her weather-beam, and fire a musket ahead, to induce her to heave to and show her colours. This and a second were disregarded; but a port was opened and a gun run out and brought to bear on the boat, which caused the officer to pull into her wake, when part of the crew of the brig commenced firing musketry, while the others got the gun on the poop, and pointed it at the boat.

Mr Tottenham now commenced firing as fast as the spare hand could load for him, being just able to keep way with the brig.

Four of the men on board the brig having been hit, her crew left the gun, and after firing muskets for twenty minutes, finding that they were unable to weather the land or tack without being boarded by the boat, they ran the brig on shore. Here her crew, to the number of eighteen, including three wounded men, abandoned her, leaving another mortally wounded on board.

In the course of the afternoon the brig was perceived from the mast-head of the *Hyacinth*, which stood in and anchored, and hove her off; when she proved to be of 200 tons, fully equipped for conveying about 1000 slaves, with two guns of four pounds calibre loaded, a barrel of powder, and a quantity of Langridge-shot, a number of muskets, swords, and bayonets on the deck. Almost every bullet expended in the gig was traced to the gun-carriage, or its immediate vicinity on the poop.

### A Pinnace Attacks a Slaver—1845

On the 12th of January 1845, Lieutenant Lodwick, first lieutenant of HM steamer *Growler*, Captain Buckle, who had been away for some time cruising in the pinnace on the look-out for slavers, fell in with a *felucca*, which, on seeing the pinnace, hove to. The lieutenant naturally expected that she would make no resistance, as she might have got away if she had chosen. When the pinnace, however, was within thirty yards of the *felucca*, a whole range of muskets was observed pointed over her bulwark. After this, Lieutenant Lodwick cheered his men on to get up to her before she discharged this fearful battery; but no sooner was the cheer uttered than the *felucca* opened on the boat. This was a staggerer for the British boat; but fortunately the slaver's crew fired too high (the *felucca* had now filled, and was going just as fast as the boat could pull). Lieutenant Lodwick—the rim of whose hat was shot through—at once returned the first volley with a round shot and 180 balls in a bag. A second volley from the *felucca* told with far more disastrous effect; two men were shot dead, and Lieutenant Lodwick and two men severely wounded—the lieutenant having been struck on the left knee and thigh. This left the pinnace with so few men, that, having also had six of her oars shot away, Lieutenant Lodwick was obliged to abandon the chase, and was picked up by the *Growler*, standing towards the *Gallinas*, boat and gear being literally riddled with shot.

Lieutenant Lodwick was promoted for his gallantry. The *felucca* had been chased by every vessel on the coast, and always got away clear. She was afterwards captured by a war-steamer, and bore evident marks of her conflict with the pinnace. There were about seventy men on board—English, French, and Americans—and she was commanded by an Englishman.

## Adventure of HMS Wasp—1845

As HMS *Wasp*, Captain Usherwood, was cruising in the Bight of Benin, near Lagos, on the 27th of February 1845, a strange sail was seen, and Lieutenant Stupart was immediately ordered in pursuit. At about eight o'clock in the evening he came up with her, and found her to be the *Felicidade*, a Brazilian schooner, fitted for the slave trade, with a slave-deck of loose planks over the cargo, and a crew of twenty-eight men. With the exception of her captain and another man, they were transferred to the *Wasp*; and Lieutenant Stupart, with Mr Palmer, midshipman, and a crew of fifteen English seamen, remained in charge of the prize. On the 1st of March, the boats of the *Felicidade*, under Mr Palmer, captured a second prize, the *Echo*, with 430 slaves on board, and a crew of twenty-eight men, leaving Mr Palmer, with seven English seamen and two Kroomen, on board the *Felicidade*. Several of the *Echo*'s crew were also sent on board as prisoners, with their captain. Soon afterwards Mr Palmer and his small crew were overpowered and murdered by the crew of the *Felicidade*, and an unsuccessful attempt made by the miscreants to gain possession of the *Echo*. The *Felicidade* was seen and chased on the 6th of March by HMS Star, Commander Dunlop. When she was boarded, no one was on her deck, the crew being concealed below; and on being found and questioned, they stated the vessel to be the *Virginie*, and accounted for their wounds by the falling of a spar; but there were traces of a conflict, and many tokens which proved that English seamen had been on board. She was then sent to Sierra Leone, in charge of Lieutenant Wilson and nine men.

Whilst on the passage, during a heavy squall, the schooner went over, filled, and sank, so as only to leave part of her bow rail above water. When the squall passed, the whole of the crew were found clinging to the bow rail. Some expert divers endeavoured to extract provisions from the vessel, but without success; and nothing but death stared them in the face, as the schooner was gradually sinking. Lieutenant Wilson ascertained that there were three common knives among the party, and it was resolved to make a raft of the main-boom and gaff, and such other floating materials as remained above water. These they secured by such ropes as could be cut and unrove from the rigging, and a small quantity of cordage was retained to make good any defects they might sustain by the working of the spars; a small topgallant studding-sail was obtained for a sail; and upon this miserable raft the ten persons made sail for the coast of Africa, distant 200 miles, without rudder, oar, compass, provisions, or water.

Being almost naked, and washed by every wave, their sufferings were very great. Destitute of food or fresh water, scorched by a burning sun during the day, and chilled with cold during the night, they thus remained twenty days. Delirium and death relieved the raft of part of its load of misery, two blacks being the first to sink under their sufferings.

The question naturally suggests itself, How did the survivors support life? Some persons would be almost afraid to put the question, or hear the answer. There is nothing, however, to wound our feelings, but much to admire in the admirable conduct of Lieutenant Wilson and his men during these melancholy and miserable twenty days. Showers of rain occasionally fell; they caught some water in their little sail, which they drank, and put some into a small keg that had floated out of the vessel. The sea was almost always breaking over the spars of the raft, which was surrounded by voracious sharks.

The famishing sailors actually caught with a bowling-knot a shark eight feet in length, with their bare hands, and hauled it upon the raft; they killed it, drank the blood, and ate part of the flesh, husbanding the remainder. In this way three other sharks were taken, and upon these sharks the poor fellows managed to prolong their lives till picked up (in sight of the land) in what may be termed the very zero of living misery. Lieutenant Wilson and four seamen survived, and recovered their strength. Order and discipline were maintained upon the raft; fortitude, forethought, a reliance upon Divine Providence, and good conduct, enabled these Englishmen to surmount such horrible sufferings, while the Kroomen and Portuguese sank under them.

### CAPTURE OF A SLAVER—1845

HMS *Pantaloon*, ten-gun sloop, Commander Wilson, had been for two days in chase of a large slave-ship, and succeeded in coming up with her becalmed, about two miles off Lagos, on the 26th May 1845. The cutter and two whale-boats were sent, under the command of the first lieutenant, Mr Lewis D.T. Prevost, with the master, Mr J.T. Crout, and the boatswain, Mr Pasco, some marines and seamen, amounting to about thirty altogether, to make a more intimate acquaintance with the stranger. The pirate gave the boats an intimation of what they were to expect as they neared, by opening on them a heavy fire of round shot, grape, and canister, in so spirited a style, that after returning the compliment by a volley of musketry, the boats prepared for hard work. Animated by the show of resistance, each boat now emulated the other in reaching the enemy, the pirate continuing a sharp fire as they steadily advanced, the marines as briskly using their muskets. In half a hour from the discharge of the first gun from the slaver, the boats of the *Pantaloon* were alongside; Lieutenant Prevost and Mr Pasco on the starboard, and Mr Crout, in the cutter, on the port side. The pirate crew, sheltering themselves as much as possible, nevertheless continued to fire the guns, loading them with all sorts of missiles, bullets, nails, lead, etcetera; and, amidst a shower of these, our brave sailors and marines dashed on board. Lieutenant Prevost and his party, in the two boats, were soon on the deck of the prize. The master boarded on the port bow, and, despite the formidable resistance and danger, followed by one of his boat's crew, actually attempted to enter the port as they were firing the gun from it. He succeeded in getting through, but his seconder was knocked overboard by the discharge. The gallant fellow, however, nothing daunted, was in an instant up the side again, taking part with the master, who was engaged in a single encounter with one or two of the slaver's crew. Having gained the deck after a most determined resistance, they now encountered the pirates hand to hand, when the cutlass and bayonet did the remainder of the work. Lieutenant Prevost finally succeeded in capturing the vessel, but the pirates fought desperately; and it was not until seven of their number lay dead on the deck, and seven or eight more were severely wounded, that they ran below and yielded. In the encounter, two British seamen were killed; the master and boatswain, and five others were severely wounded. Lieutenant Prevost received immediate promotion.

### An Attempt to Recapture a Prize—1847

On the 22nd of July 1847, HMS *Waterwitch*, with HMS *Rapid* in company, captured the Brazilian brigantine *Romeo Primero*, which was subsequently given in charge to Lieutenant W.G. Mansfield, RN, and four seamen, to be conveyed to Saint Helena for adjudication. Owing to adverse winds, and the unmanageable qualities of the prize, the officer in command found it necessary to alter his destination, and to bear up for Sierra Leone.

On the 11th of August, about midday, two of the crew being engaged aloft, and the others in the bunks, where the arms were stowed, the lieutenant being at the moment pulling a rope which had been recently spliced, was murderously assailed from behind by one of the prisoners, with an axe used for chopping firewood. There were four of them who were during the daytime allowed the liberty of the vessel. At the same moment, the other three prisoners furiously attacked the sailors in the bunks, who, from the unexpected nature of the assault, were driven from their post wounded and unarmed. Lieutenant Mansfield, laying hold of a piece of firewood, gallantly but unequally contended with a Brazilian armed with a cutlass. In the course of a desperate struggle, the officer received no fewer than nine wounds, more or less severe; a greatcoat which he wore being, under Providence, the means of saving him from instant death. The two sailors who had been occupied in the shrouds, having reached the deck, of course unarmed, the lieutenant, nearly exhausted by profuse haemorrhage, made a violent effort to join them, in which he fortunately proved successful, though in his progress one of the prisoners discharged at him a marine's musket, the contents of which took effect, inflicting a most dangerous wound in his head, and bringing him for an instant to the deck. Having succeeded in recovering his feet and gaining his men, he encouraged them to rush aft upon their armed antagonists—a piece of service which three of their number performed in the most daring manner; the fourth seaman (since dead) being hors de combat from his wounds, and the lieutenant himself fainting at the instant from loss of blood. The intrepidity of the three British tars rendered them more than a match for their armed antagonists, whom they speedily overpowered, one of the prisoners leaping overboard and perishing in the waves. Believing their officer to be killed, the seamen, in the excitement of the moment, were about to hurl the surviving prisoners over the gangway, when Lieutenant Mansfield, partially reviving, ordered them to be imprisoned, that their wounds should be washed, and that they should be reserved to be dealt with by the authorities at Sierra Leone.

On the 1st of September the *Romeo Primero*, the scene of this bloody encounter, entered the port. Lieutenant Mansfield, who, since the day of the conflict, had scarcely been able to stir hand or foot, was promptly conveyed to sick-quarters, and for many days his life was entirely despaired of by his medical attendants. The gallant little crew, all wounded, were also looked after in the best manner which skill and sympathy could suggest; but two were soon beyond the reach of human succour,—one dying of the direct consequences of his wounds, and the second of fever induced by them. After a fortnight of extreme danger on shore, Lieutenant Mansfield showed symptoms of recovery, and in the same year received the rank of commander.

### Attempt to Retake a Prize—1848

The *Grecian* having captured a clipper Brazilian hermaphrodite brig, with nearly 500 slaves on board, Lieutenant D'Aguilar was placed in charge of her as prize-master, with ten men, and ordered to proceed to Bahia, the sloop following him thither. The prize duly arrived, and anchored at Bahia before the *Grecian*, and not the slightest suspicion was entertained but that she was safe. In the course of the day, however, Lieutenant D'Aguilar received some hints to the effect that a combination was being made on shore among the slavers to attempt to retake the prize; and, although nothing definite was communicated, it was sufficient warning to him to be on the alert, and to take precautions which saved him and his men from being massacred. The evening passed off without disturbance; but about ten o'clock at night several boats from the shore were seen pulling for the brig, containing, it was estimated, 150 Brazilians. As they neared the prize, they were hailed, and ordered to keep off, but with some boldness they advanced alongside. The strangers having approached too near to be agreeable,

Lieutenant D'Aguilar endeavoured to check them by a discharge of musketry. This commenced a most severe conflict, the fire being returned by the pirates as they dashed alongside and attempted to board. That firmness and undaunted bravery, however, which is characteristic of British seamen, was here displayed in an eminent degree; and the Brazilians, with their overpowering numbers, were completely beaten off by Lieutenant D'Aguilar and his little band, with a loss, on the enemy's side, it is said, of upwards of ten killed and thirty wounded. As may naturally be supposed, where the contest was one at close quarters, and where each of the gallant defenders had so many assailants to wait upon, they did not come out of the melee unscathed. Scarcely one of them escaped a mark, and several of them were severely wounded. Lieutenant D'Aguilar received many hurts about the head. It subsequently transpired that it was the intention of the Brazilians to have silently got alongside the vessel, and to have secured the prize-crew. They would then have cut the cables and made sail, to land the cargo of slaves at another part of the coast. This affair was the theme of general applause in the squadron on the station.

CHAPTER 14
# The Recapture of the Emily Saint Pierre by Captain William Wilson
*1862*

The recapture of the *Emily Saint Pierre* reminds us of the fighting days of the wars with France and America, when several similar events took place; but during the whole course of English naval history we find no deed more gallant or more worthy of record. The *Emily Saint Pierre* was a large Liverpool East Indian trader, commanded by Captain William Wilson. She left Calcutta on the 27th of November 1861, with orders to make the coast of South Carolina, to ascertain whether there was peace or war. If peace had been declared, Captain Wilson was to take a pilot and enter the port of Charleston; if there was a blockade, he was to proceed to Saint John's, New Brunswick.

On the 8th of March 1862, he considered his vessel to be about twelve miles off the land, when a steamer was made out approaching. When the steamer, which proved to be a Federal vessel of war, the *James Adger*, came within hail, the *Emily Saint Pierre* was ordered to heave to, and was soon afterwards boarded by two boats, whose officers and crews took possession of her. Filling on the main-yard, they steered for the Federal squadron. Captain Wilson was now ordered into the boat, and carried on board the flagship, when he was informed by flag-officer Goldboursh that his vessel had saltpetre on board, and that consequently she was a lawful prize to the Federal

Government, but that he might take a passage on board her to Philadelphia. He replied that his cargo was not saltpetre, that his ship was British property, and that he could not acknowledge her a lawful prize.

On returning to his ship in about an hour, he found that all his crew had been taken away except the cook and steward, and that a fresh ship's company had been placed on board, consisting of Lieutenant Stone, a master's mate, twelve men, and an engineer, a passenger, fifteen in all. Having weighed anchor, they proceeded to sea. Captain Wilson felt confident of the illegality of the capture, and that if he could regain possession of his ship, he was justified in making the attempt. He had studied the characters of his cook and steward, and knew that he could trust them. He waited his opportunity. There was, however, not much time to spare. The 21st of March arrived. The commanding officer, Lieutenant Stone, had the watch on deck. It was about half-past four, and still dark, when Captain Wilson called his steward and cook into his state-room, and told them that he was resolved to regain his ship or lose his life. He asked their assistance, which they at once promised to afford. He then gave them each a pair of irons, which he had secured, and a sheet, and told them to follow him, as the moment for action had arrived. The master's mate was asleep in his berth. Captain Wilson opened the door, and walked in. After handing out his revolver and sword, he grasped the mate's hands. In an instant the gag was in his mouth, and the irons were fixed. The brave captain, with his two followers, then went to the passenger's cabin, and having taken the arms from his berth, secured him in the way they had the mate. The most difficult part of the undertaking was now to overcome the commanding officer, who, unsuspicious of danger, was walking the deck of his prize. However, retaining wonderful coolness, and undaunted by the hazard he ran, Captain Wilson went on deck, as if he had just turned out, and joined Lieutenant Stone in his walk, making some remarks as to the state of the weather. After walking for about ten minutes, he induced him to go down into the cabin to look at the chart which he had himself been examining, taking up on his way, as he followed, a belaying-pin. Now was the critical moment—the cook and steward stood in ambush behind the door. They reached the door of the after-cabin, where the chart was spread out, when, lifting up the belaying-pin, Captain Wilson told the lieutenant that if he moved he was a dead man, and that the ship should never go to Philadelphia; when the cook and steward, springing on him, had in a moment the irons on his wrists and the gag in his mouth, and he was pitched without ceremony into a cabin, and the door locked upon him. The crew had next to be mastered. Three were walking the deck, another was at the helm, and a fifth was on the look-out forward.

With truly wonderful nerve and command of voice, Captain Wilson called the three men aft, and pointing to the hatchway of the store-room, near the helm, told them that a coil of rope was wanted up. He then shoved off the hatch, and as he showed them the corner where it was, they all three jumped down. Quick as lightning he replaced the hatch, which his followers secured, while he warned the man at the helm that his life would pay the penalty if he moved or uttered a word. The look-out was then called aft, and being seized, was asked if he would assist in navigating the ship to a British port. On his declining to do so, he was handcuffed and secured in a cabin. Captain Wilson then called the watch, knowing well that they would not all come on deck together. He was consequently able to secure two before the suspicions of the rest were aroused. The third, however, drew his knife as the steward was about to seize him, when the latter shot him in the shoulder with his pistol, and he was seized. The remaining men, jumping on deck, were knocked over and secured.

Once more Captain Wilson had entire command of his ship, but with a crew of two men, neither of whom could even steer, nor were they accustomed to go aloft; while he had fifteen prisoners below, who would naturally lose no opportunity of retaking the ship. His greatest difficulties were only now beginning. What consciousness of his superlative seaman-like qualities, what perfect and just self-reliance he must have possessed, to have undertaken the task of navigating a ship completely across the Atlantic with such means at his disposal! Considerate and generous, as well as brave, as soon as he had shaped a course for England, he went below, and announced to Lieutenant Stone that the ship was his own again; but offered to take the gag out of his mouth and the irons off his wrists if he would consent to remain a prisoner in his berth, and make no attempt to regain possession of the ship.

To this Lieutenant Stone consented, and dined at table every day under guard, while the crew were supplied with an ample allowance of bread, beef, and water. Four of their number, after some consideration, volunteered, rather than remain prisoners, to lend a hand in working the ship; but as they were landsmen, they were of no use aloft. It seems surprising that Captain Wilson should have trusted them; but undoubtedly his bravery must have inspired them with such awe that they dared not prove treacherous.

But few days had passed after he had commenced his homeward passage, with his crew of six landsmen, than it came on to blow so hard that he had to close reef the topsails. Placing his cook and steward at the helm, he made the other men take reef tackles to the capstern, while he went alone aloft, lay out on the yard, passed the earrings, and tied the reef-points, keeping an eye all the time at the helm, and directing his two faithful men by signs how to steer. The wind increased till it blew a heavy gale, and the sea getting up, the tiller by a sudden jerk was carried away. He now began for the first time, perhaps, to have fears that he might not after all make his passage; but undaunted, he set to work to repair the mischief as well as he was able. His strength and energies, as well as those of his brave companions, were tried to the utmost. They had both to navigate the ship, to watch the four men who had been liberated, and to feed and attend to their prisoners.

Providence favoured them; the weather moderated, the wind was fair, and without accident Captain Wilson brought the *Emi-*

*ly Saint Pierre* into the Mersey thirty days after he had retaken her, having accomplished a passage of nearly 3000 miles. As an act of individual courage, forethought, coolness, nerve, and the highest seaman-like qualities, the recapture of the *Emily Saint Pierre* stands unsurpassed by any performed by a sailor of any period, rank, or country.

Captain Wilson received the welcome he so richly deserved on his arrival at Liverpool, from the mercantile as well as all other classes. The Council of the Mercantile Marine Service presented him with a gold medal, and silver medals with suitable inscriptions to the steward and cook; they also each of them received a purse with twenty guineas, and 170 merchants of Liverpool bestowed on Captain Wilson the sum of 2000 guineas; while numerous other presents were made by various companies, eager to show him in what high estimation his gallantry was held. His officers and crew who had been made prisoners by the Federals, on their arrival at Liverpool after their release, presented to him a valuable sextant, to show their sense of his kindness to them during the voyage from India, and of his noble conduct.

CHAPTER 15

# Arctic Exploring Expeditions

## THE NORTH-WEST PASSAGE

The discovery of a passage from the Atlantic to the Pacific Ocean has been the darling project of numberless Englishmen of science as well as navigators, from the time of Henry the Eighth down to the present day. A short account of the various expeditions, and of the adventures of the gallant men who have made the attempt, would alone fill a volume. By these expeditions, unsuccessful though they mostly were in accomplishing their object, the names of many of the bravest and best of England's naval commanders have become immortalised. Well indeed may Englishmen be proud of men such as Ross, Parry, Clavering, Lyon, Beechey, and Franklin, and of others who have in still later days exhibited their dauntless courage and perseverance in the same cause—Collinson, McClure, McClintock, Sherard Osborn, Forsyth, and many more.

Nowhere can all the noble qualities which adorn the British seaman be more fully called forth than during a voyage in the Arctic seas, and the detention to which he is subject for years together on its ice-bound shores. From the first entering these regions, dangers beset him. Suddenly he finds his vessel among immense fields of floating ice, through which he can with difficulty force a passage or escape shipwreck. Then, in the darkness of night, icebergs of vast height are seen close aboard, towering above the mast-heads, the sea dashing with fury round their bases, from which, should he not scrape clear, his destruction is certain. Sometimes, to prevent his vessel being drifted on icebergs, or the rocky shore, or fields of ice, to leeward, he secures her on the lee side of some large berg. The base of the mass beneath the water is continually melting; and, while he fancies himself secure, it decreases so much as to lose its balance, and its lofty summit bending down, it may overwhelm him in its ruins. Then, again, large masses become detached from its base, and, rising up violently from far down in the sea, strike the bottom of the vessel with terrific force, capable of driving in her planks and breaking her stout timbers. Often, also, he has to saw his way through sheets of ice, cutting out canals with untiring perseverance to gain a piece of clear water beyond. Sometimes his vessel is so tightly frozen within a field of ice that he has no power to extricate her; then the field, urged by the tides or wind, moves on at a rapid rate for hundreds of miles, till it encounters some other field or a projecting shore. Now commences a scene of horror which may well make the stoutest heart tremble. The field breaks into thousands of fragments; huge masses of many hundred tons weight, and larger than his ship, are thrown up, one on the other, rising almost as if they had life, till they tower far above the sides of his vessel, and appear ready every instant to crush her, as she lies helplessly among this icy mass of a seeming ruined world. Sometimes a huge lump, bigger than the ship herself, becomes attached to her bottom; and as the mass around her melts, it rises to the surface, and throws her on her beam-ends. Sometimes, as she is sailing in an open space, two fields suddenly close in on her. If her crew have time to cut a dock in the field nearest her, or find a bay ready formed, she may escape; if not, when the fields meet, her stout ribs are crushed in as if they were of wax, and the explorer is fortunate if he escapes to the ice with some of his boats and a few provisions and clothes before his vessel disappears, to encounter a voyage without shelter in that frigid region, till he falls in with some whale ship, or can gain its inhospitable shores. But suppose he escapes the dangers of the sea I have described, and many others, and takes shelter for the winter in some bay or gulf, ice-bound, he must remain during the winter without any communication with the rest of his fellow-creatures besides those who form his own adventurous band. The sun sinks below the horizon, and it is not seen again for months together; darkness is around him, and one dreary mass of snow covers the face of nature. The intense cold prevents him often from venturing beyond the shelter with which he has surrounded his vessel; or if he is tempted to do so, frost-bites may attack his hands and his feet, and deprive him of their use. Sometimes the Arctic explorer has had to journey for weeks together across the barren waste of ice or snow-covered ground, dragging his sledge after him, and sleeping night after night under the thin roof of a canvas tent; and, as summer draws on, often wet through from the melting snow, without an opportunity of drying his clothes. Seldom has he an abundance, and often he suffers from a scarcity, of provisions; while, if his strength fails him from illness or injury, he can scarcely hope to regain his ship alive. The first exploring expedition which was sent out during the reign of Queen Victoria was placed under the command of Sir George Back, in the *Terror*; but winter setting in early, his ship was caught by the ice, thrown on her beam-ends, and nearly destroyed. Though in a dreadfully shattered condition, she was providentially enabled to return home. It was not till the year 1845 that a new expedition by sea was determined on, and the command given, at his earnest request, to Sir John Franklin—an expedition over the fate of which for many long years hung a mysterious uncertainty, full of pain and anxiety. Notwithstanding the hazardous nature of the work in which they were to be engaged, numbers of officers and men eagerly pressed forward as volunteers to serve under the veteran Arctic explorer. The chief difficulty was in selecting the most fit among the many applicants, and happy did those consider themselves who were chosen.

The following is a list of the officers who were finally appointed to the expedition:

*Erebus*. Captain, Sir John Franklin, KCH; Commander, James Fitzjames; Lieutenants, Graham Gore, Henry T. Le Vesconte,

James William Fairholm; mates, Charles T. des Vaux, Robert O'Sargent; second master, Henry F. Collins; surgeon, Stephen Stanley; assistant surgeon, Harry D.S. Goodsir; paymaster and purser, Charles H. Osmer; master, James Reid, acting; fifty-eight petty officers, seamen, etcetera. Full complement, seventy.

*Terror.* Captain, Francis R.M. Crozier; Lieutenants, Edward Little, George H. Hodgson, John Irving; mates, Frederick J. Hornby, Robert Thomas; ice-master, T. Blakey, acting; second master, G.A. Maclean; surgeon, John S. Peddie; assistant surgeon, Alexander McDonald; clerk in charge, Edwin G.H. Helpman; fifty-seven petty officers, seamen, etcetera. Full complement, sixty-eight; making in all one hundred and thirty-eight souls.

The expedition sailed from England, May the 26th, 1845. They arrived at the Whalefish Islands, a group to the south of Disco, on the 4th of July. On the 26th they were seen moored to an iceberg, in 74 degrees 48 minutes north latitude, and 66 degrees 13 minutes west longitude, by a Hull whaler, the *Prince of Wales*, Captain Dannet. The ships had then on board provisions for three years, on full allowance, or even four, with the assistance of such game as they might expect to obtain. Everyone on board had resolved to persevere to the utmost in pushing their way through any channel which might offer a prospect of success towards the west; but the letters of Captain Fitzjames especially seemed to point clearly to Wellington Channel as the passage they would most probably first attempt. No news of the expedition having reached England up to the year 1847, some slight apprehensions began to be felt, though the general hope was that Sir John had pushed on perhaps into the Polar basin, and might make his appearance by way of Behring's Straits. However, it was thought right in 1848 to despatch another expedition to search for the missing ships. Two vessels were commissioned for that purpose, and placed under the command of Sir James Ross, an officer who has been nearer the northern and southern poles than any other human being. The ships were not ready for sea till the 12th of June. They were fitted to contend with the dangers of the Polar seas in a way no former ships had been, and every means that could be devised for the comfort and convenience of their crews were liberally supplied; while the officers and men were influenced by an earnest zeal to discover their missing countrymen, and to rescue them from the forlorn condition in which it was too probable they were placed. Such have been the motives which have induced, year after year, numbers of other gallant officers and men to volunteer their services to encounter the terrific dangers and hardships of a Polar voyage to search for Sir John Franklin and his brave followers. Who also has not heard of the noble efforts and sacrifices the late Lady Franklin made to despatch expedition after expedition in search of her gallant husband? and with what untiring zeal, and deep, earnest devotion, she and his faithful niece laboured on, month after month, and year after year, with talents, mind, and all their best energies devoted to the cause? All honour be to those noble ladies, worthy to be loved and reverenced by all who love and respect the British navy, and admire the gallant spirit which imbues it.

But to return to our narrative. Our space will not allow us to give more than a very brief sketch of the several searching expeditions which have been sent out, and the names of the ships and officers composing them.

The first, then, was that under Captain Sir J. Ross, consisting of—*Enterprise*, 540 Tons. Captain, Sir James C. Ross; Lieutenants, R.J.L. McClure, F.L. McClintock, and W.H.J. Browne; master, W.S. Couldery, acting; surgeon, W. Robertson, acting; assistant surgeon, H. Matthais; second master, S. Court; clerk, Edward Whitehead. Total complement, sixty-eight. *Investigator*, 480 Tons. Captain, E.J. Bird; Lieutenants, M.G.H.W. Ross, Frederick Robinson, and J.J. Barnard; master, W. Tatham; surgeon, Robert Anderson; mates, L. John Moore and S.G. Cresswell; second master, John H. Allard; assistant surgeon, E. Adams; clerk in charge, J.D. Gilpin. Total complement, sixty-seven.

The expedition left England on the 12th of June 1848, and reached Barrow's Straits by the end of August. Sir James Ross then endeavoured to find a passage through Wellington Channel; but it was so completely blocked up with ice that he was compelled to give up the attempt that year as hopeless. The ice closing in on the ships at an unusually early period, after running great risk of being crushed, Sir James took refuge in Leopold Harbour for the winter. Hence several expeditions were sent out on foot. Sir James Ross and Lieutenant McClintock set out in May, with sledges, each accompanied by six men, and explored the whole of the north and west coasts of North Somerset; and, being absent thirty-nine days, returned to the ships on the 23rd of June. Meantime Lieutenant Barnard started for the northern shore of Barrow's Straits, crossing the ice to Cape Hind. Lieutenant Browne visited the eastern shore of Regent Inlet, and Lieutenant Robinson the western shore, and reached several miles to the southward of Fury Beach. No traces were discovered, however, of Sir John Franklin, but every device that could be thought of was employed to let his party know of the position of the ships. At Fury Beach, Lieutenant Robinson discovered Sir John Ross' house, and much of the provisions left there by the *Fury* in 1827 still remaining, and in excellent condition. On the 28th of August the vessels quitted Leopold Harbour, where, at Whaler Point, a large supply of provisions, fuel, and a steam-launch were left, in the hopes that some of Sir John's party might visit the place. Again, from the 1st to the 25th of September, the vessels were so closely beset with ice, that it was feared they might be compelled to spend another winter in those regions, even should they escape being crushed to fragments. Happily they got clear, after drifting into Baffin's Bay, and reached England in November.

The *North Star*, an old twenty-six-gun frigate, of 500 tons, had in the meantime, in the spring of 1849, been despatched with provisions for Sir James Ross, under command of Mr J. Saunders. Having got blocked in by the ice for sixty-two days, she was compelled to winter in Wolstenholme Sound, on the western coast of Greenland.

Immediately on the return of the *Enterprise* and *Investigator* they were re-commissioned, and placed under the command of

Captain B. Collinson, with directions to proceed to Behring's Straits, to resume the search in that direction. HMS *Plover*, Commander Moore, was already there, employed in surveying the north-western coasts of the American continent.

The following were the officers appointed to them:

*Enterprise*. Captain, R. Collinson; Lieutenants, G.A. Phayre, J.J. Barnard, and C.T. Jago; master, R.T.G. Legg; second master, Francis Skead; mate, M.T. Parks; surgeon, Robert Anderson; assistant surgeon, Edward Adams; clerk in charge, Edward Whitehead. Total complement, sixty-six.

*Investigator*. Commander, B.J. McClure; Lieutenants, W.H. Haswell and S.G. Cresswell; mates, H.H. Saintsbury and R.J. Wyniatt; second master, Stephen Court; surgeon, Alexander Armstrong, MD; assistant surgeon, Henry Piers; clerk in charge, Joseph C. Paine. Total complement, sixty-six.

Mr Miertsching, a Moravian missionary, who had spent five years on the coast of Labrador, was appointed to the *Enterprise* as interpreter. The vessels sailed from Plymouth on the 20th of January 1850, and reached the Sandwich Islands on the 29th of June. Meantime the *Herald*, Captain Kellet, had been ordered up from Oahu to Behring's Straits, to assist in the search. At Petropaulski she met the Royal Thames Yacht Club schooner *Mary Dawson*, owned by Mr Shedden, who had come along the Chinese coast to Behring's Straits, also in search of Sir John Franklin. After exploring for some time in company, they were compelled by the ice to leave the Straits; but the *Plover* wintered there, while Lieutenant Pullen led a boat expedition of a most arduous nature along the northern shores of America, towards the Hudson's Bay establishment on the Mackenzie River. Sir John Richardson also led a land party from the south to the Polar seas, but was compelled to return without discovering any trace of the expedition.

In 1846, also, the Hudson's Bay Company sent out an expedition, commanded by Dr John Rae, to survey the unexplored portion of the American continent, between the farther point reached by Dease and Simpson and the strait of the Fury and *Hecla*.

In the year 1850 several expeditions were sent out. The first consisted of HMS *Resolute* and *Assistance*, Captain Ommaney, with the screw-steamers *Pioneer*, Lieutenant Osborn, and *Intrepid*, Lieutenant Cator, as tenders, under the command of Captain Horatio T. Austin, in the *Resolute*. Their chief aim was to visit Melville Island, and to explore the shores of Wellington Channel, and the coast about Cape Walker. The ships were provisioned for three years, and a transport completed their supply at Whalefish Islands.

No expedition ever left England with a greater prospect of success, all engaged in it being enthusiastically resolved to use every exertion to advance the noble cause.

The ships were commissioned on the 28th of February 1850, and left England the 3rd of May. On the 16th of June they arrived at the Whalefish Islands, where they received the remainder of their supply of provisions from the transport.

At the same time that Captain Austin's expedition was fitting out, another was arranged and placed under the command of Mr William Penny, an experienced whaling captain of Dundee, to act in concert with it. Mr Penny, by the directions of the Admiralty, proceeded to Aberdeen and Dundee, where he purchased two new clipper-built vessels, which were named the *Lady Franklin* and *Sophia*; the first in compliment to Sir John's devoted wife, the latter to his admirable niece. These vessels were placed under Mr Penny's command, with separate instructions direct from the Admiralty. The ships showed during the voyage the good judgment employed by Mr Penny in their selection, and the men acquitted themselves throughout the enterprise in a way to justify the praise bestowed on them by their associates in the ships-of-war. Mr Penny had been employed in the Arctic seas since he was twelve years old, and had commanded a whaling ship for sixteen years.

The ships left Aberdeen on the 13th of April, but did not fall in with Captain Austin's squadron till the 28th of June, off Berry Island, on the west coast of Greenland.

About the same time that the above-named ships left England, three other expeditions were despatched; one in the *Prince Albert*, under Commander Forsyth, chiefly at Lady Franklin's expense. She had a crew of twenty men. Her mates were W. Kay and W. Wilson, and Mr W.P. Snow acted as clerk. She sailed from Aberdeen on the 5th of June, and was thus the last vessel which left England that year. Another in the *Felix* yacht, with a tender—the *Mary*—under the veteran Captain Sir John Ross, at his own charge. The Americans likewise showed a generous sympathy in the fate of the missing expedition, and sent out one to aid in the search, under Lieutenant de Haven, in the U.S. brig *Advance*, and the U.S. vessel *Rescue*, commanded by Mr S.P. Griffen.

These various expeditions were to examine the different channels up which it was supposed Sir John Franklin might have endeavoured to work his way. The result of their examinations proved beyond almost all doubt that he proceeded up Wellington Channel.

Without following the ships step by step through their laborious progress across Baffin's Bay, down Lancaster Sound and Barrow's Straits, we will carry them at once to Beechey Island, which lies at the south-eastern extremity of Wellington Channel, just at its entrance into Barrow's Straits. Here, on the 27th of August, Mr Penny discovered undoubted traces of Sir John Franklin. Here, accordingly, the ships assembled to prosecute the examination. Dr Sutherland, who went out in the *Lady Franklin*, gives the following account of the interesting event:

> Traces were found to a great extent of the missing ships: tin canisters in hundreds, pieces of cloth, rope, wood—in large fragments and in chips; iron in numerous fragments, where the anvil had stood, and the block which supported it; paper, both written and printed, with the dates 1844 and 1845; sledge marks in abundance; depressions in the gravel, resembling wells which they had been digging; and the graves of three men who had died on board the missing ships in January and April 1846. One of the shore party was despatched with this intelligence to Mr Penny, who immediately came on shore, accompa-

nied by Sir John Ross, Commander Phillips of the *Felix*, Sir John's vessel, Commander De Haven and Lieutenant Griffiths of the American expedition, which had joined our ships in Barrow's Straits, and other officers. There were unequivocal proofs that the missing ships had spent their first winter in the immediate vicinity of Beechey Island. A finger-post was picked up, which we at once supposed had been made use of to direct parties to the ships during winter, if they should happen to have lost their way in a snowstorm. Captain Parry adopted the same precautions around his winter quarters at Melville Island; and it is not improbable some of the posts may be found, after a lapse of thirty years. Our ideas were, that the ships had wintered in a deep bay between Beechey Island and Cape Riley, which we called *Erebus* and Terror Bay.

Immediately adjacent to the supposed position of the ships, we found the site of a large storehouse and workshop, and smaller sites, which were supposed to have been observatories and other temporary erections. Meat-tins to the amount of 600 or 700, and a great number of coal-bags, one of which was marked 'T-e-r-r-o-r,' were found. *But there were no papers found anywhere that had been left by the missing ships.*

This station, in the opinion of Captain Penny, was occupied by Sir John Franklin's party until the 3rd of April 1846, if not longer, as a look-out up Wellington Channel, to watch the first opening of that icy barrier which seems so frequently to block it up.

No record, however, was left to show in what direction the bold explorers had proceeded. With deep regret, therefore, that no further information could be gained, the various vessels continued the search. Captain Forsyth had, however, before this returned in the *Prince Albert* to England, with news of an interesting discovery made by Captain Ommaney, of some articles left by Sir John Franklin on Cape Riley. He reached Aberdeen on the 22nd of October, having been absent somewhat less than four months.

Early the next year the *Prince Albert* was again despatched, under the command of Mr Kennedy, an old Arctic explorer; but he was unable to effect more than to prove where Sir John Franklin and his followers were not.

Captain Austin's ships were constantly placed in great peril as they proceeded on their voyage. An officer on the *Assistance* writes:

> The *Assistance* was hemmed in by the ice in the centre of Wellington Channel, and was in such imminent danger of being crushed to pieces, that every preparation was made to desert her. Each person on board was appointed to a particular boat, provisions were got on deck, and every two men were allowed one bag between them for spare clothes, attached to lines which were passed through the upper deck, ready to be pulled up at any moment. One day the vessel was raised six feet out of the water by the pressure of the ice; and it became so probable that she would fall on her broadside, that the men were employed with shovels and pickaxes in smoothing a place on the ice for her to lie upon.

Again, on the 6th, a large floe came down upon them with great violence, and, pressing the vessel against the land ice, lifted her several feet out of the water. Everyone rushed on deck, with the exception of the carpenter, who coolly sounded the well to ascertain the depth of water in the hold. For some hours the ship was in danger of being driven on shore; the ice continued to grind and pile up round her, while all the ice-anchors were laid out, one of which was wrenched in two by the tremendous strain, and thrown high up into the air. The wind, however, providentially changed, the ice slackened, and they were safe. At length, while Captain Austin's squadron were secured for the winter in a field of ice between Cornwallis and Griffiths Islands, Mr Penny and Sir John Ross reached Assistance Harbour, where they wintered. A variety of means were taken to amuse the crews during the depth of winter; and, as soon as spring began, exploring parties went out in every direction.

We cannot trace the progress of the several parties in boats and sledges. Their persevering struggles serve to prove the existence, at all events, if that were required, of the heroic endurance of hardships, the indomitable courage, the invariable cheerfulness under the most depressing trials, and the unconquerable ardour, in spite of every obstacle, characteristic of British seamen. About 2000 miles altogether were traversed by the different parties. Mr Penny made every effort to ascend Wellington Channel; but his success was trifling compared to his unwearied endeavours. When his sledge was stopped by open water, and after incredible labours a boat was brought to the spot, thick-ribbed ice had collected to impede its progress. All the efforts of the heroic explorers were in vain. Lieutenant De Haven's ships returned to the United States, after enduring many hardships; and Captain Austin, Sir John Ross, and Mr Penny came back to England in the autumn of 1851.

Another year, however, was not allowed to pass before a further expedition was entrusted to the command of a talented officer, Sir Edward Belcher. The *Assistance* and *Resolute* were again commissioned, and, with the *Pioneer* and *Intrepid* screw-steamers, were placed under his orders, many of the officers who before accompanied Captain Austin volunteering their services. Captain Kellet, who had returned home in the *Herald*, was appointed to command the *Resolute*.

They proceeded early in the spring for Wellington Channel, and, favoured by an open season, part of the squadron entered that mysterious inlet, with a favourable breeze, in high health, and with buoyant hopes that they were about to carry succour to their long-lost countrymen—how soon, like those of many others, to meet with disappointment! Up that very channel, it has since been ascertained, the expedition under Sir John Franklin had gone, but had been compelled, as those in search of it soon were, to return southward.

In the meantime, Commander Inglefield, who had first gone out in the *Isabel*, commissioned the *Phoenix* steam-sloop, with the *Lady Franklin* as a sailing-tender, and proceeded to Baffin's

Bay. Mr Kennedy again went out in the *Isabel*, and the Americans sent forth the well-known expedition under Dr Kane, whose narrative must be read with the deepest interest by all, and his early death, the result of the hardships he endured on that occasion, sincerely deplored.

While Sir Edward Belcher in the *Assistance*, accompanied by the *Pioneer*, proceeded up Wellington Channel, Captain Kellet in the *Resolute*, accompanied by the *Intrepid*, leaving the *North Star* with stores at Beechey Island, continued his voyage to Melville Island, which he reached after encountering many dangers, and where he was frozen up at Bridport Inlet, on the 11th of September 1852.

We before narrated how the *Enterprise* and *Investigator* left England in January 1850, and, proceeding round Cape Horn, the latter reached the Sandwich Islands in June, and sailed again for Behring's Straits the day before the arrival of her consort. The *Investigator* had a remarkably quick passage to Behring's Straits; and after communicating with the *Herald*, Captain Kellet, off Cape Lisbourne, and exchanging signals with the *Plover*, which vessel wintered in those seas, she pursued her course easterly along the north coast of North America, and passed Point Barrow under press of sail on the 5th of August. Thus it will be seen that several ships as well as land parties were engaged in the search for the long-lost crews of the *Erebus* and *Terror* at the same time—from the east and west as well as from the south.

Since the 5th of August 1850, no tidings had been received of Captain McClure and the *Investigator*, till the time that Captain Kellet, who last saw him in the west, had once more made his way into the Arctic Ocean from the east, and was now commencing his long winter imprisonment at Bridport Inlet, Melville Island, in September 1852. The only time that exploring parties can travel is during daylight in the early autumn or in the spring. The spring is most fitted for crossing the Frozen Sea, before the ice breaks up and the cold has become less intense. In the autumn of 1852, Lieutenant Median, of the *Resolute*, was despatched by Captain Kellet to explore the coast of Melville Island to the west, and to form depots of provisions, as were other parties in different directions. On his return, passing through Winter Harbour, in Melville Island, at no great distance to the west of Bridport Inlet, what was his surprise and satisfaction to find in a cairn, a record, with a chart of his discoveries, left by Captain McClure on the previous May, stating that he should probably be found in Mercy Harbour, Banks' Land, unless he should be able to push on through Barrow's Straits, which it seemed very unlikely that he could have done. This was the first evidence to the new explorers of the actual existence of a continuous channel from the Atlantic to the Pacific—that there exists a North-West Passage.

Most tantalising was it, however, to them to know that at that season they could not possibly venture across to meet their countrymen. Indeed, the gallant McClure expressly forbade them in the document they had discovered. "Any attempt to send succour will only increase the evil," were his words. The winter passed rapidly away, but it was not till March that Captain Kellet considered it prudent to send an expedition across the Straits to where he supposed the *Investigator* was to be found.

We will now trace the progress of the *Investigator*, from the time she was last seen passing Point Barrow under a press of sail.

She made the ice on the 2nd of August, and, more than once being nearly caught by it, she reached Cape Bathurst by the 30th. Rounding it, she stood east and north, passing the south of Baring Island, which was called Cape Nelson. She then reached a channel with Baring Island on the west, and another land on the east, to which the name of Prince Albert's Land was given, when, on the 30th of September, she was fairly frozen in. Prince Albert's Land was taken possession of on the 8th of October, in the name of Her Most Gracious Majesty, by Captain McClure, with a party of officers and men, who landed, and planted a staff with a flag to it on the shore. On their return to the ship, they found that the land and sea ice had separated, and they were alarmed with the prospect of having to remain on shore during the whole of an Arctic autumn night. Happily, their signals were at last seen, and a party, with two of Halkett's inflatable boats, was sent to their assistance. In consequence of the excessive roughness of the ice, no other boat could have been got across. "By these means a large party were relieved, who were without tents, clothing, fuel, provisions, or in any way provided to withstand the severities of a Polar night, with the thermometer eight degrees *minus*." We take the opportunity of advising that all vessels should be provided with one or more of these admirable contrivances. They may be of any size, from that in which one man alone can sit, to one capable of carrying fifty people. One might always be kept on deck, which could be launched in a moment should a man fall overboard. By this means numberless lives might be saved.

Captain McClure, feeling assured that the ship was immovably fixed for the winter, started with a sledge party on the 21st, to proceed to the north-east, in the hopes of discovering Barrow's Straits; and, after travelling for upwards of seventy miles, they had the intense gratification, on the 26th of October, of pitching their tents on its shores. The next morning, before sunrise, he and Mr Court ascended a hill, 600 feet in height, whence they could command a view of forty or fifty miles over the Straits, though the opposite shore of Melville Island could not be discerned. They found, however, by their observations, that Sir Edward Parry had very correctly marked the loom of the land on which they stood; and that thus the long-vexed question was solved, and that, whatever others might have done, or might be doing, they had, at all events, found a watery way from the Pacific to the Atlantic Oceans.

They reached the ship again on the 31st, narrowly escaping destruction in a fog, when Captain McClure had to wander about during a whole night on a floe, with the thermometer from five to fifteen degrees below zero. And now the first winter of the *Investigator* was commenced in those ice-bound regions. By the middle of April, expeditions were sent out in all directions, and depots of provisions established for the relief of the long-lost companions of Sir John Franklin.

Both sides of the Prince of Wales' Straits were thoroughly explored, as was Baring Island and Prince Albert's Land as far as its southern shore, known as Wollaston Land,—a continuous coast-line being thus laid down along the whole southern shore of Barrow's Straits, and that of the north shore of the American continent, united with the discoveries of previous explorers. This, it will be remembered, was the winter of 1850-51.

When the short summer once more returned, Captain McClure made every endeavour to get the ship to the north-east, through the Prince of Wales' Straits into Barrow's Straits, but in vain. So closely was the ice packed at the north-east end, that, after running great hazard of shipwreck, he was compelled to give up the attempt on the 16th of July, when only twenty-five miles distant from Barrow's Straits, and bearing up, he ran to the south and west round Baring Island. The voyage off the west coast of that large island was full of danger, the ship frequently narrowly escaping being cast away, till at length, with a fair breeze, she entered Banks' Straits, which, leading into Melville Sound, may be looked upon as the western end of Barrow's Straits. They were but some eighty miles distant from Barrow's Straits, with every prospect of gaining them, and being able the following season to return home, when a heavy barrier of ice rose before them to intercept their progress. Backward they were driven into a deep bay, to which the name of the Bay of Mercy was given, as an acknowledgment of the merciful way in which they had been preserved from so many dangers. They had actually been only five days under weigh after leaving their winter quarters in Prince of Wales' Straits.

As in the previous season, their time was fully occupied in making exploring expeditions in all directions, and in shooting excursions. With the exception of about three weeks in January, when it was too dark to shoot, enough game was killed to enable them to enjoy a meal of fresh meat three days in the fortnight.

On the 11th of April, Captain McClure, with Mr Court, second master, and a sledge party, started to cross the ice on sledges, to visit Winter Harbour, in Melville Island. Soon after leaving the ship a thick fog came on, and continued for several days, so that their destination was not reached till the 28th.

We must picture to ourselves the sort of work these brave men had to go through, to do full justice to their perseverance and courage,—day after day travelling on, dragging their sledges across the frozen strait, often in the face of biting winds, encamping night after night with simply a tent to shelter them and a spirit-lamp only with which to cook their food or to afford them warmth. Yet thus, during that eventful period in the history of Arctic discovery, were many hundred British seamen employed in different portions of the icy ocean, all nobly engaged in the search for their lost countrymen and brother sailors. Not only for month after month, but year after year,—the only interruption being the dark, long night of mid-winter, and the brief period of summer navigation,—when, amid icebergs and ice-fields, whirled here and there, tossed by storms, and urged impetuously on by currents, they forced their way onward, in the hope of gaining the open ocean in another hemisphere.

At Winter Harbour Captain McClure found a large fragment of sandstone, with this inscription—"His Britannic Majesty's ships *Hecla* and *Griper*, Commanders Parry and Lyddon, wintered in the adjacent harbour during the winter of 1819-20. A. Fisher, *sculpsit*." Lieutenant McClintock had left a notice of his visit on the previous year on the same fragment, and protected it by a large cairn. In this cairn Captain McClure now deposited his own despatches, giving a plan of the way he intended to proceed under the various circumstances which might occur. One portion especially is worthy of notice.

After stating his intention of visiting Port Leopold, in Barrow's Straits, and of leaving there information of the route he purposed to pursue, he says: "Should no intimation be found of our having been there, it may be at once surmised that some fatal catastrophe has happened, either from being carried into the Polar Sea, or smashed in Barrow's Straits, and no survivors left. If such should be the case, it will then be quite unnecessary to penetrate farther to the westward to our relief, as, by the period that any vessel could reach that port, we must, from want of provisions, all have perished; in such case I would submit that the officer may be directed to return, and by no means incur the danger of losing other lives in quest of those who will then be no more." Admirable indeed is the calm courage with which he contemplated that fearful contingency which we now know too well overtook the expedition of which he was in quest, and his generous anxiety that no more valuable lives should be sacrificed in searching for him. Accomplishing in ten days what occupied eighteen upon the outward trip, the party reached the ship on the 9th of May. Summer was approaching. Some deer and musk oxen were shot. By the 10th of August the frozen-up mariners began to entertain the joyful hopes of being liberated. Lanes of water were observed to seaward, and along the cliffs of Banks' Land there was a clear space of six miles in width extending along them as far as the eye could reach; and on the 12th the wind, which had been for some time from the northward, veered to the south, which had the effect of separating the ice from that of the bay entirely across the entrance. Every moment they were in expectation of their release, and then a few days' sail would carry them into Barrow's Straits, and perhaps into Baffin's Bay itself. Shortly, however, the wind changed to the northward, the ice again closed: in vain they waited for it to open.

On the 20th the temperature fell to 27 degrees, and the entire bay was frozen over. The ice never again opened, and the usual preparations were made for passing a third winter in those Arctic seas. It is wonderful to observe how officers and men kept up their spirits, and how cheerfully they bore their trials and privations. They had for a year been placed on two-thirds allowance of provisions; the consumption was still further decreased, to enable them to exist another eighteen months. The winter was severe, but passed away without sickness; and now Captain McClure informed his crew that it was his purpose to send a portion home in a boat by Baffin's Bay. The intended travellers were put on full allowance, and all preparations were made for their starting on the 15th of April.

One day towards the end of March, Captain McClure and his first lieutenant were taking their daily exercise on the floe near the ship, when they saw running towards them a person whom they supposed to be one of their own men chased by a bear. They hurried on, when, to their surprise, they discovered that he was a stranger, his face so blackened by the smoke from the oil-lamp that his features could not be recognised. "Who are you? Where are you come from?"

"Lieutenant Pim—*Herald*—Captain Kellet," was the answer. Wonderful indeed it seemed; for Lieutenant Pim was the last person with whom the captain of the *Investigator* had shaken hands in Behring's Straits. It was some time before Lieutenant Pim could find words to express himself, when he announced that he was ahead of his party, who had crossed from the winter quarters of the *Resolute* in Bridport Inlet, Melville Island. Captain McClure then set out with a party of officers and men to visit the *Resolute*, which ship was reached on the 19th of April 1853, after traversing a distance of 170 miles.

Great was the satisfaction of the two gallant captains at thus again meeting. It was finally resolved that a portion of the crews of both ships should be sent home, while the remainder should stay in the hopes of extricating them during the coming summer. As, however, many of the *Investigator*'s crew were suffering from scurvy, only a small number were able to continue the journey westward, under command of Lieutenant Cresswell and Lieutenant Wynniett.

On the 2nd of June they arrived on board the *North Star*, Captain Pullen, at Beechey Island. The distance was 300 miles, and it had taken them four weeks to perform the journey.

On the 8th of August the *Phoenix* screw-steamer, Captain Inglefield, arrived. At that time Captain Pullen had been away a month up Wellington Channel, to communicate with Sir Edward Belcher. By the time he returned, the season had so much advanced, that it was decided to send back the *Phoenix* with Lieutenant Cresswell and his party. On the 4th of October they landed at Thurso, and on the 7th of October arrived at the Admiralty, with the announcement of the safety of the *Investigator*, and the tidings that the geographical question of the existence of the long-sought-for North-West Passage had been satisfactorily solved.

We must now turn briefly to narrate the fate of the numerous exploring vessels left in the Arctic regions at the setting in of the winter of 1853-54.

Before we do so, we must, however, give a brief account of the progress made by the persevering and brave Captain Collinson.

When, in 1850, Captain McClure succeeded in reaching the ice through Behring's Straits, the *Enterprise*, from having been somewhat longer on her voyage, was not so fortunate, and was compelled to winter in Port Clarence. Hence the *Enterprise* again sailed on the 10th of July 1851, to push her way eastward along the American coast, visiting the islands which form the northern shore of the channel. Here he found several depots and marks left by Captain McClure in the spring or in the previous autumn. The *Enterprise* finally was frozen in, in a sheltered harbour in Prince Albert's Land, near the entrance of Prince of Wales' Straits.

Several long and hazardous expeditions were performed on foot with sledges during the spring of 1852, both north and east, being out between forty and fifty days. Again putting to sea, the *Enterprise* passed through Dolphin and Union Straits and Dean's Straits eastward. By the 26th of September the *Enterprise* reached Cambridge Bay, when she was again frozen in, to pass her third winter in the ice—one of the most severe ever experienced in those regions. During the next spring, that of 1853, Captain Collinson, with his Lieutenants Jago, Parkes, and other officers, were employed in pushing on their laborious explorations in the direction where they hoped some traces of their long-lost countrymen might be found. In latitude 70 degrees 3 minutes north and longitude 101 degrees west they fell in with a cairn erected by Dr Rae, from which they obtained the first intimation that any parties had preceded them in the search, and their observations tended to corroborate his, namely, that the ice, *except in extraordinary seasons, does not leave the east coast of Victoria Land.*

Little did Captain Collinson know that from the shore on which he stood, as he looked eastward, he gazed on the very ice-field in which the *Erebus* and *Terror* had been beset, and that amid it, not many miles distant, the brave, the noble Franklin had breathed his last—that it was during an extraordinary season the two exploring ships had entered the icy snare, from which they were never to be released.

But we are anticipating the events of our deeply interesting and melancholy history.

Captain Collinson and his companions reached their ship on the 31st of May, after an absence of forty-nine days. It will be thus seen, that in justice the honour should be awarded to Captain Collinson and his followers, equally with Captain McClure and his, of having discovered the North-West Passage. Indeed, it is believed that it is only by the way he came, if any passage is practicable, that a ship could get round from the east to the west.

On the 10th August the *Enterprise* once more put to sea, steering westward. The Straits were found free of ice till they were abreast of the mouth of the Coppermine River, where they were detained till the 23rd. They passed Cape Bathurst on the 31st, again encountering ice; Herschel Island on the 5th of September; and, after overcoming various obstacles, were finally fixed for the winter on the west side of Camden Bay.

The season passed mildly away. In the spring more expeditions were made, and visits received from the Eskimo. The ship was not free till the 20th of July. She reached Port Clarence on the 21st of August; and at length Captain Collinson was able to send home despatches announcing the safety of his ship, officers, and crew.

We are inclined to consider Captain Collinson's voyage, with the light of the information subsequently given us, not only as the most remarkable of all the Arctic voyages, but as guided by the greatest wisdom, and executed with a courage, forethought, and perseverance unsurpassed. He may well claim the honour of being "the first navigator who took a ship of 530 tons through the narrow Dolphin and Union Straits and Dease's Strait, ice-strewn and rocky as they are, in safety to Cambridge Bay (105 degrees west), preserved his men in health through three winters, and finally brought them home in health and his ship in safety."

We must now return to Sir Edward Belcher's expedition. The greatest service it rendered was through Captain Kellet, by whose means the brave Captain McClure and his crew were rescued from their perilous position. We left the *Resolute* and *Intrepid* on the northern side of the Strait, frozen up in Bridport Inlet, in the spring of 1853. Although a northern gale drove them to sea during the summer, when they drifted about for eighty-seven days helplessly in the pack till off Cape Cockburn, on the 12th of November they were again frozen in; and the *Investigator*, also remaining fixed, was abandoned, the officers and crew spending the winter on board the *Resolute*. The *Assistance* and *Pioneer* being likewise frozen in, Captain Kellet received orders from Sir Edward Belcher to abandon his part of the squadron; and on the 26th of August the two last-named ships were also abandoned, the officers and crews arriving safely on board the *North Star* on the following day at Beechey Island. Fortunately the next day the *North Star* met the *Phoenix* and Talbot, when all the ships returned to England.

All due praise must be awarded to the gallant officers and men of the expedition, who exerted themselves heroically in the great cause they had undertaken. An Arctic passage was discovered; McClure and his followers performed it on the ice, probably the only way in which it ever will be performed; but the most important Arctic mystery was still unsolved—the fate of Franklin remained undiscovered. It was only known where he was not. As if to teach all those engaged in that well-arranged, powerful expedition a lesson of humility, the discovery was reserved for others with far humbler means at their disposal.

CHAPTER 16

# Voyage of the Fox

None of the numerous expeditions sent forth to discover traces of Sir John Franklin's expedition afford matter of greater interest than that of the little yacht the *Fox*, while it has surpassed all in successfully clearing up the mystery which for ten long years or more hung over the fate of that gallant Arctic explorer and his brave companions.

The *Fox*, a screw-steamer of 177 tons, was the property of Lady Franklin, and the command of her was confided to Captain McClintock, RN, who had already made several Arctic voyages. He had as officers, Lieutenant Hobson, RN, and Captain Allan Young, a noble-minded commander of the mercantile marine; with Dr Walker as surgeon, and Mr Carl Petersen as interpreter. She was prepared at Aberdeen for her arduous undertaking, and sailed 1st of July 1857. She entered Baffin's Bay, and had got as far north as Melville Bay, on its north-west shore, when she was beset by the ice early in September, and there blocked up for the winter.

Soon after midnight on the 25th of April 1858, she was once more under weigh, and forcing her way out from among huge masses of ice thrown in on her by the ocean swell. Repeatedly the frozen masses were hurled against the sharp iron bow, causing the vessel to shake violently, the bells to ring, and almost knocking the crew off their feet. On one occasion the ice stopped the screw for some minutes. Anxious moments those—"After that day's experience I can understand how men's hair has turned grey in a few hours," says Captain McClintock.

Touching at the Danish settlements to refit, and at Pond's Bay, the little *Fox*, narrowly escaping destruction, at length reached Beechey Island on the 11th of August. Here a tablet was erected to the memory of Sir John Franklin and his officers and crew, and the *Fox*, having filled up with stores and coals from the depot there, left again on the 16th.

On the 18th she had run twenty-five miles down Peel's Straits, the hopes of all raised to the utmost, when a pack of ice appeared, barring their farther progress. Putting about, she visited the depot at Port Leopold, where boats and an abundant supply of all sorts of articles were found, which, in case of the destruction of their own vessel, would afford the explorers a fair prospect of escape.

Far different was the condition of Arctic explorers now, than it had been when Franklin sailed on his fatal expedition. Then they had to depend entirely on their own resources; now, through the sagacity and forethought of those who sent them forth, depots of provisions and boats and sledges, and even huts, had been provided, to afford every possible means of escape should any disaster overtake their ships.

Captain McClintock, on leaving Leopold Harbour, sailed north down Prince Regent's Inlet, but in vain attempted to force a passage through any channel to the east. At last he returned some way north to Bellot's Straits, discovered by Mr Kennedy, and called after his unfortunate companion, Lieutenant Bellot, of the French navy, who lost his life when belonging to Sir Edward Belcher's expedition. He passed some distance through Bellot's Straits, and the *Fox* was finally beset, on the 28th September, in a beautiful little harbour in them, to which the name of Kennedy Harbour was given.

Depots were now established by travelling parties to the north-east, some eighty miles or more from the ship, and all preparations made for prosecuting their interesting search in the spring. This commenced the winter of 1858-59, the second passed by the *Fox* in the ice.

On the 17th February, Captain McClintock started with Mr

Petersen and one man, Thompson, on a long pedestrian expedition, with two sledges drawn by dogs. Lieutenant Hobson set off about the same time, as did also Captain Young,—all three expeditions in different directions, towards the south; the first two accomplished several hundred miles to King William's Island.

Great indeed were the trials and hardships they underwent in these expeditions. Day after day they trudged on, employed for two hours each evening, before they could take their food or go to rest, in building their snow huts, exposed to biting winds, to snow and sleet, and often to dense fogs.

On one occasion one man alone of a whole party escaped being struck by snow-blindness; and he had to lead them with their packs, and to guide them back to the vessel. How terrible would have been their fate had he also been struck with blindness!

On the west coast of King William's Island, which is separated by a broad channel from the mainland of America, they fell in with several families of Eskimo, among whom numerous relics of the Franklin expedition were discovered. The most interesting were purchased. Farther north, on the west coast, a cairn was found, within which was a paper with the announcement of Sir John Franklin's death, and with the sad statement, written at a subsequent period, that it had been found necessary to abandon the ships and to proceed to the southward.

A boat on runners also was found with two skeletons in her, and another skeleton at a distance—all too plainly telling a tale which shall be narrated hereafter. The Eskimo also said that they had seen men sink down and die along the shore; and that one ship had gone down crushed by the ice, and that another had been driven on shore. With this terrible elucidation of the long-continued mystery, only partly cleared up before by Dr Rae, they began their return journey.

On the 19th of June Captain McClintock reached his ship, the ice having begun to melt with the increased warmth of the weather. August arrived, and the explorers began to look out anxiously for the breaking up of the ice.

At last, on the 10th, a favourable breeze drove the ice out

of the bay, and the trim little *Fox*, under sail and steam, merrily darted out of her prison, and hurried north towards Barrow's Straits. She reached Baffin's Bay, and, touching at the Danish settlements, arrived in the English Channel on the 20th of September, having made the passage under sail in nineteen days from Greenland.

### THE FATE OF SIR JOHN FRANKLIN'S EXPEDITION

The last intelligence which had been received of the *Erebus* and *Terror* was from the whalers in July 1845, at Melville Bay. Thence the expedition passed on through Lancaster Sound to Barrow's Straits, and entered Wellington Channel, the southern entrance to which had been discovered by Sir Edward Parry in 1819. Up by it the ships sailed for 150 miles, when, being stopped by the ice, they returned south by a new channel into Barrow's Straits, and passed the winter of 1845-46 at Beechey Island. In 1846 they proceeded to the south-west, and ultimately reached within twelve miles of the north entrance of King William's Land.

Here they spent the winter of 1846-47, as far as can be known, in the enjoyment of good health, and with the intention and hope of prosecuting their voyage to the westward through the only channel likely to be open along the northern shore of America, and from the known portion of which they were then only ninety miles distant.

On Monday the 24th May 1847, Lieutenant Gore, with Mr Des Voeux, mate, and a party of six men, left the ship, and proceeded for some purpose to King William's Island, where, on Point Victory, he deposited a document stating that Sir John Franklin and all were well. This document was afterwards visited by Captain Crozier, and a brief but sad statement of after events written on it. In less than three weeks after that time, the brave, kind, and well-beloved commander of the expedition, Sir John Franklin, had ceased to breathe, as Captain Crozier states that he died on the 11th of June 1847. Who can doubt that his life was taken by a merciful Providence before he could become aware of the dreadful doom about to overtake his gallant followers?

A STRONG PARTY MUST HAVE BEEN DESPATCHED WITH A BOAT ON A SLEDGE

Probably Lieutenant Gore returned from that journey of exploration, as Captain Crozier speaks of him as the late Commander Gore, showing that on the death of their chief he had been raised a step in rank; but not long to enjoy it—he having among others passed away. The command of the expedition now devolved on Captain Crozier; but who can picture his anxiety and that of his officers and men, as the summer of 1847 drew on—the sea open to the north and south, but the ships immovably fixed in the vast mass of ice driven down upon them from Melville Sound? How bitter must have been their grief and disappointment when August and September passed away, and they found that they must pass another winter, that of 1847-48, in those regions! We know, too, that the ships were only provisioned up to 1848.

Painfully that dreary winter must have passed away, and sad must have been the feelings of Captains Crozier and Fitzjames when they came to the resolution of abandoning the ships, by which a high sense of duty had induced them hitherto to remain.

Up to 22nd April 1848, the total loss by deaths had been nine officers and fifteen men. On the 22nd April 1848, Captains Crozier and Fitzjames, with their officers and crews, consisting of 105 men, abandoned their ice-bound ships, and landed on the 25th on King William's Island, and started the following day for Back's Fish River, which runs through the Hudson's Bay territories from the south.

Their hope was that they might, voyaging up that river, at length reach some of the Hudson's Bay Company's trading posts. That they reached the mouth of Fish River we have melancholy evidence. Here they probably encamped, and, when the season advanced, proceeded some way up, but, finding the difficulties of the navigation insurmountable, they returned to the mouth of the river, with the intention perhaps of proceeding along the coast to the westward through the North-West Passage, which they now knew for a certainty to exist. Before, however, they could do this, it was necessary to send to the ships for stores and any provisions which might have remained on board.

For this purpose a strong party must have been despatched with a boat on a sledge, showing that they started rather early in the summer season, before the Straits were frozen over, or late in the spring, when they might expect to have to return by water. They greatly overrated their strength. When still eighty miles from the ships, they left the boat with two or more invalids in her, and a variety of valuables, hoping to reach the ships more speedily, and to return to her. One or more of those left with the boat attempted to follow, and dropped by the way. Some, perhaps, reached the ships, and attempted to regain the boat; but the greater number, overcome with hunger, disease, and cold, fell on their northward journey, never to rise again.

Two skeletons were found in the boat; and one, supposed to be that of a steward, between her and the ships. Of the ships, one was seen by the Eskimo to go down, while the other drove on shore with one body only on board, probably that of a person who had died during the final visit. Certain it is that no one regained the boat on their return journey to the south. Plate and vast quantities of clothing were found along the route, showing that on leaving the ships the hapless men considered themselves capable of considerable exertion; and as they carried a large amount of powder and shot, they undoubtedly hoped to maintain themselves by means of their guns.

In vain did the main body at the mouth of Back's Fish River wait the return of their shipmates. Week after week, month after month, passed by—they did not appear. How long they remained encamped on this bleak and barren coast it is difficult to determine. If the account received by Dr Rae is to be credited, it was not till the spring of 1850 that the survivors of that gallant band made a last desperate attempt to push their way inland, and sank down, as had their companions in suffering many months before them. Thus perished the whole of that gallant band of true-hearted seamen, who, with high hopes and spirits, had left England five years before in the prosecution of an undertaking which they had every reason to believe would so greatly redound to the honour and glory of

England, and to their own high renown. The task was accomplished; a knowledge of the North-West Passage was obtained. Their lives were sacrificed in the attainment; but they won names imperishable in English naval history, and gave another example of the undaunted courage, hardihood, and perseverance of British seamen.

CHAPTER 17

# The Expedition to the North Pole
## 1875

Since the numerous expeditions connected with the search for Sir John Franklin, England had sent forth none towards the North Pole. Other nations, in the meantime, had been making efforts to reach the long-desired goal. Influenced by the representations of numerous officers and other scientific men interested in Arctic discovery, the British Government at length came to the resolution of despatching some ships under the command of naval officers, who were to penetrate through Smith's Sound, to ascertain whether an open Polar sea existed, and to endeavour to reach the North Pole.

Two screw-steamers, the *Alert* of 751 tons, and the *Discovery* of 668 tons,—being strengthened by every means science could devise for resisting the Polar ice,—were fitted out, and Captain Nares was selected to command the expedition. Commander Markham, who had considerable experience, was appointed to act under him on board the *Alert*. Captain Nares and Commander Markham were the only two officers in the expedition who had previously crossed the Arctic Circle, but all the others were selected for their known high character and scientific attainments.

The other officers of the *Alert* were Lieutenants Aldrich, Parr, Giffard, May, and Sub-Lieutenant Egerton. Various important duties connected with the scientific objects of the expedition were undertaken by them. Dr Colan, the fleet surgeon, was known as a good ethnologist; Dr Moss, in addition to other scientific attainments, was an excellent artist. Captain Fielden went as ornithologist; Mr Wootton, the senior engineer, was an officer of experience; Mr White was the photographer of the *Alert*; and Mr Pullen, the chaplain, was a botanist. Besides the officers, the complement of the *Alert* was made up of petty officers, able seamen, marines, and others, forty-eight in all, some of whom were well able to assist the superior officers in their scientific duties. Christian Neil Petersen, a Dane, who had served in the expedition of Dr Hayes, was engaged as interpreter and dog-driver on board the *Alert*.

The *Discovery* was commanded by Captain Henry Stephenson. His active staff consisted of Lieutenants Beaumont, Rawson, Archer, Fulford; Sub-Lieutenant Conybeare; Doctors Ninnis and Coppinger; engineers Gartmel and Miller; assistant paymaster Mitchell, a photographer and good artist. Mr Hodson was the chaplain, and Mr Hart the botanist.

Their scientific duties were divided like those of the officers of the *Alert*. HM steamship *Valorous* was at the same time commissioned by Captain Loftus Jones to accompany the exploring ships up Davis' Straits as far as Disco, where she was to fill them up with the coals and provisions which she carried for the purpose. She was an old paddle-wheel steamer of 1200 tons, and was but ill fitted to withstand the ice she was likely to encounter in those seas. Loud cheers from thousands of spectators rose in the air, as, on the 29th of May 1875, the three ships steamed out of Portsmouth harbour and proceeded towards Bantry Bay, which they left on the 2nd of June for their voyage across the Atlantic. Heavy gales were met with, which tried the gear of the ships, the *Alert* and the *Discovery* each losing a valuable whale-boat, besides receiving other damage. The *Valorous* reached Godhaven on the 4th of July, and the *Alert* and *Discovery* arrived there on the 6th. Some days were spent here in transferring the coals and stores brought out by the *Valorous* to the two exploring ships—the *Alert* receiving also twenty-four dogs, which had been provided by the Danish Government. The ships then proceeded, accompanied by the *Valorous*, to Riltenbenk, where the *Discovery* received her twenty dogs, and an Eskimo named Frederik, who came on board with his kayak.

On the 17th of July the *Alert* and *Discovery* steamed northward on their adventurous expedition, while the *Valorous* proceeded towards the Disco shore, where, from its coal cliffs, she was to supply herself with fuel.

A fog coming on hid the ships from each other. After running through a perfectly clear sea for some distance, the weather being fine, Captain Nares determined to take his ships through the middle ice of Baffin's Bay, instead of passing round by Melville Bay. On the 24th of July the pack was entered, but the floes were rotten, and at first not more than 250 yards in diameter. As the ships advanced, the ice became closer, and the floes of much larger circumference, making it necessary to look out for channels. The commanders were constantly in the crow's nests, and succeeded at length in carrying their ships through, in the space of thirty-four hours, although not without some scratches, and having to put on full steam.

They found the entrance to Smith's Sound perfectly clear of ice, none drifting southward, although there was a fresh northerly breeze. The scene of the wreck of the Polaris was visited, and either the log, or a copy, of the ill-fated vessel discovered. The next point touched at was Cape Isabella, on the 29th of July. Here a cairn with a small depot of provisions was erected, at an elevation of 700 feet from the water, by the crew of the *Alert*, while the *Discovery* pushed forward. On the 30th of July the *Discovery* was beset off Cape Sabine, by a close pack five or six miles broad. The *Alert*, having bored through it, joined her, and both ships spent three days, sometimes getting under weigh and attempting to escape, until the 4th of August, when the pack moving forward enabled them to round Cape Sabine. Proceeding twenty miles farther along the south side of Hayes Sound, they put into a snug harbour, near which was discovered a valley with abundance of vegetation, and traces of musk oxen. Finding, however, that there was no channel in that direction, they bore away to the eastward, towards Cape Albert. Here a clear space of water appeared along the shore of the mainland; but the coast affording no protection, they ran into the pack, with the expectation of forcing their way through. In this they were disappointed, and, unable to extricate themselves, they were drifting at a fearful rate towards an iceberg. The *Discovery* seemed to be in the greatest danger, but suddenly the floe wheeled round, and the icy mountain was seen tearing its way through the surface ice directly down on the *Alert*. Her destruction seemed inevitable, when, at the distance of scarcely a hundred yards, the iceberg turned over, the floe splitting up, when the ship, although nipped, made her escape. They both then got round in the wake of the iceberg. For the next twenty-four hours they were struggling towards the shore, through ice four feet thick, amidst bergs of 300 feet in diameter, although only from twenty to forty high. At length successful, they reached, on the 8th of August, the land of Victoria. Thus they pushed forward, sometimes struggling with the ice, and boring their way through the packs, at others making progress by an open space near the shore. So closely-packed was the ice, that the channel by which the ships advanced was often immediately closed astern, so that they would have found it as difficult to return as to proceed northward.

On the 25th August, after many hairbreadth escapes, a sheltered harbour was reached on the west side of the channel in Hall's Basin, north of Lady Franklin's Sound, in latitude 81 degrees 44 minutes north. Here the *Discovery* was secured for the winter, while the *Alert*, as it had been arranged, pushed onwards, for the purpose of proceeding as far as possible through the supposed open Polar Sea, and reaching, some might have vainly hoped, the Pole itself.

After rounding the north-east point of Grant's Land, instead of discovering, as had been expected, a continuous coast leading a hundred miles farther towards the north, the *Alert* found herself on the confines of what was evidently a very extensive sea, but covered as far as the eye could reach by closely-packed ice of prodigious thickness. Through this ice it was at once seen that it would be impossible to penetrate. The ship, indeed, herself was placed in the greatest peril, for the ice was seen bearing down upon her while she lay unable to escape, with a rock-bound coast to the southward, and no harbour in which to seek for refuge.

Happily she was saved by the extraordinary depth to which the ice sank; for the mass grounding on the beach, formed a barrier inside of which she was tolerably safe. We can well enter into the disappointment of those who expected to have found the long-talked-of open Polar Sea, instead of which ice, evidently of great age and thickness, the accumulation, it might be, of centuries, and resembling rather low floating icebergs massed together, than the ordinary appearance of salt-water. When two vast floes meet, the lighter portions floating between the closing masses are broken up and thrown over their surface, sometimes to the height of fifty feet above the water, forming a succession of ice-hills of the most rugged description.

Although Captain Nares saw at once the almost impracticable character of the ice in the direction of the Pole, and which there was every probability would prove continuous, he resolved, as soon as the weather would allow, to despatch a sledge party in the desired direction. The supposed Polar Sea was appropriately named the "Palaeocrystic Sea," or "Sea of Ancient Ice."

The ice hitherto met with was seldom more than from two to ten feet in thickness; that which was now stretched before them was found to measure from eighty to one hundred and twenty feet in depth, its lowest part being fifteen feet above the water-line. This enormous thickness was produced in consequence of its being shut up in the Polar Sea, with few outlets by which it could escape to the southward, the ice of one season being added in succession to that of the previous year.

The two ships were now in their winter quarters,—the *Alert* off the coast of Grant's Land, with a bleak shore to the southward, and to the north a vast wilderness of rugged ice, extending in all probability to the Pole, in latitude 82 degrees 27 minutes, many miles farther than any ship had ever attained; while the *Discovery* was seventy miles off, in a harbour on the coast of Greenland, inside Smith's Sound, in latitude 81 degrees 45 minutes. Lieutenant Rawson, with a party of men, had come on board the *Alert* in order to convey notice of her position to the *Discovery*. He made two determined attempts to perform the journey between the two ships without success, owing to the ice remaining unfrozen till late in the autumn in Robson's Channel. He and his men had therefore to pass the winter on board the *Alert*. As soon as the safety of the *Alert* was secured, sledge parties were sent on along the shore to the southward and westward, with boats and provisions for the use of the travelling parties in the spring, under the command of Commander Markham and Lieutenant Aldrich. The latter advanced three miles beyond Sir Edward Parry's most northward position, and from a mountain 2000 feet high sighted land towards the west-north-west; but no land was seen to the northward. On their return journey, which lasted for twenty days, most of the people were frost-bitten in the feet.

The winter was passed by the officers and crews of the two ships much in the same way. Banks of snow were heaped round the vessels, and the decks covered ten feet thick with snow to keep out the cold from below, the only apertures being those required for ventilation or egress. The interiors of the ships being warmed by hot-water pipes, a comparatively comfortable atmosphere below was maintained. The time was passed by holding schools, with theatricals, penny readings, and games of all sorts. As soon as travelling was possible, on the 12th of March, Lieutenant Rawson and Mr Egerton, accompanied by Neil Petersen and his dog sledge, set off from the *Alert* to communicate with the *Discovery*, the temperature being at this time forty degrees below zero. Two days after leaving the ship Petersen was taken ill. A camp was pitched, but, as he showed no signs of recovering, the officers determined to return. At the utmost risk to themselves they succeeded in retaining heat in the body of the sufferer, and were thus able to bring him alive to the ship; but his feet, which they were unable to protect, were so severely frost-bitten that it was found necessary to amputate both of them, from the effects of which operation he died two months afterwards. The following week, the two officers with fresh men set out and succeeded in reaching the *Discovery*, thus relieving those on board of the anxiety they had felt in regard to her consort's safety. During the first week in April, the exploring parties, with sledges from both ships, started off in various directions. The party selected to make the desperate attempt to reach the North Pole was under the charge of Commander Markham and Lieutenant Parr. Such was the rough nature of the ice, that a road had to be formed in many places by pickaxes before an advance could be made, even with light loads. The sledges having thus to go backwards and forwards over the same road, the advance was very slow, averaging not more than a mile and a quarter each day. Unable to obtain any fresh provisions, their food was of a character not calculated to maintain their health, and consequently ere long they were all attacked by scurvy. Notwithstanding this, the gallant men pushed on, until on 12th May they planted the British flag in latitude 83 degrees 20 minutes 26 seconds north, leaving only 400 miles between them and the North Pole—many miles farther to the north than any explorers had hitherto succeeded in gaining. The distance made good was 73 miles only from the ship, but in order to accomplish it 276 miles had been travelled over. Commander Markham saw clearly that by proceeding farther he should run the risk of sacrificing the lives of his people. Thus, with a heavy heart, he determined to go back.

The return journey was attended by even greater difficulties than the advance. From the time of their start in April to their return in June, the days had been spent in dragging the sledges over a desert of ice-hills, which resembled a stormy sea suddenly frozen; half the time the men facing the sledges, and hauling forward with their backs in the direction they were going. On getting to within 30 miles of the ship, so large a number were suffering from scurvy, that Lieutenant Parr gallantly volunteered to set out alone to obtain relief. Happily he succeeded, after much difficulty, in arriving, and help was immediately despatched, the officers and men vying with each other in dragging forward the sledges. Unhappily one man had died before assistance had arrived. Of the rest, only two officers and three men were able to work; three others painfully struggling on rather than add to the difficulties of their companions. The remainder, being perfectly helpless, were carried on the sledges.

Another party sent out by the *Alert* proceeded to the west under Lieutenant Aldrich, and, after exploring 220 miles of coast-line, they also were attacked by scurvy. Not returning at the time appointed, relief was sent to them. Lieutenant Aldrich and one man alone, out of a crew of seven, remained at the drag-ropes. Numerous expeditions had been sent out also by the *Discovery*, one of which proceeded along Greenland and suffered greatly. When met by a party, under Lieutenant Rawson, sent out to their assistance, they were found dragging forward four of their helpless comrades, two at a time, advancing only half a mile a day. Two of the men died just as Polaris Bay was reached, opposite Discovery Harbour.

Other exploring expeditions were made in various directions. Captain Stephenson made two trips across Hall's Basin to Greenland. When at Polaris Bay he hoisted the American ensign and fired a salute, while a brass plate, which had been prepared in England, was fixed on Hall's grave. On the tablet was the following inscription:—"Sacred to the memory of Captain C.F. Hall, of the U.S. Polaris, who sacrificed his life in the advancement of science, on 8th November 1871. This tablet has been erected by the British Polar Expedition of 1875, who, following in his footsteps, have profited by his experience."

No inhabitants were seen in the neighbourhood of the ships' winter quarters, but ancient Eskimo remains were traced on the west side of Smith's Sound up to latitude 81 degrees 52 minutes. From thence they crossed it at the narrowest parts of the channel to Greenland. It seems surprising that animal life should exist so far north; but that it does so was proved, six musk oxen having been shot at the *Alert*'s winter quarters, besides fifty-seven others near Discovery Grave. In the same neighbourhood, although not, unfortunately, until the summer had commenced, a seam of good coal, easily worked, was discovered by Mr Hart, the naturalist. It is remarkable that the aurora was far less magnificent than in more southern latitudes. Of the numerous expeditions sent out by the *Discovery*, several were exposed to extreme danger, while nearly the whole of the men engaged in them suffered from scurvy. One expedition had been despatched to explore North Greenland with a lifeboat. In this party Lieutenant Rawson with four men had become detached, when, with the exception of the lieutenant and a marine, they were attacked with scurvy. One of the men died on the way. Happily they were met by Dr Coppinger, by whose assistance they were greatly restored; an Eskimo, also, being successful in shooting seals, supplied them with fresh food. Dr Coppinger, feeling anxious about the North Greenland party, set out with the Eskimo in a dog sledge, and found them in a most exhausted condition; everything had been left behind, and four were so crippled with scurvy that they were being dragged on by two others, who were only slightly attacked. When the doctor arrived they had not a particle of food, and must inevitably have succumbed. One of the party died the morning after their arrival at Hall's Rest, to which they had been dragged. So critical was the condition of the sufferers, that an officer and two men were despatched in a dog sledge to communicate with the ships; but, as the ice was already breaking up, it was with the greatest difficulty that the channel was crossed in about three days. On their arrival, the captain immediately set out with a relief party. Great anxiety was felt for another party under Lieutenant Beaumont, which was absent far longer than had been expected. He had with him a whale-boat, in which he and his people were driven far up the Sound, and it was not until the ships were on the point of returning home that they were picked up.

The above brief account may give some faint idea of the hardships and sufferings endured by the officers and men of the expedition, as well as of their courage and perseverance.

At length the icy barrier which had enclosed the *Alert* for so many long months began to break up; but there appeared not the slightest indication of a passage opening up to the northward by which the desired goal could be reached. Captain Nares felt fully confident that the sea before him had for centuries remained frozen, and would continue for ages more in the same condition. His crew were all, more or less, suffering from scurvy.

As much resolution and moral courage is often exhibited in retreating as in advancing. Captain Nares saw that to remain longer in the Polar Sea, in the vain attempt to carry out the object of the expedition, would not only be useless, but would in all probability prove destructive to the lives of his gallant followers. Steam was accordingly got up, and the *Alert*, boring her way through the ice, succeeded in again entering Smith's Sound. Early in August she got within ten miles of the *Discovery*; but for some time being prevented moving farther south by the ice, an officer was despatched overland to direct Captain Stephenson to get ready for sea. Not, however, until the 28th of August could the *Discovery* force her way out of her ice-bound harbour.

It often appeared as if all their efforts to get free would be baffled, but by dint of constant watchfulness for an open channel, by boring and blasting the ice before them, and often running full tilt at the mass which impeded their progress, they forced their onward way, until at length the open sea was gained. The Arctic Circle was recrossed on the 4th of October, exactly fifteen months after it had been crossed on the northward voyage.

Happily the *Pandora*, Captain Allan Young, who had gone in search of the expedition, was met with, and returned with the ships. Heavy gales were encountered in the Atlantic, when they were all separated. The *Alert* reached Valencia harbour, in Ireland, on the 27th of October, and the *Discovery*, Queenstown, on the 29th, soon after which they both returned to Portsmouth.

Besides Neil Petersen, three men, George Porter, James Ward, and Charles Paul, seamen, died of scurvy. The scientific results of the expedition are considerable; and the gallant men engaged in it have fully maintained the high reputation of British seamen for courage, perseverance, high discipline, hardihood, and endurance.

Chapter 18

# Memoir of Commodore James Graham Goodenough

To die in the path of duty, whatever that duty may be, is as honourable as to fall when engaged on the field of battle, or on the deck in fight with an enemy; and for either lot, British officers have ever shown themselves ready.

Among those of whose services the country has lately been deprived, none stood higher in the estimation of all who knew him than Commodore James Graham Goodenough. A brief notice of his career may induce others to follow his example. He was the second son of the Dean of Wells, was born in 1830, and sent at the age of eleven to Westminster School, of which his father had once been headmaster. He there gained the character he ever maintained of a brave, noble, and kind-hearted boy, who hated all evil doings or evil things. He was diligent and successful in his studies, and was beloved by all his companions.

In 1844 he joined HMS *Collingwood* as a naval cadet, and in her proceeded to the Pacific station. Here he spent four years, gaining from his messmates the same warm regard he had won from his schoolfellows. Ready for the performance of every duty, he was the leader among his companions on all occasions. He was a good linguist, and equal to the best in navigation and seamanship, as well as in all exercises. His chief characteristic was the thought of others rather than himself. When the *Collingwood* was paid off, he joined the *Cyclops*, commanded by Captain *Hastings*, and in her continued some time on the coast of Africa. He was promoted to the rank of lieutenant in 1851, passing the best examination at college. In that rank he served on board the *Centaur*, the flagship on the Brazilian station. He next served, during 1855, on board the *Hastings*, commanded by Captain Caffin, a Christian officer, whose advice to his young midshipmen when joining is worthy of being noted: "If you are a Christian, nail your colours to the mast and fight under them; you will be sure, in the end, to overcome your opponents!" While belonging to the *Hastings*, he was gazetted as having served with the rocket-boats at the bombardment of Sveaborg. After commanding the gunboat *Goshawk*, he proceeded to China, where he joined the *Calcutta*, flagship; and was gazetted on four occasions: for the capture of a large snake-boat from pirates in the Canton River, for being thrice in action in boats for the destruction of Chinese war-junks, for gallant services at the assault and capture of Canton, and for services on shore at the capture of the Chinese forts in the Peiho River. He now obtained the rank of commander, and returned for a brief time to England. After this he had for three years the command of the *Reynard*, on the China station. He next served as commander on board the *Revenge*, in the Channel squadron, and in 1863 was promoted to the rank of captain. During a residence on shore of about eighteen months he married. In 1864 he was sent by the Admiralty to America to visit the dockyards of the United States, and, at the end of that year, he went out to the Mediterranean as captain of the *Victoria*, flagship of Sir Robert Smart.

For five years, until 1870, he was in command of the *Minotaur*. The high esteem in which he was held was shown by his having been selected to assist in the revictualling of Paris after the Prussian siege, and also in distributing the peasant relief fund, when, accompanied by his wife, he gained the affection of all with whom he came in contact.

In 1871 the Admiralty again employed him to visit and report on the naval dockyards of Russia, Austria, Italy, and France,— another proof of the confidence reposed in him.

At length, on the 22nd of May 1873, he was appointed to

command HMS *Pearl*, as commodore on the Australian station. He went out with the determination of doing his utmost for the advancement of science and for furthering the cause of humanity. In the duties he had undertaken he was engaged for nearly two years, during which, while cruising through various parts of the Western Pacific, he never failed when visiting islands inhabited by savage races to endeavour by every means in his power to establish with them a friendly intercourse. On the 12th of August he had landed at Carlisle Bay, on the island of Santa Cruz, accompanied by an interpreter, through whose means, according to his usual plan, he was engaged in communicating with the natives, when, after a conference with some who appeared to have no hostile intentions, as he was in the act of stepping into his boat, a savage, a few yards off, shot a poisoned arrow, which struck him in the side. The example thus set was followed by the other natives, and several of the British were wounded. The boats immediately returned to the ship, but, notwithstanding the efforts of the surgeons to counteract the effects of the poison, the commodore felt that death was approaching. His great anxiety during the following days of intense suffering was to impress the principles by which he had been guided on those serving under him. As he lay in his cabin and his last hours were passing, not a murmur escaped his lips. The only regret he expressed was that he had not strength enough to praise God sufficiently for all His mercies. His chaplain writes:

> The day before his death, believing that he would not live out the night, he had all his officers summoned to his bedside, where, in lovely and loving words, he spoke of the truth and the infinite love of God, and the readiness he felt to go. He had a word for each—a word of love—as, at his request, each kissed him and said good-bye. He then caused himself to be carried on to the quarter-deck and placed on a bed there, the ship's company being assembled to hear his last words to them. He earnestly desired that no revenge should be taken on the natives of Santa Cruz. In these last words to the men he spoke to this effect: 'We

cannot tell their reason, perhaps they had been injured by white people, but we cannot communicate with them, not knowing their language; perhaps some day, it may be twenty or thirty years hence, some good missionary, some Christian man, may go among them and find out why they did this.' His heart was full of God's love to himself. He spoke of this love, and exhorted all to love God, telling them how he had loved them all, even when having to punish them, seeing good in them to love. Many such words were spoken before he said good-bye, blessing them all in the name of God. He passed away in perfect peace at 5:30 p.m., on Friday the 20th of August 1875. Thus died, in the performance of his duty, as true and noble a sailor as any of the gallant officers who have graced our naval annals. The two young seamen, Smale and Rayner, who had been wounded at the same time as the commodore, died within a few hours of him.

CHAPTER 19
# The Abyssinian Expedition
*1867*

Far to the south of Egypt, beyond Nubia, lies a little known and mysterious country now called Abyssinia, formerly a part of Ethiopia, the wonderful kingdom of the renowned Prester John and once of the Queen of Sheba.

Bounded on the north by the Eastern Soudan, on the east by a stretch of sterile, uninviting ground varying in width to the Red Sea from a dozen to at least two hundred miles, and a sort of "no man's" land unless claimed in a measure by Egypt and in a kind by Italy in these latter days; adjacent in the south to the broad lands of the warlike Gallas tribes, and approached from the west by the barren Southern Soudan,—Abyssinia has from time immemorial been the arena of rebellions, of intertribal hostilities, of inroads by neighbouring tribes, of attacks by civilised powers. Least of all has the land produced signs of progress in the arts of peace. Its mountains, towering to heights of 8000, 10,000 and 13,000 feet, have been the hiding-places of cruel robbers, of deposed chiefs, of disappointed insurgents; and its valleys have rung with countless cries of dying men in hotly contested battles.

Abyssinia has throughout the ages been divided into provinces, although the greatest authority has been nominally centred in one royal personage, or Negus. In the fact of these divisions, or principalities, we have largely the secret of continual disturbance. Jealousy has been responsible for much. The three principal provinces are Amhara, Tigre, and Shoa; the first being in the centre, with Tigre in the north, and Shoa in the south. Gondar is the capital of Amhara, Adowa is the main town of Tigre, and Amkobar is the most important place in Shoa. The prince, or governor, of each province, is known as *Ras*, a term we often find in reference to Abyssinian matters.

In the seventh century of the Christian era, 200 years after the country had passed the zenith of its power and glory, the Mohammedans swept like a great avalanche upon Abyssinia, stifled but did not utterly destroy Christianity, which had been introduced in the middle of the fourth century of the era in which we live; and maintained such a strong influence, that for century after century the whole land was in darkness and ignorance; and though the Christian religion has remained, it is in a debased and corrupt form. Europe knew nothing of Abyssinia worth the name for ages. Then a princess of Judah, Judith, prosecuted designs upon poor Abyssinia, sought out the members of the reigning family, and would have caused each one to be slain. Fortunately, a young prince was carried off to a place of safety. Coming to maturity, he ruled in Shoa, while for nearly half a century Judith reigned in the north. In the year 1268 *a.d.* the true royalists were restored to power in the whole kingdom.

When the warrior-mariners of Portugal were searching for new empires in every sea and upon every continent, rumours reached them of a kingdom somewhere, at the head of which was Prester John. This was just prior to the dawn of the fifteenth century.

Filled with wonder at the reports that reached them, and curious to solve the mystery that enshrouded Prester John and his wonderful kingdom, the Portuguese went on making their searches, under Pedre de Covilham, of renown, fixed upon Abyssinia, entered it, and secured the friendship of the chief ruler. Strange to relate, the Portuguese made no serious attempt to add Abyssinia to their dominions—possibly they did not think the task worth the trouble and expense; but they maintained some degree of power over the people through their religion, an influence whose effects were seen by Bruce and by other travellers of scarcely a hundred years ago—one not obliterated by tribal warfare and by a terrible, merciless coming of the Gallas from their country in the south.

In the year 1818 was born in Kaura, a child to whom the name Lij Kassi was given—a lad whose uncle was then governor of that part of Abyssinia. The boy grew to be wilful, self-reliant, and very ambitious; it is even said that he set himself out to be the elect of God, who should raise his country to a glory equal to that of Ethiopia of old. There was a prophecy indeed, "And it shall come to pass that a king shall arise in Ethiopia, of Solomon's lineage, who shall be the greatest on earth, and his powers shall extend over all Ethiopia and Egypt. He shall scourge the infidels out of Palestine, and shall purge Jerusalem clean from the dealers. He shall destroy all the inhabitants thereof, and his name shall be Theodoras." Whether Lij Kassi really pretended to be the elect of Heaven, the Messiah, or not, certain it is that when he had fought very bravely to found a state of his own, and had defeated the prince of Tigre in pitched battle, he gave himself out to his followers and to all Abyssinia as Theodore, king of Ethiopia, and was crowned under that name in his thirty-eighth year.

The ambition of Theodore was still boundless. He gathered an increased following, conquered tribe after tribe in Abyssinia proper, and prosecuted a most successful crusade in the country of the Gallas, subduing descendants of those who had wrought havoc in his native land from time to time, and established himself at a place nearly a mile square, and 9000 feet above the level of the sea. The town is known to us as Magdala.

Gondar was still the capital of Abyssinia, and to it and the country generally Theodore invited Europeans. Ambitious as he was, and warlike, the king—for Theodore had become the acknowledged ruler of the nation—was anxious to develop the resources of his kingdom, and that his people should be taught trades and industries. He was intelligent enough to see that Abyssinia could not be a great country if its natives were not imbued with ideas of civilisation, and if its products were not purchased by foreigners and their wares imported to the interior. Many merchants and artisans in search of employment under another flag went out to Abyssinia, therefore, and found employment; while consuls, or representatives, of European powers were appointed, and welcomed by Theodore to his court.

The British consul, Mr Plowden, was killed by a rebel force in March 1860, while on his way to the port of Massowah upon the coast; and so grieved was Theodore that he commissioned a superior body of his soldiers, not only to subdue the offending tribes, but to seek out the murderers of Mr Plowden and to punish them. This was done, and the king was greatly pleased when the British Government freely acknowledged he was in no sense to blame for the massacre. They sent out Captain Cameron to succeed the unfortunate Plowden, and presents were carried from our Queen. Theodore was delighted, further, to receive Protestant missionaries from England, and to show other tokens of friendship for *Britannia*.

A great change came over Theodore's conduct at length. His temper was soon ruffled, his pride was unbearable, he practised cruelties upon his people, and he became cold towards England, more particularly when months passed away and he received no answer to a letter sent to the British Government. So wroth was the king when he heard that Cameron was going to Egypt—a country Theodore disliked—that he ordered the arrest of the British consul and two missionaries, named Sterne and Rosenthal. They were thrown into a dungeon, in the year 1863. Great indignation was aroused in England. When, however, it was known that Theodore had some grounds for thinking that he had not been treated with full courtesy, Mr H.J. Rassam, then at Aden, was sent with Lieutenant Prideaux and Dr Blaine on an embassy to Theodore, taking with them friendly letters from the British Government, together with handsome presents; and it was expected that upon their arrival and explanation the prisoners would be released.

The king at first received them courteously, but, his mood soon changing, they too were seized and thrust into prison. The

British Government in vain endeavoured to procure their release; but finding this impossible, an expedition was prepared.

As the Red Sea lies under the jurisdiction of the Indian Government, it was at Bombay that the preparations were made, and the command was given to Sir Robert Napier, then commander-in-chief of the Bombay army, with Sir Charles Staveley second in command. Vast numbers of ships were taken up for transport, 30,000 animals were purchased in India, Arabia, Egypt, and the Mediterranean, and 15,000 troops received orders to embark. An advance party under command of Colonel Merewether, arrived at Zula, a tiny village in Annesley Bay, and preparations were at once commenced for the disembarkation of the troops and stores upon their arrival. HMS *Satellite* and other men-of-war also arrived in the bay, and the work of making the piers and preparing store-houses commenced. The construction of the piers, and the duty of landing the stores, fell upon the naval force, and were admirably performed, the manner in which the Jacks worked under a blazing sun eliciting the warmest encomiums from the military officers. Water was terribly scarce, and the boilers of the men-of-war were kept constantly at work distilling for the use of the transport animals and troops.

When the expeditionary force marched inland a Naval Brigade of eighty men with two rocket tubes, commanded by Captain Fellowes of the *Dryad*, was organised. These marched forward, and speedily took their place with the advanced division, under General Staveley. Their arrival was warmly greeted in the camp, their cheerfulness and good-humour here, as during the Indian Mutiny, rendering the men of the Naval Brigade great favourites with the soldiers. Their camp was a sort of rendezvous, and round the fires many a cheerful song was sung, many a joke exchanged, after the day's work was over.

Theodore had retreated, upon the news of our advance, to Magdala, a natural fortress of immense strength situate 400 miles from the coast. At Antalo, half-way up, a halt was made for three weeks, to allow stores to be accumulated. Here, fortunately, large quantities of provisions were procured from the natives, and numbers of little cattle hired for transport; for the want of water upon landing, and a terrible disease which broke out among the horses in the passes up to the plateau land, had disorganised the transport train, and immense as was the number of animals, it proved wholly incapable of transporting the stores for so large a force. At Senafe, at Adigerat, and at Antalo, strong fortified camps were erected, and bodies of troops left to overawe the king of Tigre, who, although professing to be our ally, could not have been depended upon had misfortune of any kind befallen us.

The march from Antalo led over a mountainous country almost bare of habitations, and the fatigues endured by the men were very great. The climate, however, proved exceedingly healthy, and although the heat by day was great, at night the air was cool and bracing, and in some places even sharp cold was experienced. From the plateau of Dalanta, some 15 miles from Magdala, a view of the fortress was obtained, and after a day's halt the advanced column was ordered to move forward. It consisted of the 4th Regiment, a regiment of Punjabis, one of Beloochees, and the Naval Brigade.

The march commenced at daybreak. The road was extremely difficult, and the men suffered greatly from want of water. The baggage had proceeded up a valley under the charge of the Beloochees and a baggage guard of men of the 4th Regiment, the rest of the column marching along the hill, so as to protect it from a flank attack. It had been intended that the column of baggage should not emerge from the valley upon the plateau of Aroge until the troops had arrived there for its protection. Owing to some misapprehension, however, upon the part of Colonel Phayre, who commanded it, the Beloochees were marched up on to the plateau before the covering force arrived there, and while the column of baggage was still in the valley. A continuation of this led direct to Magdala, and Theodore seeing it there, apparently unprotected and open to attack, ordered his men to advance and seize it.

The fortress of Magdala consists of three hills. Magdala itself, the strongest of the three, upon which the royal town is situate, lay behind the other two, and, except across a wide neck separating it from them, was inaccessible, as upon its other three sides it rose almost precipitously from the plain. The two hills in front were called Sallasye and Fala. As there was no intention of attacking until the second division had reached the spot, the troops were ordered to lie down, and an hour or two passed in inactivity. Then, with telescopes, a stir could be seen upon the top of Fala, where several guns were in position. Presently there was a flash, a pause for a second or two, and then the sound of a ball whistling through the air. This fell near the Beloochees, who were lying with piled arms on the plateau. Almost simultaneously a great body of men were seen descending by the road which led from the neck connecting the hills of Fala and Sallasye. When the head of this body reached the plateau it broke up, and was seen to be composed of great numbers of natives, headed by many chiefs on horseback.

Sir C. Napier at once gave orders for the 4th to advance. Thirst and fatigue were forgotten in a minute, and at a swinging trot the 4th passed to the front. The next order was for the Naval Brigade to advance to a knoll which commanded the plateau, and to open fire with their rockets upon the crowd of advancing enemies.

The moment was critical, the head of the baggage train had just reached the plateau from the ravine below, and there was a doubt whether the enemy would not be upon it before the troops could come to its assistance. The sailors were but a short time in laying their tubes, and a cheer broke from the troops as the first rocket whizzed out across the plateau. The roar and rush of this strange, and to them unknown, missile caused an instant halt of the advancing crowd of Abyssinians. The horses of the chiefs swept round and round, and scampered hither and thither in wild affright. The footmen paused, and for a moment it seemed as if the attack was coming to an end. Rocket after rocket whizzed out; but as the Abyssinians soon saw that the destruction wrought by these missiles bore no proportion whatever to the noise they made, they speedily recovered themselves, and advanced bravely to the attack.

The delay, short as it was, had, however, enabled the 4th to come into line, and as the Abyssinians advanced they opened a heavy fire of musketry upon them with their breechloaders, which were here for the first time used by British soldiers in actual warfare. For a few minutes the Abyssinians stood bravely against the storm of shot; then, leaving the ground scattered with dead and wounded, they turned and made towards the fortress.

In the ravine itself the combat had been more serious. There a large number of Abyssinians, coming straight down from Magdala, fell upon the baggage train. The company of the 4th under Captain Roberts, forming the baggage guard, defended themselves and their charge gallantly. Fortunately many of the mules were loaded with ammunition. These were broken open, and the contents served out; and the men were consequently enabled to keep up a steady stream of fire upon their opponents. These, however, pressed gallantly forward, and did not give way until the Punjabis, advancing to the edge of the plateau, took them in flank, and, pouring volley after volley among them, drove them up the hillside with a loss of more than 500 killed. This body was estimated at 2000 strong, and it is questionable whether any of them returned to Magdala.

As the enemy upon the plateau retreated, the Naval Brigade moved forward and took up a fresh position, and sent their rockets into the crowd as they ascended the path to their fortress, and then, turning their aim at the guns upon its edge, near which Theodore was himself standing, sent their rockets up with so accurate an aim that the guns were speedily deserted. King Theodore himself was greatly moved by these strange implements, and asked Mr Rassam, whom he had placed near him, if they were allowed in civilised warfare. In all, the fight cost the Abyssinians 800 killed and 1500 wounded, besides the 1500 whose retreat to the fortress was cut off.

The effect of this encounter upon Theodore was immense. Hitherto he had looked upon himself as invincible, and believed that he should defeat the English without the least difficulty. This view was also held by all the people through whom we had marched upon our way. In Abyssinia it is the priests only who wear head-gear, and the people viewed the helmets of our soldiers as signs that, if not absolutely clerical, they were at least men of a peaceful disposition. Our close formation, too, had altogether failed to impress them, and the reports which had been forwarded to Theodore had no doubt confirmed his belief that we were not formidable as opponents. The complete defeat of his army on the plateau of Aroge, in which his most trusted general, Fitaurari Gabriye, was killed, completely shook him, and among his people the disinclination to renew the combat with men armed with such wonderful weapons was complete. The Abyssinians, indeed, complained that we did not fight fair; their custom being that a line of men should advance, discharge their pieces, and then retire, after which the opposite side did the same. Then when the battle had gone on for some hours, the party that had lost most men retired. The steady advance of the British troops, and the incessant fire which they kept up, struck them as opposed to all rules of fairness.

Theodore now sent down to inquire what terms would be given him; but the reply was that nothing short of unconditional surrender could now be granted, but that if he would send down his captives, and submit, his life should be spared, and honourable treatment given him. He now sent down a large herd of cattle, and these were, somewhat unfortunately, received, for there is no doubt that the reception was, in accordance with Abyssinian customs, a sign that hostilities would come to an end, and the following morning the whole of the captives were sent into camp. Theodore again asked for terms; but was again informed that unconditional surrender could alone be accepted.

By this time the second division had arrived upon the scene, and a strong force prepared to attack the stronghold of the Abyssinian king. The Gallas, the hereditary enemies of the Abyssinians, had come up in great numbers and encircled the fortress behind, rendering all escape in that direction impossible, for although the fortress could not be attacked from the rear, there existed two or three narrow paths by which escape was possible.

On the night before we attacked, Theodore attempted to escape in this manner; but finding the Gallas everywhere in force, he returned to his citadel and prepared to defend it to the last. His army was now, however, determined to offer no further resistance. Cowed by the terrible slaughter at Aroge, and seeing that the power to order wholesale executions had now passed out of the tyrant's hands, the whole of the chiefs and their followers declared that they would no longer obey his orders, and only some twenty or thirty faithful men remained with him.

The 33rd Regiment led the assault, and advanced up the steep road by which the enemy had before descended to the attack. Fala and Sallasye were covered with natives, and at every moment an attack was expected upon us, although messages had been sent down by the chiefs saying that they rendered their submission. The 33rd, however, gained the top of the hill without a shot being fired, and there some 15,000 or 20,000 persons were seen sitting quietly down. Orders were given to disarm the men, and they and their families were then suffered to leave, and the force moved over the shoulder of Sallasye towards Magdala itself.

A small party of officers and others, riding on in advance, came, at the edge of the shoulder connecting Sallasye with Magdala, upon some fifteen of Theodore's guns, which he had not had time to take with him into Magdala. At the same moment a party of horsemen, among whom the natives recognised Theodore himself, came down the steep path from the fortress, and rode about on the plateau, brandishing their arms and shouting defiance. The officers dismounted, and finding some cases of ammunition with the guns, turned these upon Theodore, and speedily drove him and his companions up into the fortress again.

Presently the 33rd and Naval Brigade arrived on the spot, as well as Penn's Battery, and fire was opened upon Magdala by the guns and rockets. Soon some of the conical thatched houses which covered the top of Magdala were in flames, and after half an hour's fire the 33rd advanced to the attack. As they ascended the steep hill, shots were fired from the inside. The 33rd replied by thrusting their muskets through the loopholes; others climbed up a steep shoulder, from which they commanded the back of the gate. The defenders were shot down, and the English soon entered the place. A few shots more only were fired, and one of these proved fatal to the Abyssinian king. Whether he killed himself, or whether he was shot, will ever remain a disputed question. But the general opinion was that he fell by his own hands. Certain it was that the shot entered his mouth and passed out at the back of his head.

The work of the expedition was now over. Great numbers of native prisoners, many of whom had been detained in Magdala for years, were released; the huts dignified by the name of the Palace were fired; and soon nothing remained of the royal town save blackened ashes. The expedition then turned its face to the sea, which it reached just in time. Had it been a few days later, the rains, which had already commenced, would have filled the passes, and confined the troops prisoners on the plateau land until their subsidence.

The result of this expedition gave great satisfaction at home, and a peerage was conferred upon the able and fortunate commander, under the title of Napier of Magdala.

CHAPTER 20

# The Ashanti War
## 1874

Seven years after the Abyssinian campaign another African war broke out, this time upon the western coast.

Here, at a short distance above the line, lies the British colony of Cape Coast. The town, known as Cape Coast Castle, had been in the possession of the English for centuries, and a large tract of country down the sea coast, and extending back 80 miles to the river Prah, was under their protectorate.

North and west of the Prah were the Ashantis, a warlike race, who had gradually conquered and absorbed all their neighbours. The rites and ceremonies practised by the kings at Coomassie, their capital, were of the most savage and bloodthirsty nature, rivalled in this respect only by the neighbouring kingdom of Dahomey. At coronations, funerals, or other state occasions, it was customary to immolate hundreds of victims, and in order to supply this demand constant wars were undertaken. The Ashantis had for the most part kept up their connection with the sea through Elinina, a town situate some seven or eight miles from Cape Coast Castle. This place belonged to the Dutch; but a short time before, it had been handed by them to us in exchange for some positions farther up the coast. This caused much offence to the Ashantis, who maintained that Elmina was tributary to them, the Dutch having been in the habit for very many years of sending an annual present, or, as the Ashantis regarded it, tribute.

The Ashantis had some grounds for their belief that they

could overcome any force that the English could send against them, for in the year 1824 an expedition, headed by the governor, Sir Charles Macarthy, had crossed the Prah against them, and had been surrounded and cut to pieces, only three men escaping. As this defeat had never been avenged, the Ashantis were justified in the belief that they were capable of overrunning our country; and in 1873 a large force crossed the Prah and fell upon the villages of the Fantis, as the natives of this part under British protection are called. The natives of the protectorate having for very many years been prevented from fighting among themselves, had lost all their national virtues of bravery, and the consequence was that they were utterly unable to withstand the advance of the Ashantis.

The only forces at the command of the governor were some companies of the 2nd West India Regiment, a body of Fanti police, and a small force of Houssas, an extremely brave and warlike people living near Lagos, ready at all times to enlist where fighting is likely to go on. This little force was commanded by Lieutenant Hopkins; but, when the Ashantis approached, the great body of our Fanti allies, after fighting for a few hours, fled, and Lieutenant Hopkins, being unable with so small a force to withstand the approach of the enemy, fell back. The Ashantis took possession of Dunquah, and thence threatened both Elmina and Cape Coast Castle. The castle itself was originally strong, and was still in sufficiently good repair to resist any attack that the enemy were likely to make upon it, but the town was entirely incapable of defence; and had the Ashantis pushed on after their victory, there can be little doubt that both Cape Coast and Elmina would have fallen into their hands.

Fortunately, however, HMS *Baracouta*, Captain Freemantle, arrived upon the spot, and a body of 110 marines under the command of Lieutenant—Colonel Festing, of the Royal Marine Artillery, was landed. Martial law was proclaimed. The inhabitants of the native town of Elmina rose; but the *Baracouta* bombarded the place, and set it on fire, and the natives retired to join their Ashanti friends in the woods. These were now approaching the town; and Colonel Festing landed with the marines and marine artillerymen, a party of bluejackets belonging to the *Baracouta*, *Druid*, *Seagull*, and *Argus*, under Captain Freemantle, some men of the 2nd West India Regiment, and a body of Houssas. The Ashantis, some 2000 in number, marched boldly along, and attempted to outflank the position occupied by the English.

In this they would have succeeded had not Lieutenant Wells of the *Baracouta* opened fire upon them with a very heavy fire of Sniders on the part of his tars. The head of the column was arrested, and Colonel Festing, advancing upon them with his main force, opened fire, and thus, attacked both in front and on the flank, the Ashantis fled, leaving 200 killed. Several other skirmishes took place. Lieutenant Gordon, who had raised a body of Houssas, did excellent service, and formed a redoubt at the village of Napoleon, about five miles from Cape Coast. Except, however, within range of the guns of the forts, the whole country was in the hands of the Ashantis.

It was now evident that a force which was estimated at 20,000 could not be driven out from the vast woods which covered the whole country as far as the Prah, with so small a force as that at the disposal of the authorities, and it was determined by the Home Government to send out an expedition to deliver the protectorate of its invaders, and to chastise the Ashantis on their own ground. In the meantime the *Simoom* arrived on the coast with a strong body of marines and marine artillerymen, and Commodore Commerell came up from the Cape of Good Hope and took the command of the naval portion of the forces.

He determined to ascend the Prah with the boats of the squadron, to see what facilities that river offered as a means of advance into the interior, and to communicate with the chiefs upon the bank. He had ascended the river only about a mile and a half when a very heavy fire was suddenly opened upon him by the enemy concealed in the thick bush which lined the banks. The commodore himself was badly wounded; Captains Luxmore and Helden were also severely hurt; and 4 men killed and 16 wounded. The boats returned at once to the *Rattlesnake*.

The town of Chamoh, which stood at the entrance of the Prah, was the next day bombarded and burnt.

Several other skirmishes occurred; but as we were not in a position to take the offensive, and the Ashantis appeared indisposed to renew their attacks upon Elmina or Cape Coast, things remained quiet until the arrival of Sir Garnet Wolseley, with some twenty English officers, in the *Ambriz*. No troops had been sent with him, as it was considered that the situation might have changed before he reached the coast, or that upon his arrival there he might find the force of marines and bluejackets, with the aid of the 2nd West India Regiment, another wing of which had come down from Sierra Leone, sufficient for the purpose.

He found, however, that the situation was far too serious: that the Fantis were utterly untrustworthy; and that with so small a force he could make no impression upon the great Ashanti armies gathered in the woods. Two regiments of natives were, however, enrolled, the one under Lieutenant-colonel Evelyn Wood, the other under Major Russell, each of them numbering some 300 or 400 men. It was decided that the advance into Ashanti should be attempted from two different points. At the southern point of the colony, where the River Volta forms the frontier of the territory, Captain Glover, formerly of the Royal Navy, was commissioned to raise a large native force. Upon the opposite side of the Volta the people were in alliance with the Ashantis, and unless a strong demonstration had been made at this point, they might at any moment have crossed the river and attacked the protectorate from the east.

The first operation undertaken by Sir Garnet Wolseley was an attack upon several of the villages near Elmina, occupied by the Ashantis. The most perfect secrecy was maintained as to the plans, for it was certain that the enemy were accurately informed of all our doings. It was given out that Sir Garnet intended to go down to Accra, some 50 miles down the coast, and many of his officers at the time of embarkation believed this to be the true state of the case.

On board ship all preparations had been made for landing,

and before daybreak the men-of-war were off Elmina. The boats were at once lowered, and the marines and bluejackets disembarked. At Elmina they were joined by several companies of the 2nd West India Regiment in garrison there. A large number of native bearers were also in readiness, these having been sent off the night before, with orders to bring back stores.

Morning was just breaking when the force moved forward. For the next three hours no resistance was met with. One village found deserted was burnt.

As they passed along through the bush, the Houssas, who had been drilled by Captain Rait, RA, kept up a tremendous fire, yelling and shouting. But as their aim was quite wild and half the guns fired into the air, much ammunition was wasted. Captain Freemantle with the sailors then made for the left of the wood so as to divert the enemy's attention. A heavy fire was poured in upon them by the natives, who were completely hidden from our men.

The marines and bluejackets pushed on steadily in the direction of a village which lay in the centre of the wood. The natives, who were assembled in large numbers, kept up a heavy fire from the roofs of the huts. As Captain Freemantle was advancing to find a better place for the gun, he was wounded by a slug, which passed right through his arm, but fortunately was able to continue directing the gun. The Houssas under Captain McNeill were doing little good by their indiscriminate firing, and indeed it was a matter of some difficulty to keep them together. Colonel McNeill was severely hit in his arm, and subsequently had to return to England from the effects of the wound.

A combined movement was made upon the enemy, who retreated from the village before the dashing of the bluejackets.

From this village the force marched to the sea coast, whence a portion continued their way some four miles farther, and attacked and carried another village, where the Ashantis made a somewhat obstinate defence. The force here was embarked by the boats of the squadron, while the remainder marched back to Elmina. The distance marched by the seamen and marines who had been up all night, was no less than 21 miles, under a burning sun. In the course of the march several deep swamps, where the water came over the men's knees, had to be crossed. The paths were everywhere difficult in the extreme, and yet no man fell out, and only four were admitted to hospital upon the following day.

The next engagement took place near Dunquah, where Colonel Festing commanded the force. Sallying out to attack a large body of Ashantis, he inflicted considerable damage upon them; but their numbers were so strong, and they fought with such determination, that he was obliged to fall back. Lieutenant Wilmot, who commanded eight Houssas of the artillery, was early in the fight wounded in the arm, but continued at his post until, an hour later, he was shot through the heart. A few days afterwards another indecisive fight of the same nature took place.

A position of much importance, lying some three miles off the main road, was the village of Abrakrampa. This place had been a missionary station, and contained a church and several houses, besides the village huts. It lay in the heart of the forest, and at night the sound of the war-drums of the Ashantis could be plainly heard. The post was commanded by Major Russell, with his black regiment, and he had with him a body of seamen and marines. As, however, the amount of fever among the white men on shore was very great, and the naval officer in command, Captain Freemantle—for Commodore Commerell had been obliged to return to the Cape from the effect of his wound—was anxious that his men should not remain upon shore, orders were sent up to Major Russell to march the marines and seamen down to the shore. Fortunately, however, an hour or two before the men were to start, the news arrived that the Ashantis were advancing to attack the camp.

A breastwork had been thrown up round the village, and the church was converted into a sort of keep, platforms having been raised inside to the level of the upper windows, through which the marines and seamen could fire at the advancing enemy. When, from the noise in the woods, Major Russell became assured that the news was true, he sent a messenger to Cape Coast for assistance, and prepared to repel the attack. The Ashantis advanced with great bravery, but were driven back by the rapid fire kept up upon them from the breastworks and church, and presently fell back into the woods again. They, however, continued to beleaguer the place, occasionally showing in great masses.

Directly the news reached Cape Coast every available seaman and marine was landed from the ships, and at seven in the morning the column started. The distance was about 15 miles, and the heat tremendous. An hour's rest was allowed at a village where the road for Abrakrampa turned off from the main line, and at the end of that time the great proportion of our men were sufficiently recovered to continue their march. They made a long detour, so as to avoid coming down by the road by which the Ashantis would naturally expect them to advance, and in which they would have been engaged in a fight in the thick of the forest. They therefore arrived at Dunquah without firing a shot.

It was then late in the evening. The following morning the black troops advanced into the forest, and reported that the Ashantis were in full flight. The garrison then sallied out, and found that the village occupied as the Ashanti headquarters had been deserted, and that the enemy had left. They still, however, lingered in large numbers in the woods near, for a party of Fantis were fallen upon, and many were killed.

The force of bluejackets and marines, together with the 2nd West India Regiment, now advanced towards the Prah, the Ashantis hastily retreating, and no more fighting took place.

Thus the invasion of the protectorate was defeated, and the invaders driven across their frontier, with a loss admitted by themselves of several thousands, before the arrival of a single soldier from England, solely by the naval forces, aided by the one black regiment upon the spot. The West Indians were placed in garrison upon the Prah, and the bluejackets returned to their ships.

In December the 42nd, a battalion of the Rifle Brigade, and the 23rd Fusiliers arrived. It was found, however, that it was impossible to provide transport for so large a force, and the 23rd were therefore re-embarked, together with a battery of Royal Artillery which had also come out. Two hundred of the Fusiliers, however, subsequently re-landed and marched to the front.

On the 1st January the disembarkation took place, and the 42nd Highlanders and Rifle Brigade marched for the front, the Naval Brigade having gone up a week previously. On the 20th the bridge across the Prah was completed by the bluejackets and engineers, under the command of Colonel Home. Lord Gifford, in command of a party of native scouts, first went forward, and was followed by Wood and Russell's native regiments. These pushed forward without opposition, and gained the crest of the Adansi hills. The King of Ashanti was now seriously alarmed, and sent in three German missionaries and a French merchant, whom he had retained for some time as prisoners.

Short as the time had been that the force was on shore, already large numbers were suffering from sickness, and out of the total European force of 1800 men, 215 were already unfit for duty.

Without opposition the force arrived as far as Fommanah, a large village 30 miles from Coomassie. Here letters were received from the king, asking for peace. Sir Garnet Wolseley, however, demanded that hostages consisting of leading members of the king's family should be given up as proofs of his sincerity. The king, however, who was in reality only trying to gain time, took no notice of the demand, and the advance continued.

At the village of Borborassie, a few miles farther, the Ashantis offered their first resistance. The place was carried with a rush by the Naval Brigade, a company of Fusiliers, and some of Russell's regiment. Captain Nicol, who led the advance, was killed.

Information was now gained that the enemy was posted in great force near the villages of Amoaful and Beckquah, and here a battle was expected to take place. Owing to the number of garrisons left at the various posts upon the road, Wood's regiment was now reduced to three companies only, Russell's to four companies. These regiments took their place in the line in the rear of the Naval Brigade.

The plan of battle was that the 42nd were to form the main

attacking force, and were to drive the enemy's scouts out of Agamassie, a little village two miles in front of Amoaful, situate in a dense wood. After carrying the village, they were to move straight on, extending to the right and left, and if possible advance in a skirmishing line through the bush. The right column, consisting of half the Naval Brigade and Wood's regiment, was to cut a path out to the right, and then turn parallel with the main road, so that the head of the column should touch the right of the skirmishing line of the 42nd; the left column, consisting of the other half of the Naval Brigade, was to proceed after a similar fashion on the left. The Naval Brigade, it should be said, was commanded by Commodore Hewett. The company of the 23rd was to go behind the head-quarter staff, and the Rifle Brigade to remain in reserve. Thus, could this plan of battle have been carried out, the whole would have formed a hollow square, the right and left columns protecting the 42nd from any of those flanking movements of which the Ashantis were always so fond.

Upon the preceding evening Major Home, advancing from the village of Quarman, at which the head of the column had halted the night before, cut a wide path to within 50 yards of the village of Agamassie, and ascertained that that village was held by a small body only.

The 42nd went on in advance, and with a rush carried the village. For a minute or two the fire lulled, and then from the circle of woods lying around it, a tremendous fire broke out upon them. The first shot was fired a few minutes before eight. The 42nd gradually made their way forward; but some delay elapsed before the Naval Brigade could take up the two positions assigned to it, for Agamassie was but a tiny village, and this was so encumbered by the troops, and with the bearers of the hammocks and ammunition, that movement was difficult in the extreme. The noise was prodigious, the Ashantis using very heavy charges of powder. Close to the village Captain Buckle of the Royal Engineers was shot dead as he led his men, cutting a path into the forest from which the Ashanti fire was pouring out.

For an hour but little advance was made, the Ashantis holding their ground most tenaciously. The two bodies of the Naval Brigade were accompanied by parties of Rait's artillerymen with rockets, but the fire of these and the Sniders was insufficient to clear the way. Even after an hour's fighting, the Ashantis still held the bush, not 200 yards from the village, and two companies of the Rifle Brigade were sent up the left-hand road to keep the line open. The wood was so thick that the Naval Brigade were unable to make much way, and were forced to lie down and fire into the dense bush, from which the answering discharges came incessantly, at a distance of 20 yards or so. The air above was literally alive with slugs, and a perfect shower of leaves continued to fall upon the path.

In the wood, all just views of direction were lost. The sailors complained that the 23rd or the 42nd were firing at them, and the 42nd and 23rd made the same complaint of the Naval Brigade. In fact, from the denseness of the wood, and the general and continuous roar of musketry, it was impossible to gain any just ideas of direction.

Colonel Macleod, who commanded the left column, presently found the resistance in front of him cease; but he knew nothing of the position of the 42nd, with whose left he should have been in touch.

The 42nd were having a hard time of it. They were well handled by Major Macpherson, who was in command. For a time they succeeded in forcing the enemy back, but coming to a swamp between two rises, their advance was for a time completely arrested. Not an enemy was to be seen; but from every bush on the opposite side the puffs of smoke came thick and fast, and a perfect rain of slugs swept over the ground on which they were lying. Captain Rait, assisted by Lieutenant Saunders, brought his gun—for from the narrowness of the path he was able to bring only one into action—well to the front of the 42nd, and poured round after round of grape into the enemy, until their fire slackened a little, and the 42nd again advanced. At the top of the hill the Ashantis made again a desperate stand. Here the gun again did good service, and at last the regiment fought their way over it, the enemy contesting every foot. Another rush was made, and the regiment then burst through the wood into the open clearing in which the large village of Amoaful was situate. Out of 450, they had 9 officers and 104 men wounded. For a short time the Ashantis kept up a fire from the houses; but the 42nd soon drove them from the village, and all further resistance at this point was at an end.

The right-hand column, too, had suffered severely. Colonel Wood received a slug in the left breast, and 6 naval officers and 20 men were also wounded. Captain Luxmore, RN, was in command here. A company of the Rifle Brigade had been sent out to strengthen them, when all at once, just when the battle appeared over, the Ashantis made a tremendous effort to turn our flank and to retake the village of Agamassie. The Rifles in reserve sprang to their feet and advanced to meet them, and for a while the roar of musketry was as heavy as it had been during the day. Then, after an hour's fighting, Sir Garnet Wolseley gave the word to advance. The men of the Rifle Brigade sprang forward, and in five minutes the Ashantis were in full retreat. Altogether, including the natives, the number of British casualties exceeded 250.

The force slept at Amoaful, and the next day the Naval Brigade, with Russell's regiment and Rait's battery, supported by the 42nd, moved off the main road to attack the neighbouring village of Beckquah, which was the capital of one of the most powerful of the Ashanti kings. As the narrow road entered the clearing, the enemy opened a tremendous fire upon them. Lord Gifford rushed forward, followed by his scouts. The Houssas, who were next behind, for once hung back; but the sailors, who came next, sprang forward over the Houssas, and entered the village. The natives, encouraged by the smallness of our force, fought strongly; and as there were over a thousand fighting men in the village, we should have suffered heavily had not the lesson given the day before of the white men's superiority stood us in good stead; and as the Houssas and other companies of Russell's regiment now poured in, the enemy speedily lost heart and fled.

The troops were placed in position to defend the place from any attack from the bush, and the sailors, provided with port-fires, set fire to the town from end to end.

Next day the advance began, the orders being that every man was to receive four days' rations, and each regiment take its own provision and baggage. The advance began at seven o'clock. The road was found strewn with the litter cast away by the retreating enemy. The road was very difficult and boggy. Streams had to be bridged in many places by the engineers, and it took six hours to move as many miles. At one village on the way, a thousand of the enemy assembled to make a stand; but their defence was feeble, and Russell's regiment carried the place at a rush.

Upon reaching the village of Agamemmoo, the general sent back for the baggage. This did not arrive until nearly four o'clock, and it was then too late to move on in the night. The clearing was a small one, and so close had the troops to lie, that the whole width and length of the street was paved with human bodies. The next day there was fighting during the whole march, the Ashantis having placed several ambushes. The streams and swamps were even more frequent than upon the day preceding, and eight hours were occupied in going six miles, when the camp halted on the river Dah. A flag of truce came in, but as the king did not send the hostages required, preparations were made for an advance at daybreak in the morning. The engineers set to work to bridge the river, and Russell's regiment waded through, and bivouacked upon the opposite bank.

The night was tremendously wet; but the troops moved forward in high spirits in the morning. The fight commenced as soon as the column had crossed, and was a repetition of that of Amoaful. Lieutenant Saunders, in the front, with his gun cleared the way with grape. The Bonny men, who were in advance, would at last go no farther, and Lieutenant Eyre, adjutant of Wood's regiment, to which they belonged, was killed.

The Rifles then came forward, and very slowly the advance was continued until the head of the column was within 50 yards of the village. Then the Rifles gave a cheer, and with a sudden rush cleared the way to the open, and carried the village. In the meantime the whole column was engaged in repelling a series of flank attacks. These attacks were most gallantly persevered in by the Ashantis, who at times approached in such masses that the whole bush swayed and moved as they poured forward. Their loss must have been extremely large, for our men lined the road and kept up a tremendous Snider fire upon them. Our own casualties were slight, the road, like almost all roads in the country, being sunk two feet below the level of the surrounding ground; consequently the men were lying in shelter, as behind a breastwork.

The Naval Brigade at one time inflicted great slaughter upon the foe, by remaining perfectly quiet, until the enemy, thinking that they had retired, advanced full of confidence, cheering, when a tremendous fire almost swept them away.

It took us, altogether, nearly six hours from the time our advance began until the rear-guard had gained the village, a distance of only a mile and a half. Coomassie was still six miles off, and had the Ashantis continued to fight with the same desperation, we should not have reached Coomassie that night.

The instant the baggage was all in the village, the advance again began.

At first the Ashantis fought with great determination. But our men pushed steadily forward, and then, advancing at a double, the foes, scared by the onslaught, gave way, and fled at the top of their speed. The whole force now pushed forward, and without further opposition crossed the pestilential swamp which surrounds Coomassie, and entered the town.

The king and the greater portion of his fighting men had retired, and as the provisions were running short, and the force greatly weakened by the number of wounded and of men who had dropped with fever, it was impossible to pursue him in the bush. After a day's halt, the blood-stained capital was burnt, and the army retired to the coast.

CHAPTER 21

# Spirited and Gallant Exploits

### A Remarkable Rescue

The following account is given in the words of Admiral Castle:

In the year 1837, I commanded HMS *Pylades*, on the East India station. We were on our return home, by the way of the Cape of Good Hope, when, on the 8th of May of that year, we were off Cape L'Agulhus. It was blowing a heavy gale of wind, with a tremendous sea running, such a sea as one rarely meets with anywhere but off the Cape, when just at nightfall, as we were taking another reef in the topsails, a fine young seaman, a mizen-topman, James Miles by name, fell from the mizen-topsailyard, and away he went overboard. In his descent he came across the chain-span of the weather-quarter davits, and with such force that he actually broke it. I could scarcely have supposed that he would have escaped being killed in his fall; but, as the ship flew away from him, he was seen rising on the crest of a foaming wave, apparently unhurt. The life-buoy was let go as soon as possible, but by that time the ship had already got a considerable distance from him; and even could he reach it, I felt that the prospect of saving him was small indeed, as I had no hope, should we find him, of being able to pick him out of that troubled sea; and I had strong fears that a boat would be unable to swim, to go to his rescue, should I determine to lower one. I was very doubtful as to what was my duty. I might, by allowing a boat to be lowered, sacrifice the lives of the officer and crew, who would, I was very certain, at all events volunteer to man her. It was a moment of intense anxiety. I instantly, however, wore the ship round; and while we stood towards the spot, as far as we could guess, where the poor fellow had fallen, the thoughts I have mentioned passed through my mind. The sad loss of the gallant Lieutenant Gore and a whole boat's crew a short time before, about the same locality, was present to my thoughts. To add to the chances of our not finding the man, it was now growing rapidly dusk. As we reached the spot, every eye on board was straining through the gloom to discern the object of our search, but neither Miles nor the life-buoy were to be seen. Still, I could not bring myself to leave him to one of the most dreadful of fates. He was a good swimmer, and those who knew him best asserted that he would swim to the last. For my part, I almost hoped that the poor fellow had been stunned, and would thus have sunk at once, and been saved the agony of despair he must be feeling were he still alive. Of one thing I felt sure, from the course we had steered, that we were close to the spot where he had fallen. Anxiously we waited,—minute after minute passed by,—still no sound was heard; not a speck could be seen to indicate his position. At least half an hour had passed by. The strongest man alive could not support himself in such a sea as this for so long, I feared. Miles must long before this have sunk, unless he could have got hold of the life-buoy, and of that I had no hope. I looked at my watch by the light of the binnacle lamp. 'It is hopeless,' I thought; 'we must give the poor fellow up.' When I had come to this melancholy resolve, I issued the orders for wearing ship in a somewhat louder voice than usual, as under the circumstances was natural, to stifle my own feelings. Just then I thought I heard a human voice borne down upon the gale. I listened; it was, I feared, but the effect of imagination; yet I waited a moment. Again the voice struck my ear, and this time several of the ship's company heard it. 'There he is, sir! There he is away to windward!' exclaimed several voices; and then in return they uttered a loud hearty cheer, to keep up the spirits of the poor fellow. Now came the most trying moment; I must decide whether I would allow a boat to be lowered. 'If I refuse,' I felt, 'my crew will say that I am careless of their lives. It is not their nature to calculate the risk they themselves must run.' At once Mr Christopher, one of my lieutenants, nobly volunteered to make the attempt, and numbers of the crew came forward anxious to accompany him. At last, anxiety to save a drowning man prevailed over prudence, and I sanctioned the attempt.

The boat, with Mr Christopher and a picked crew, was lowered, not without great difficulty, and, sad to say, with the loss of one of the brave fellows. He was the bowman; and, as he stood up with his boat-hook in his hand to shove off, the boat give a terrific pitch and sent him over the bow. He must have struck his head against the side of the ship, for he went down instantly, and was no more seen. Thus, in the endeavour to save the life of one man, another was already sent to his long account. With sad forebodings for the fate of the rest of the gallant fellows, I saw the boat leave the ship's side. Away she pulled into the darkness, where she was no longer visible; and a heavy pull I knew she must have of it in that terrible sea, even if she escaped destruction. It was one of the most trying times of my life. We waited in suspense for the return of the boat; the minutes, seeming like hours, passed slowly by, and she did not appear. I began at length to dread that my fears would be realised, and that we should not again see her, when, after half an hour had elapsed since she had left the ship's side on her mission of mercy, a cheer from her gallant crew announced her approach with the success of their bold enterprise. My anxiety was not, however, entirely relieved till the falls were hooked on, and she and all her crew were hoisted on board, with the rescued man Miles. To my surprise I found that he was perfectly naked. As he came up the side, also, he required not the slightest assistance, but dived below at once to dry himself and to get out of the cold. I instantly ordered him to his hammock, and, with the doctor's permission, sent him a stiff glass of grog. I resolved also to relieve him from duty, believing that his nervous system would have received a shock from which it would take long to recover. After I had put the ship once more on her course, being anxious to learn the particulars of his escape, as soon as I heard that he was safely stowed away between the blankets, I went below to see him. His voice was as strong as ever; his pulse beat as regularly, and his nerves seemed as strong as usual. After pointing out to him how grateful he should feel to our Almighty Father for his preservation from an early and dreadful death, I begged him to tell me how he had contrived to keep himself so long afloat. He replied to me in the following words:—'Why, sir, you see as soon as I came up again, after I had first struck the water, I looked out for the ship, and, getting sight of her running away from me, I remembered how it happened I was there, and knew there would be no use swimming after her or singing out. Then, sir, I felt very certain you would not let me drown without an attempt to pick me up, and that there were plenty of fine fellows on board who would be anxious to man a boat to come to my assistance, if you thought a boat could swim. Then, thinks I to myself, a man can die but once, and if it's my turn to-day, why, there's no help for it. Yet I didn't think all the time that I was likely to lose the number of my mess, do ye see, sir. The next thought that came to me was, if I am to drown, it's as well to drown without clothes as with them; and if I get them off, why, there's a better chance of my keeping afloat till a boat can be lowered to pick me up; so I kicked off my shoes, and then I got off my jacket, and then, waiting till I could get hold of the two legs at once, I drew off my trousers in a moment. My shirt was soon off me, but I took care to roll up the tails, so as not to get them over my face. As I rose on the top of the sea, I caught sight of the ship as you wore her round here, and that gave me courage, for I felt I was not to be deserted; indeed, I had no fear of that. Then I knew that there would be no use swimming; so all I did was to throw myself on my back and float till you came up to me. I thought the time was somewhat long, I own. When the ship got back, I saw her hove to away down to leeward, but I did not like to sing out for fear of tiring myself, and thought you would not hear me; and I fancied also that a boat would at once have been lowered to come and look for me. Well, sir, I waited, thinking the time was very long, and hearing no sound, yet still I could see the ship hove to, and you may be sure I did not take my eyes from off her; when at last I heard your voice give the order to wear ship again. Then thinks I to myself, now or never's the time to sing out. And, raising myself as high as I could out of the water, I sang out at the top of my voice. There was a silence on board, but no answer, and I did begin to feel that there was a chance of being lost after all. "Never give in, though," thinks I; so I sung out again, as loud, you may be sure, as I could sing. This time the answering cheers of my shipmates gave me fresh spirits; but still I knew full well that I wasn't safe on board yet. If I had wanted to swim, there was too much sea on to make any way; so I kept floating on my back as before, just keeping an eye to leeward to see if a boat was coming to pick me up. Well, sir, when the boat did come at last, with Mr Christopher and the rest in her, I felt strong and hearty, and was well able to help myself on board. I now can scarcely fancy I was so long in the water.' I was much struck with the extraordinary coolness of Miles. He afterwards had another escape, which was owing less to his own self-possession, though he took it as coolly as the first. On our passage home, the ship was running with a lightish breeze and almost calm sea across the Bay of Biscay, when Miles was sent on the fore-topgallant-yard. By some carelessness he fell completely over the yard, and those aloft expected to see him dashed to pieces on the forecastle. Instead of that, the foresail at that moment swelled out with a sudden breeze, and, striking the bulge of the sail, he was sent forward clear of the bows and hove into the water. A rope was towing overboard. He caught hold of it, and, hauling himself on board, was again aloft within a couple of minutes attending to his duty, which had so suddenly been interrupted. On his arrival in England, Lieutenant Christopher received the honorary silver medal from the Royal Humane Society for his gallant conduct on the occasion of saving Miles' life.

## Two Courageous Swimmers—1838

HMS *Seringapatam*, Captain Leith, was lying off the island of Antigua, in August 1838, when, on Sunday, the 26th of that month, eight of her officers, three of whom were youngsters, and all belonging to the midshipmen's berth, with a gentleman, a resident in the island, and two seamen, started away from the ship in a pinnace on a cruise. Their intention was to go down to Falmouth Bay, situated about two miles to leeward of English Harbour, where the ship was, and to beat back. The afternoon was very fine, and everything seemed to promise them a pleasant excursion. Having spent a short time in Falmouth Harbour, they hauled their wind, and made three or four tacks on their way back to the ship. The boat, however, made little or nothing to windward, in consequence of the wind being very light. Forgetful of the sudden squalls which visit those latitudes, the merry party of young officers seemed to have kept but a bad look-out to windward; for, while standing in on the starboard tack, the boat was taken by a sudden squall. The helm was put down; but the boat not coming up to the wind so as to lift the sails, she was capsized under every stitch of canvas. She, however, went over so gradually, that all hands had time to creep to windward and seat themselves on the gunwale. The sails prevented her from turning bottom up, and at the same time protected them in some measure from the breaking of the sea. What seems very extraordinary is, that not one of the party, officers or seamen, had a knife in his pocket, so that they had no means of cutting away the rigging and righting the boat. As soon as they had settled themselves on the side of the boat, they had time to look about them, and to consider their perilous position. They were fully two miles from the shore, whence it was scarcely possible anyone should have observed the accident, and they were an equal distance or more from the ship; thus the current might carry them far away before anyone could come to their assistance. A sea might get up and wash them off the wreck; or sharks might attack and devour them, for the boat's gunwale was only six inches awash. Not a sail was in sight; and all felt convinced that if some unforeseen assistance did not come to their aid, they must perish. Despair was well-nigh taking possession of the bosoms of all the party. Silent and melancholy they sat on the wreck, meditating on their fate. All were young. Life, with all its fancied charms and anticipated pleasure, had a few short moments previously been before them; and now, death in all its terrors—slow, lingering, and agonising—stared them in the face. One only of the whole party was a good swimmer, Mr W.R. Smith, and he was a very bold and strong one. He looked at the shore: two miles was a long distance to swim, with a full consciousness, too, that those deep waters swarm with those terrific monsters of the deep, the seamen's just dread—the hideous, shark.

"Well," said Smith at last, looking wistfully at the distant shore, "I feel that I ought to try, as it is the only chance of saving all hands; and I think I could have managed it if I had had but a companion, but it's a long way to go alone through the silent water."

"If that is your only reason, Smith, why, I will try and keep you company," said Palmes, another midshipman, who had hitherto sat silent, not complaining like some of the rest. "I am not much of a swimmer, and I don't feel as if I could ever get to shore. However, it's a good cause, and I'll do my best."

Thus it was speedily settled, for there was no time to be lost. The two noble adventurers, having bid farewell to their shipmates, whom Palmes, at all events, never expected to see again, threw off their jackets and shoes, and struck away together from the wreck. The prayers of those they left behind followed them, for the safety of all depended on their success. Smith swam steadily and strongly, and Palmes made amends for his want of strength and skill by his courage and spirit. Still, before they got half-way to the shore, the courage of one of them was to be sorely tried. As Smith swam along, he felt his legs strike against something, and, looking down into the clear water, he saw, to his horror, two enormous sharks swimming past him. As yet they had not noticed him; and fortunate was it for both of the brave fellows that they had kept on their trousers and socks, for had the monsters seen the white flesh of their naked feet, they would to a certainty have fixed on them as their prey. With admirable presence of mind, Smith kept this dreadful fact to himself, lest the knowledge of it should still further unnerve his companion, who already was almost exhausted by his exertions. At this time they were still full a mile from the shore, which, to their anxious eyes, appeared still farther off.

"Smith, my dear fellow," exclaimed Palmes, "I can swim no farther. Do you push on, and leave me to my fate."

"Not I, my lad," answered Smith. "Cheer up, man; we'll yet do well. Here, rest on me for a time; but don't cease striking out."

Suiting the action to the word, he came alongside and supported his companion; but he did not tell him why he urged him to keep striking out. Again they struck out together, and Palmes seemed somewhat recovered; but once more his strength forsook him, and he fancied himself incapable of proceeding. Still Smith did not lose courage; but he saw the necessity of keeping their limbs moving, lest the dreadful sharks should be tempted to lay hold of them. Palmes had fully as much moral courage as his companion, but he was his inferior in physical strength; yet, feeling that not only his own life and that of Smith, but that of their nine fellow-creatures remaining on the wreck, depended on their reaching the shore, nerved him to further exertions.

Those only who have swam for their lives, when the arms have begun to ache, the knees refuse to bend, and the breath grows short, can tell the feelings of the two gallant young men, but more especially those of the brave Palmes. Spurred on by Smith, each time that he grew faint and weary, he nerved himself for fresh exertions. At last, as they strained their eyes ahead, the shore seemed to come nearer and nearer. They could distinguish the sandy beach and the green herbage beyond. On a sudden, before even he expected it, Smith felt his foot touch the shore. With a joyful exclamation of thankfulness, he grasped Palmes by the hand, and aided him to wade on to the dry land. No sooner had they emerged from the water, than, overcome with fatigue, poor Palmes sank down on the beach, where he lay for some time unable to move. We fain would believe—nay, we are certain—that they both offered up in their hearts a silent thanksgiving to the Great Being who had thus mercifully preserved them from the perils of the deep. But the gallant Smith, while rejoicing in his own preservation and that of his friend, did not forget the shipmates he had left floating on the wreck. As soon as he had recovered sufficient strength to move, he hurried off to the nearest habitation, to give information of the accident, and to procure a boat to go to their assistance. Already much time had been lost. It was half-past four when the accident occurred, and they had been two hours in reaching the shore, so that darkness was now rapidly approaching, which, of course, would increase the difficulty of finding the wreck. The instant Palmes was able to move, he also got up and went in search of a boat. He procured one, with a crew to man it, while Smith took charge of another; and they immediately started in search of their shipmates. Meantime information of the sad accident had been conveyed on board the

*Seringapatam.* The kind heart of the captain was much grieved when he heard of it, for he could not but fear that the remainder of the party had perished. From him, downwards to the smallest boy in the ship, everybody was most painfully anxious about them. He instantly despatched boats in all directions to search for the missing party. All sorts of reports were flying about on board; and as sharks were known to abound, it was feared by the seamen that they might have destroyed their young shipmates. The night also became very bad: the wind rose, and threatened to increase; the sea got up with it, thick clouds collected, and the white-topped waves added to the gloominess of the night, while the rain came down in torrents, and the lightning burst forth in sharp and vivid flashes, increasing the dangers to be apprehended. The boats of the *Seringapatam* took different directions, each officer commanding shaping the course he thought most likely to bring him up to the wreck. Some of the searching boats went in a wrong direction altogether, being misled by a pilot as to the direction the current took. Hour after hour passed by, and no sign of the wreck was perceived; and both those on board, and many of those in the boats, began to despair of success. As they looked out through the darkness, they fancied they could hear the voices of their shipmates at a distance, imploring aid, or that they saw their figures on the bottom of the boat amid the surrounding gloom. We shall, however, follow the *Seringapatam*'s barge, commanded by her gunner. He knew the set of the current; and, as soon as he shoved off from the ship's side, he ran directly down to leeward along the coast, at the distance he understood the boat had been capsized, he being thus better able to calculate the direction in which she would have drifted. His purpose was then to beat back again, thus entirely covering the ground where the wreck must be. On his way down he fell in with the shore-boat, commanded by Mr Smith, who, at once approving of his plan, joined him in the search. By their calculations, the boat would have drifted some five or six miles to leeward, and would be drawn rather off shore. They were right; and about the very place where they expected, she was discerned still floating as Smith had left her. With anxious hearts they pulled up to her. Five only of the nine were seen still clinging to her. The other four had too probably given themselves up to despair. The crew of the barge cheered, and were answered with a faint hail from those they had come to save, almost sinking from exhaustion.

"Where are the rest?" exclaimed Smith, as he saw their diminished numbers.

"Only a short distance inshore of us," was the answer. "They have not left the wreck five minutes."

"Alas! but in those five minutes the poor fellows may have sunk fathoms down, or been grasped by the jaws of the hungry sharks," thought Smith, as he instantly pulled away in the direction indicated.

His four shipmates were found not far apart, each of them lashed to an oar, and striking out as well as they could for the shore; but, strange to say, only one of them could swim at all.

It was then past nine o'clock, making nearly five hours that the poor fellows had held on to the boat, with all the horrors of death staring them in the face; for of course they were not aware that Smith and Palmes had reached the shore, and indeed had begun to fear that they were already numbered with the dead. Their pleasure, and—we believe, their gratitude—was increased when they discovered that both had escaped, and had been the means under Providence of preserving their lives.

Their sufferings had been very great. When the storm came on, they expected every moment to be washed from the wreck; and, to add to their horrors, a shark had been for most of the time lying between the masts of the pinnace, his fiery eyes glaring up at them, and watching them, as about soon to become his prey. Had it not, indeed, been for Smith's coolness and skill as a swimmer, and for the generous daring of Palmes, in all human probability every soul must have perished. The circumstances we have narrated having been represented to the Royal Humane Society, the silver medallion of the Society, with a complimentary letter, was sent out, and presented on the quarter-deck of the *Seringapatam*, by Captain Leith, to each of the two young officers, in the presence of the whole ship's company,—a suitable and gratifying reward for their gallantry, in addition to that their own consciences could not fail to afford.

Some years after the events I have just described, Mr W.R. Smith, having reached the rank of lieutenant, belonged to HMS *Endymion*. On the 4th of February 1847, she was at anchor off Sacraficios Island, near Vera Cruz. The night of the 4th was excessively dark, and a strong current was running past the ship, when Mr West, mate, slipped his foot from the gangway, and fell into the sea, striking his head against the ship's side. On the cry of "A man overboard!" which was instantly raised, Lieutenant W.R. Smith and others rushed on deck; but, owing to the excessive darkness and the strong current, no object could at first be seen floating. At length something white was perceived at a distance, when Lieutenant Smith immediately plunged into the water, and struck rapidly out towards it. On reaching the object, he found it to be Mr West, who was lying quite motionless, though, from his head sinking under water, he would speedily have been deprived of life. Lieutenant Smith at once raised his head above water, and kept him floating until by repeatedly calling he attracted a boat to his assistance, when he and his companion were carried on board. The crew were thickly clustering on the rigging to see them return, and from among them another man missed his footing and fell overboard from the main-chains. Mr Smith, who saw the accident, not knowing whether the man could swim, instantly plunged in again to his assistance, but found, on reaching him, that he was perfectly able to keep himself afloat till the boat could arrive to pick him up.

### Rescue of a Boat's Crew—January 1840

HMS *Wolverine* formed one of the African squadron, and was commanded by the brave and kind Commander Tucker. She had been cruising off the coast, when, on the 15th of January 1840, she anchored off the river Brass, or Saint John, one of the mouths of the far-famed and mysterious Niger. Captain

Tucker had made himself thoroughly acquainted with the coast, as well as with the modes of proceeding of the slave-dealers and of the slavers, and he was thus enabled to capture a very large number of vessels, though, with single-minded purpose, as his object was to stop the slave trade, he endeavoured to take them before they got their slaves on board. Soon after the brig had brought up, about four miles from the shore, Captain Tucker ordered the boats to be hoisted out, and to be fitted for service during an absence of three days. While this work was going forward, a canoe was observed paddling off from the shore towards the ship. On her coming alongside, she was found to contain two natives of great consequence, it seemed, judging from their costume,—that is to say, if scarlet dresses, or rather wrappers round the loins, and ornamented caps, might be admitted as tests of rank. They came up the side without hesitation, and, after some cross-questioning, they informed Captain Tucker that they had seen a fine schooner, under American colours, up the river Nun, and that from her appearance and movements there could be no doubt that she was a slaver. The promise of a reward induced them, with negro eagerness, to undertake all Captain Tucker proposed,—to act as spies, and to bring further information about the vessel, and then to perform the part of pilots in conducting her, when captured, down the river. This information, which it was hoped was correct, hurried the departure of the boats. Lieutenant Dumaresq took charge of the pinnace, as commanding officer of the expedition; Mr Arthur B. Kingston, then a mate, had the cutter; and Mr Thorburn, another mate of the *Wolverine*, went in the gig. Water, provisions, and arms having been placed in the boats, and all being ready, they shoved off from the ship at half-past ten in the morning. Lieutenant Dumaresq had one of the black pilots in his boat, and Mr Kingston had the other with him. Sometimes sailing when there was a breeze, and at others, when it fell light, the crews, eager for work of some sort, pulling away with a will, they soon reached the mouth of the River Brass. The river is here pretty broad; its banks, as far as the eye can reach, covered with tall mangroves, their dark foliage imparting a sombre and almost funereal aspect to the scenery. After the boats had pulled about ten miles up the Brass, they reached a sort of natural canal which connects the Brass with the Nun. On passing through this, they entered the Nun, when they hove to for dinner,—a meal not at all unwelcome after their long pull. The crews being refreshed, they again bent to their oars, and proceeded about 30 miles up the Nun. Darkness now rapidly came on, and they were no longer able to see ahead, nor had they been able to discover anything of their looked-for prize. On questioning their black volunteer pilots, the worthy gentlemen seemed very uncertain, not only whether the slaver had sailed, but where she had been and where they then were. One declared that they had come much higher up than where she was last seen, and that she had probably been sheltered from their observation in one of the numerous creeks which run through the banks of the river. In this dilemma a council of war was held, and at first it was proposed to retrace their steps, till the elder of the black pilots offered to take a small canoe they had with them higher up the river, to ascertain whether or not the slaver was there. This proposal being agreed to by Lieutenant Dumaresq, the two negroes pulled away, and were soon lost in the darkness, not without some slight misgivings as to whether or not they would ever return. However, to pass the time during the absence of the negroes, they piped to supper. A small portion only of the ship's biscuit and salt pork had been discussed, and a glass of grog had just been served out all round, when the canoe was seen gliding at full speed out of the darkness, the dip of her paddles just breaking the stillness of the night.

"Well, my men, any news of the slaver?" asked the lieutenant in an eager whisper, for the return of the canoe gave him hopes that a prize was at hand.

"Ship live there," answered the elder black, in the clear and distinct tones in which his race can speak, but still only in a whisper.

No sooner was this announcement made than the oars were got out simultaneously, and, at a word from Lieutenant Dumaresq, the boats went ahead like magic. Not a word except the necessary ones of command was uttered. Everyone knew the importance of silence. The three boats, urged on by their eager crews, advanced abreast at full speed. Ten minutes, or little more, were sufficient to show the dark outline of a schooner, her masts and spars relieved against the starry sky. Silent as the grave, the boats pulled on, their oars so carefully dipped, that scarcely a splash was heard. Those on board the schooner slept, or seemed to sleep, for not a sound was heard from her decks. A slaver's crew, however, conscious of the risks they are running in their nefarious traffic, are seldom off their guard, and the British seamen were fully prepared for a reception with a shower of grape and musketry. Yet, without a thought of the consequences, on getting close to her, on they dashed with a cheer, and in another instant were alongside and scrambling up her sides. So unexpected had been their attack, that not an attempt at resistance was made; and, to the no small delight of Lieutenant Dumaresq and his followers, they found themselves in possession of a fine little schooner, which proved to be the *Lark*, with a crew of no less than thirty Spaniards. They were first all properly secured and sent down below, with orders to behave themselves, and a hint that if they did not, it would be the worse for them.

A slaver's crew have a right, it is understood, to try and retake their vessel without being treated as pirates and hung in case they do not succeed, or are afterwards captured; so it becomes necessary to keep a very sharp look-out after them. Her papers were at the same time secured, and, on her circumstances being investigated, not a doubt remained as to her character.

Bending sails, and getting all ready for an early start, occupied some time, when, the watch being set, with strict orders to keep a wakeful eye on the prisoners, the rest of the party lay down on the sails, and were soon sound asleep.

At early dawn all hands were roused up, and the schooner was very soon got under weigh. There was little or no wind to fill her sails, so the boats' crews had to tow her down the river, hoping to find a breeze, as they got near its mouth, to take her out. Nine miles of their distance had been thus accomplished, when, at about seven o'clock, as she was passing through a long reach of the River Nun, a sail hove in sight, which was soon discovered to be a rakish two-topsail schooner. She stood boldly on up the river towards the *barracoons*, either not observing the little *Lark*, or, at all events, not suspecting into whose hands she had fallen. Lieutenant Dumaresq on this instantly ordered the man-of-war boats to be hauled up alongside of the schooner on the opposite side to that on which the stranger was approaching, so that she should not observe them, and, by taking fright, endeavour to make her escape. At the same time, the pinnace and gig were manned and held in readiness (the crews being well armed) to board the schooner, Mr Kingston receiving orders to remain in charge of the *Lark* with the cutter's crew. On slowly came the stranger, the light wind only just enabling her to stem the current. She seemed totally unconscious of the neighbourhood of her enemies. On a sudden something seemed to awaken her suspicions; and Lieutenant Dumaresq, judging that the best time had arrived for taking possession, shoved off and pulled towards her as fast as the crews could lay their backs to the oars. Mr Kingston meantime was left in command of the *Lark*, with the cutter's crew; Mr Thorburn accompanied their leader. Away went the boats. The stranger now for the first time was aware of her danger, or rather certainty of capture, unless she could blow the approaching boats out of the water; but she could have had but slight hopes of doing so with any chance of ultimate success, as she saw that the *Lark* was in the hands of her enemies, and she could not tell how many people might be remaining on board to avenge the destruction of their comrades. Still, slavers, when they have seen a chance of success, have often fought desperately; and the cutter's crew on board the *Lark* watched with deep interest the approach of the two boats to the big schooner, not knowing what moment she might open her fire on them; but the slaver's crew had not even the brute-like courage to induce them to fight in defence of their accursed calling, and, without firing a shot, they allowed the two boats to come alongside. Once having a firm hold of the slaver's chains with their boat-hooks, the British seamen very quickly scrambled on board. The crew, who were chiefly Spaniards, made no opposition, nor did a number of other people, who, dressed in shore-going clothes, announced themselves as passengers. There was certainly a wonderfully sea-going look about them, though they all seemed very anxious to leave the vessel as fast as possible. Now, as the consequences of detaining people against their will are often very disagreeable, Lieutenant Dumaresq, whatever might have been his suspicions, thought it best to allow the gentlemen to take their departure. It was afterwards discovered that the fellows, who were all of them belonging to the slaver's crew, took on shore a very considerable number of doubloons, which form in general the most valuable portion of a prize, unless she has her cargo of slaves on board; the slave-vessel herself and her stores rarely sell for much. What was called head-money has of late years been reduced to one-fourth of what it was formerly. The new prize proved to be the *Asp*, a fit name for a slaver, though she was now effectually deprived of her sting. As soon as she was thoroughly overhauled, and all her forthcoming papers secured, the Spanish crew were sent below, and the man-of-war's boats began towing the two schooners down the river. It was laborious work, after the incessant labour for so many hours the men had gone through; but a prize tows easily, and the gallant fellows cheerfully bent to their oars. Thus the two vessels proceeded on rapidly between the mangrove-covered banks of the river. By five p.m. the entrance of the Nun appeared in sight, and preparations were instantly made for crossing the bar,—I must rather say bars, for there are three, one within the other, at some distance apart; and over them, when the current sets out and the wind blows in, the sea breaks with great violence, so that, under those circumstances, the crossing them, even in a decked vessel, is a work of very considerable danger. On this occasion appearances were far from favourable: the wind was foul, and blowing very strong; a heavy sea was breaking over the bars, its incessant roar seeming like a warning not to venture into its power; while evening was rapidly closing in, the coming darkness threatening to increase the difficulties to be encountered. Still Mr Dumaresq was unwilling to expose his followers to the baneful atmospheric influences of another night spent within the mouth of the river, or to the chances of attack from any of the slavers' friends who might be in the neighbourhood, and who would always be ready to win back a prize at any sacrifice of the lives of the captors; though that was a contingency not likely to happen. He was rather influenced, probably, by his anxiety to secure his prizes, and to report his proceedings to his superior officer. The schooners had anchored just inside the inner bar, and all the necessary preparations having been made, and the tide serving, they again got under weigh. Mr Dumaresq led in the *Asp*, directing Mr Kingston to follow in his wake. This Mr Kingston did, approaching the bar on the starboard tack, the *Lark* having the cutter towing astern, and her own boat, which could not be hoisted up on account of the tackles being unrove, and a net full of vegetables being worked athwart the davits. Neither could her boat be got on board, on account of the crowded state of the decks. As the *Lark* drew close to the bar, the appearance of things in no degree mended. Hands were placed in the chains, who kept the lead constantly going; and, as the water shoaled, the schooners had to tack repeatedly, wearing sometimes, as the heavy swell threatened otherwise to prevent their coming round. From the first, Mr Kingston had but little confidence in the black volunteer pilot who had accompanied him on board the *Lark*; and now, though he urged him by threats to perform the duty he had undertaken, and tried to stimulate him to exertion by reminding him of his promised reward, he only answered, "This is no my bar!" and finally threw himself down on the deck under the bulwarks, refusing to take any further charge of the vessel. It must be remembered that the boats had entered the *Niger* by the Brass River, the bar of which was his bar, and that he had bargained to act as pilot through its mouth, so that there was ample excuse for the poor wretch; this, however, in no degree lessened the danger of the position in which the little *Lark* was placed.

It was now perfectly dark and very squally, while nothing was visible to mark the course the vessel should pursue but the phosphorescent light of the breakers stretching across the bar from shore to shore; while to all appearance there seemed to be reef only beyond reef, destruction on which it was scarcely possible the schooner could escape. Though the *Lark* was pressed to the utmost, the *Asp* soon distanced her; and though Lieutenant Dumaresq showed lights, they were of little or no use in guiding her course. Squall after squall struck the little schooner; and, as she heeled over, it sometimes appeared that she would never again rise, or be able to beat out through the tremendous surf which came rolling in. At length Mr Kingston judged it wise to shorten sail, which he forthwith did, having set only his mainsail, jib, and fore-and-aft foresail, a fore-trysail. He also sent a good hand on the fore-yard to look out for any break which might happily appear in the white wall of surf which came rolling in over the surrounding shoals. The little *Lark* had now reached the innermost of the three bars, and was pitching into the seas, which came foaming up and rolling over her decks. She had the cutter towing after her, and astern of that was the schooner's boat. That very soon began to fill, and finally swamped, when it became necessary to cut her adrift. This was done, and she quickly disappeared. At about a quarter to eight a blue light was observed close to windward; and as the *Lark* was wearing off the heaviest part of the bar, some voices were heard hailing her. It was soon discovered that they proceeded from the pinnace, which had apparently several hands in her. Again they hailed, imploring to be picked up, stating, as far as could be understood, that they had broken adrift from astern of the *Asp*, with the gig, which was lost; and from the words which reached the *Lark*, Mr Kingston was very much afraid that several lives were already sacrificed, while it seemed too probable that those in the pinnace would share the same fate, unless he could manage to get near them to take them on board. There was not a moment to spare. The pinnace, it must be understood, was inside the *Lark*, higher up the river, the *Lark* having passed her after she had broken adrift from the *Asp*. In another minute she would have drifted among the breakers, when the destruction of all on board would be sealed. To pick her up under weigh was almost impossible; and, with the tide and heavy sea, the schooner could not be steered with any degree of certainty even near her; and could even this be done, the probabilities were that she would be swamped before the men could be got out of her. The young officer therefore saw that but one course only was open for him to pursue with any chance of success, and that involved immense risk both to the vessel and his people. To think is to act with a British seaman in a case of emergency. He saw that to intercept the boat he must anchor; and, having both anchors clear, and a hand by the weather one all along, he ordered it to be let go, though he had but two fathoms at the time under the vessel's keel, while the surf from the second bar was curling up round the vessel's sides, threatening to make a clear sweep of her decks. His order to let go was perhaps not understood, or the Spanish crew, some thirty in number, seeing what was about to be done, and expecting instant destruction in consequence, endeavoured to impede it; at all events, he had to rush forward and cut the stoppers with an axe, which he luckily had at hand.

The schooner brought up all standing, the sea at the same instant making a terrific breach over her; but the helmsman was a good hand, and sheered her over to the exact spot the pinnace must pass. The whole was the work of a moment. The boat drifted near, a rope was hove into her, and providentially caught by the nearly exhausted crew. She was hauled alongside, her people being got out, while some fresh hands went down into her and secured her with her own cable and the end of the schooner's main-sheet. At the same time the schooner's fore-sheet was passed into the cutter as a preventer. Four men were saved from the pinnace. They stated that she and the gig had been towing astern of the *Asp*, with two hands in each, when, on crossing the inner bar, they both broke adrift together. Instead, however, of the two men in the pinnace getting into the gig, which they might have managed, those in the smaller got into the larger boat, fancying they would be safer, when they found themselves totally unable to pull her against the tide, or to guide her to shore. The *Lark* very soon after this began to drive, when the other anchor was dropped under foot, while they veered away on the larboard cable. She now held, but the breakers made a clean breach over her decks, washing adrift the numerous casks, loose spars, fowl-coops, and a variety of other things; and in addition, what was worse than all, a large scuttle-butt of palm-oil. Meantime, to increase the confusion and danger, the cutter and pinnace were striking the stern and quarters of the vessel with great force, often coming as far forward as the main-chains on both sides. The Spaniards had from the first been very unruly, and they now gave symptoms of an intention of breaking into open mutiny. In addition, therefore, to the variety of other duties the British seamen were called on to perform, it became necessary for them to keep their arms in readiness, to repel any sudden attack the fellows might venture to make on them for the purpose of regaining the schooner. The palm-oil, also, which is like very thick red mud, had coated the whole deck from before the foremast nearly as far aft as the mainmast, making it more slippery even than ice, so that no one could either stand or walk on it. The water, also, had no effect on its greasy composition, and as there were no ashes on board to strew over it, one part of the deck became almost separated from the other. The Spaniards were evidently watching their opportunity, and kept eyeing the British seamen with no friendly intentions. They were four to one of them, and though deprived of their muskets and cutlasses, they had still the long knives in their belts, without which no Spaniard ever thinks his costume complete. The wretches kept up such a hubbub, and did so much to impede the work of the vessel, that some of them very nearly got shot, as a hint to the rest of what they might expect if they proceeded to extremities. The gallant young officer himself had little fear of what they might venture to do, as, considering the dilemma the vessel was placed in, surrounded by shoals, with heavy breakers close at hand, and in thick darkness, they could scarcely hope to get out to sea and escape that way, or, if they returned up the river, to avoid recapture should they regain possession of the vessel. In obedience, however, to his written instructions, he kept some of his people under arms to watch the fellows. For full half an hour the little schooner lay in this way, it being expected every instant that her anchors would part, when a roller, more severe even than the others, threw the cutter on board on the larboard quarter, breaking the bunk adrift and capsizing it. As the vessel rose again, the boat fell aft and immediately filled, when she was of necessity cut adrift to prevent her doing more damage; and as soon as this was done she sank. Shortly after this the squalls began to become less frequent, and the breakers moderated gradually; an opening, also, was seen in the line of sparkling foam from the fore-yard; so Mr Kingston resolved to make sail and to get out of the river. He contrived to weigh the starboard or lee anchor, after very many fruitless attempts to do so on account of the heavy surges; but as it was found impossible to purchase the weather one, it was slipped, and the schooner wore round under her jib in a quarter less two fathoms. A sharp-sighted seaman stood on the fore-yard, from whence he conned the vessel,—the lead kept going as before. The mainsail was then set, and the schooner stood out towards the opening which appeared in the surf. She obeyed her helm readily, the rocks and shoals were avoided, and at length the outer bar was safely passed. At about ten p.m. she came up with the *Asp*, anchored a short distance outside. Lieutenant Dumaresq stood with speaking-trumpet in hand, and hailed the *Lark*. "I'm glad you've got out safe; but I fear four of my poor fellows are lost, and our two boats."

"They're safe on board, and I have your boat in tow," was the answer. A loud congratulatory cheer from the British seamen on board the *Asp* signified their satisfaction at the success of Mr Kingston's gallant exploit. He then anchored, and, going on board the *Asp*, was further thanked and congratulated by his superior officer; who had not only given up all hopes of the people in the pinnace and gig having escaped, but of the *Lark* herself, as his own vessel had had a most perilous passage across the bars. She had struck three times, in one of which shocks the boats had broken adrift. The two schooners again weighed and ran down to the *Wolverine*, lying off the Brass, ten miles distant. On their arrival, Mr Kingston had the satisfaction of receiving the warmest approval of his excellent commander for the gallantry and judgment he had displayed. The vessels were afterwards sent to Sierra Leone, where they were condemned and cut up.

Mr Kingston having taken the *Lark* schooner to Sierra Leone, where she was condemned, was appointed to HMS *Saracen*, which soon afterwards arrived there. From that place the *Saracen* sailed for the River Gambia, soon after the 2nd of March.

On the evening of the 13th of the same month, while on her passage there, when it was blowing fresh, with a heavy cross sea, a lad aged nineteen, named John Plunket, fell overboard from the main-topgallant-yard. In falling he struck against the topsail-yard and the sweeps stowed on the quarter, and was bleeding at the mouth and almost senseless when he reached the water. The lad could not swim, and his death seemed inevitable; when Mr Kingston, who was on the quarter-deck, without a moment's hesitation sprang overboard, exclaiming to his commander as he ran aft, "Send a boat as quick as you can, sir—I'll save him."

He struck out bravely towards the poor lad, but before he could reach him he sank. A cry of horror arose from all on board, for they thought the lad was lost, though every exertion was made to get a boat in the water to pick up Mr Kingston. Plunket, however, again rose, and Mr Kingston grasping hold of him, supported him above water, though with much difficulty, as the lad, who bled profusely from the mouth and nostrils, convulsively clung round him, and almost dragged him down to the bottom. Fortunately, he released himself from the clutch of the now senseless youth, and continued to support him by swimming and treading water. For fear of exhaustion, he afterwards threw himself on his back, and, placing the head of his almost inanimate shipmate on his chest, he kept him up for a quarter of an hour, till a boat reached them and took them on board.

On another occasion, while on the coast of Africa, in a spot where sharks were known to abound, Mr Kingston leaped overboard after another lad who had fallen into the water. Fortunately the life-buoy was let go at the same time, and, wisely catching hold of it, he towed it up to the sinking youth, and providentially preserved his life.

CHAPTER 22

# Gallant Deeds

HUMANITY OF LIEUTENANT BREEN, RN
—MEDITERRANEAN, 1850

That the seamen of the British navy are as humane as they are brave we have numberless examples to prove. The following is one of numerous instances in which they have risked and often sacrificed their lives for the good of others, and should on no account be passed over.

As one of the boats of HMS *Ganges*, forming part of the British fleet in the Piraeus, with Lieutentant Breen, Mr Chatfield, midshipman, and 16 men, was returning from the shore, laden with water, she was swamped and turned over just half-way between the *Queen* and the east point of the island of Lypso.

Mr Breen, Mr Chatfield, and most of the men, immediately struck out for the island, and reached it. The gale increased, and the cold became so intense that their clothes were frozen stiff upon them. In the morning they could see the fleet, but were unable to draw attention to themselves by the signals they were making. One of the men suffered so much from the cold that Lieutenant Breen generously stripped off his coat and put it on him. As the day closed, most of the men retired into a cave; but Mr Breen separated himself from the others, and was no more seen. On board the *Ganges* it was thought that they had not put off from shore; but next night it was known that they had set out, and a boat was sent to search. As she was passing by Lypso at dawn on the third day, the wrecked boat was accidentally descried on the beach. Mr Chatfield and half a dozen men were found in the cave in a torpid state; Mr Breen was found dead, crouched under a bush, and ten seamen were missing. There is little doubt that poor Mr Breen lost his life from his generous act in favour of the suffering seamen. The survivors found in the cave all recovered.

### Gallantry Exhibited in Preserving Life —Captain Wasey, RN—1860

On the 22nd of January 1860, the schooner *Ann Mitchell* went ashore near Fleetwood. A new lifeboat, not long before placed there by the National Lifeboat Institution, was immediately launched, when Captain Wasey, Inspecting Commander of the Coast Guard, to encourage the men, went off in her. A strong tide was running in, and a hard gale blowing from the west-north-west. It was night. Stronger and stronger blew the gale, the sea breaking terrifically on the shore and over the hapless vessel. A small steamer was got ready, and took the lifeboat in tow. Even thus but slow way was made in the teeth of the gale, the tide, and the raging sea. Still the steamer persevered. Slowly she gained ground, and at length, having got to windward of the wreck, the tow-rope was cast off, and the boat proceeded alone on her work of mercy. She got within a few yards of the wreck, when a tremendous sea rushing in, struck her and filled her, breaking some of her oars. At that moment it seemed as if the lifeboat herself was doomed to destruction. She was but small, pulling only six oars, and scarcely fitted for the arduous work in which she was engaged. Captain Wasey now anchored, and attempted to veer her down to the wreck, but the strong tide running defeated his intention. The anchor being then weighed, another attempt was made to board the vessel to leeward; but a heavy sea striking her, she was thrown over altogether, her masts falling within a few feet of the lifeboat, whose brave crew thus narrowly escaped destruction. Again, therefore, Captain Wasey determined to anchor to windward, and once more to veer down. This time success attended the efforts of the lifeboat's crew, lines being thrown on board of the wreck and secured. One of the people from the schooner then threw himself into the sea, and was hauled into the boat; but unhappily the others appeared to be either fearful or unable to follow his example; and, from the pitchy darkness and the noise of the sea and wind, it was impossible to communicate intelligibly with them. Captain Wasey learned from the man saved, that three persons remained; one—the master—had his back hurt, and another—a boy—his leg broken. While endeavouring to carry out their humane purpose, a heavy sea broke over both vessel and boat, carrying away the lines, and sweeping the boat some 300 yards to leeward. Many seamen might have despaired of regaining the wreck, but the men of the lifeboat, encouraged by their gallant leader, pulled up once more, in the hopes of saving the poor fellows on the wreck. Great was their disappointment, however, on again getting alongside, to discover that the last heavy sea had washed them all off. Captain Wasey and his gallant followers having done all that men could do, had at length to return to the shore with one only out of the four people who had formed the crew of the *Ann Mitchell*. They had been thus occupied for nearly nine hours of a dark winter's night, with untiring exertion and exposure. The lifeboat had been launched at six p.m. on the 22nd, and did not return to the shore till forty minutes past two a.m. on the 23rd.

Their labours in the cause of humanity were, however, not over for that day. Soon after daylight broke, it was reported to Captain Wasey that another vessel had apparently sunk on the shoals which surround and extend to a long distance from the port of Fleetwood. Rising without a moment's hesitation, he summoned John Fox, chief boatman of the Coast Guard, and coxswain of the lifeboat, with some other men, and two of his former crew, James Turner and John Aspingal, fishermen. The lifeboat was once more afloat, and, towed for two hours against a strong tide and heavy sea by the steam-tug, she at length reached the wreck, which proved to be the schooner

*Jane Roper*, of Ulverstone. Her crew, consisting of six men, were in the rigging, crying out for aid. Captain Wasey and his men happily succeeded in getting them all on board, and in landing them safely at Fleetwood.

On the 19th of February, while it was blowing a heavy gale from the north-north-west, with squalls, the schooner *Catherine*, of Newry, went on shore, when again Captain Wasey went off in the lifeboat, and succeeded in saving all the crew.

On 20th October 1861, the same brave officer, taking command of the lifeboat, was instrumental in saving the lives of 16 persons from the barque *Vermont*, of Halifax, Nova Scotia, wrecked on Barnett's Bank, three miles from Fleetwood. For these and various other similar services he has received several medals and clasps from the Royal National Lifeboat Institution.

### Gallantry of Lieutenant Boyle, RN.

Lieutenant the Hon. H.F. Boyle, RN, chief officer of the Coast Guard at Tenby, distinguished himself in the same humane manner.

At daybreak on the 2nd of November, the smack *Bruce*, of Milford, anchored, being totally dismasted, about three miles east of Tenby. It was blowing a furious gale from the west-south-west, and the sea, running very high, threatened every instant to overwhelm the smack, or to drive her on the rocks. Lieutenant Boyle, immediately on seeing her condition, embarked in the Tenby lifeboat, and pulled off towards the unfortunate vessel. Her crew, three in number, were found in an almost exhausted state, and taken into the lifeboat, which then made for the small harbour of Saundershott, four miles distant.

On the 9th of November, at nine p.m., the commencement of a dark cold night of that inclement season, a large brig was observed to go on shore in Tenby Bay. The lifeboat, manned by her usual varied crew of coastguardsmen and fishermen, under the charge of Robert Parrott, chief boatman of the Coast Guard, who acted as coxswain of the lifeboat, at once proceeded through a tremendous sea towards her, the wind blowing a gale

SHE REACHED THE VESSEL UNDER SAIL

from the south-west. The vessel was discovered to be on shore, in a peculiar position, on a rocky reef, so that she could only be approached from windward. The lifeboat's anchor was accordingly let go, with the intention of being veered down to the wreck, but a heavy roller striking the boat, carried away the cable and broke three of her oars.

Finding it then impossible to close with the vessel, in consequence of her peculiar position and the heavy sea breaking over her, the lifeboat returned to Tenby, and Lieutenant Boyle and his crew proceeded to the spot with all haste by land with the rocket apparatus. Several efforts were made before the party succeeded in sending a line over the wreck. At length perseverance crowned their efforts, a line was thrown, and caught by the crew on the wreck; a stouter rope was next hauled on board, and by its means, in the course of three hours, the whole of the crew, who would otherwise have met with a watery grave, were safely landed. The silver medal of the Lifeboat Institution was awarded to Lieutenant Boyle, and the second-service clasp was added to the medal received on a former occasion by Robert Parrott.

## Lowestoft Lifeboat

Few boats have been the means of saving more lives from destruction than that of the lifeboat belonging to Lowestoft, on the Suffolk coast. We will mention a few instances to show the way in which the seamen and boatmen of that place have risked their lives for the sake of those of their fellow-creatures. On the 26th of October 1859, the schooner *Lord Douglas* parted from her anchors in a heavy gale from the south, and foundered off the village of Carton, on the Suffolk coast; the crew, as she went down, climbing into the rigging, where they lashed themselves.

The Lowestoft lifeboat proceeded under sail to the spot, and, having anchored to windward of the wrecked vessel, succeeded in getting lines down to the crew, who were then drawn from the masts safely on board, and were landed at Carton. So heavy was the gale, that she split her foresail in the service. Scarcely had the lifeboat returned from saving the crew of the *Lord Douglas*, than another schooner, though lying with three anchors ahead, drove ashore at Carton. A foresail was borrowed, and the lifeboat again started on her mission of mercy. She reached the vessel under sail, and happily succeeded in rescuing all the crew; but having split her borrowed sail, she was compelled to run in for Yarmouth beach. Here the shipwrecked crew were hospitably received at the Sailors' Home.

Again, on the 1st of November, the screw-steamer *Shamrock*, of Dublin, ran on shore on the Holme Sand during a heavy gale from the south-west. As soon as the position of the unfortunate vessel was discovered, the lifeboat was launched, and proceeded under sail to the spot. The sea was breaking fearfully over the mast-head of the steamer, repeatedly filling the lifeboat. To increase the danger, an expanse of shoal-water lay close to leeward of the wreck, so that had the lifeboat's cable parted, her destruction and that of her crew might have followed. Fully aware of the risk they ran, they persevered, as brave men will, in spite of danger to themselves; and, sending lines on board the wreck, the whole crew, not without considerable difficulty, were hauled on board.

### Bravery of Joseph Rogers, a Maltese Seaman —25th October 1859

No one will forget the dreadful loss of the *Royal Charter* on the Welsh coast, when, out of 490 souls on board, not more than 25 persons came on shore alive; but many may not recollect that it was owing, under Providence, to the bravery, presence of mind, and strength of one man that even these few were saved. When the ship struck on the rocks, the sea instantly broke over her with fearful violence, filling the intermediate space between her and the shore with broken spars and fragments of the wreck; while the waves burst with fury on the hard rocks, and then rushed back again, to hurl with redoubled force on the iron shore the objects which they had gathered up in their forward course. Pitchy darkness added to the horror of the scene and the danger to be encountered by the hapless passengers and crew of the ill-fated ship. Among the ship's company was a Maltese, Joseph Rogers—a first-rate swimmer, as are many of the inhabitants of the island in which he was born. To attempt to swim on shore in that boiling caldron was full of danger, though he might have felt that he could accomplish it; but the difficulty and danger would be far greater should the swimmer's progress be impeded by a rope. In spite of that, thinking only how he might save the lives of those on board the ship to which he belonged, taking a line in hand, he plunged boldly into the foaming sea. On he swam; the darkness prevented him from being seen, but those on board felt the rope gradually hauled out. Anxiously all watched the progress of that line, for on the success of that bold swimmer the lives of all might depend. If he failed, who could hope to succeed? At length they felt it tightened, and they knew that it was being hauled up by many strong hands on shore. Now a stout rope was fastened to the line, and that being hauled on shore was secured, and a cradle was placed on it. No time was to be lost. The large ship was striking with terrible violence on the rocks, it appearing that every instant would be her last. One after the other, the people on board hastened into the cradle—as many as dared to make the hazardous passage. Ten, fifteen, twenty landed—the twenty-fifth person had just reached the shore, when, with a horrible crash, the ship parted, breaking into fragments, and 454 persons were hurried in a moment into eternity. Even Rogers, brave swimmer as he was, could not have survived had he attempted to swim among those wreck-covered waves. For his heroic courage the National Lifeboat Institution awarded the gold medal to Rogers and a gratuity of 5 pounds.

## Remarkable Instance of Endurance of a Crew of British Seamen

A small fishing smack, with a crew of five people, was wrecked off Bacton, near Great Yarmouth, on the 27th of November 1859. The poor men were in the rigging, without food or drink, for 60 hours before they were rescued from the mast of their sunken vessel, to which they had been clinging for more than

60 hours. For three nights and two days they held on to this uncertain support, about 8 feet above the raging sea, without food, and almost without clothing. One of the men took off his shirt and held it out as a signal of distress, till it was blown from his feeble grasp. The vessel struck upon the Harborough Sand on Friday evening at nine o'clock, and they were not rescued till ten o'clock on Monday morning—a case of most remarkable endurance. The vessel was but a small one, a smack with four hands. The fourth hand, a boy, climbed the mast with the others, and held on till the Saturday, when he became exhausted, and, relaxing his hold, slipped down into the sea. One of the men went down after him, seized him, and dragged him up the mast again; but there was nothing to which to lash him, and no crosstrees or spars on which to rest; so that during the night, when almost senseless with cold and fatigue, the poor boy slipped down again, and was lost in the darkness. On Sunday they were tantalised with the hope of immediate succour. A vessel saw their signals and heard their cries, and sent a boat to their relief; but after buffeting with the wind and tide, they had the mortification to see her give up the attempt, and return to the vessel. Then it was that black despair took possession of them, and they gave themselves up for lost; but clinging to their frail support for an hour or two longer, they heard a gun fire. This gave them fresh courage, for they took it to be a signal, as in fact it was, that their case was known, and an attempt would be made to save them. The vessel stood in and communicated with the shore, and a boat put off to search for them; but they were such a speck on the ocean, that, night coming on, they could not be seen, and the boat returned to shore. For the third night, therefore, they had still to cling on, expecting every moment that the mast would go over and bury them in the deep. On the Monday morning the Bacton boat made another attempt, fell in with them at ten o'clock, and landed them at Palling, more dead than alive, whence, as soon as they could be moved, they were brought to the Yarmouth Sailors' Home, their swollen limbs, benumbed frames, and ghastly countenances testifying to

the sufferings they had undergone. At this Home the poor men remained several weeks, receiving every attention from the officers of the establishment.

To conclude our short account of the services of lifeboats, we may state that in the year 1860 the lives of no less than 326 persons were saved by those stationed on the British coast, every one of which would have been lost.

We will give another example, to exhibit more clearly the nature of the work the brave crews undertake.

In the early part of that year, as the day closed, it was blowing a heavy gale off Lyme-Regis. About eight o'clock at night the alarm was given that a vessel was in distress in the offing. It was pitchy dark; indeed, the intense darkness, the strong gale, and the heavy surf on shore were enough to appal any man entering the lifeboat. After some short delay, however, the boat was manned by a gallant crew—her coxswain, Thomas Bradley, being early at his post. Tar barrels were lighted up on shore, and the boat proceeded on her mission of mercy. So truly awful was the night, that nearly everyone on shore believed she would never return again. However, after battling with the fury of the storm, and after an absence of about an hour and a half, the lifeboat did return, laden with the shipwrecked crew of three men of the smack *Elizabeth Ann*, of Lyme-Regis.

CHAPTER 23

# A Brush With an Ironclad

On the 29th of May 1877 two British corvettes, the *Shah* and the *Amethyst*, were engaged in the only encounter at sea in which Her Majesty's ships have been engaged, (with the exception of fights with slavers) for very many years, and this conflict was the more remarkable inasmuch as their opponent was an ironclad. Peru is the land of revolution and revolt against authority. Such a rising took place in the last week of May. Pierola, the leader, had as his friends the officers of the Peruvian ironclad the *Huascar*, and this vessel pronouncing in his favour, put to sea with him on board. The Peruvian Government at once sent news of the mutiny on board this ship to Admiral de Horsey, and also notified that they would not be answerable for the proceedings of those on board. The *Huascar* put into Perajua, and took coal from an English depot there; she then put to sea, stopped two British steamers and took coal also from them. As this was an act of piracy on the high sea, Admiral de Horsey determined to engage her whenever he met her.

On the 28th of May the *Huascar* appeared off the port of Iquique. Her boats disembarked a portion of her crew, and after a fight with the Peruvian troops, they captured the town. A few hours after that the Peruvian squadron, consisting of the ironclad *Independencia*, the corvette *Unica* and the gunboat *Pilsomayo*, arrived, and it was resolved to engage the *Huascar*. The fight lasted for an hour and a half, and then darkness came on and the *Huascar* steamed away.

The next morning she met the *Shah* and the *Amethyst*. Admiral Horsey sent an officer on board the *Huascar* to demand her surrender. Pierola refused, and upon the return of the officer to the *Shah*, the battle at once commenced.

The *Huascar* was built for the Peruvian Government by Messrs. Samuda, and was a turret-ship mounting two 300-pounder guns in her turret. She had also two 40-pound pivot-guns. The *Shah* and *Amethyst* were unarmoured cruisers, but in point of number of guns they were superior to the ironclad. The fight lasted for three hours. The *Huascar*'s smoke-stack was pierced, and damage done to her deck beams, but the metal of the British guns were not heavy enough to pierce the armour. In the course of the fight the *Shah* launched a Whitehead torpedo against the ironclad, but it failed to strike her. The British ships were ably handled, and received no serious damage in the encounter; and after a three hours' engagement the *Huascar* steamed away and made for a Peruvian port. As this was the first time that unarmoured vessels had ventured to engage an ironclad of modern type, every credit is due to the gallantry of our seamen, although they were unsuccessful in their attempt to capture or sink their opponent.

CHAPTER 24

# Gallant Deeds Performed by Naval Men

### DEATH OF CAPTAIN BROWNRIGG—1881

This officer had greatly distinguished himself by the energy and success with which he had carried on operations against the slaving dhows during the term of his command on the Zanzibar coast. On the 27th of November 1881 he started in the steam pinnace of the *London*, accompanied by his steward, a native interpreter, and a writer, with a crew consisting of a coxswain, Alfred Yates, three seamen, and three stokers. Captain Brownrigg was going upon a tour of inspection among the boats engaged in repressing the slave trade, and the various depots. On his way he examined any *dhows* he met which he suspected to contain slaves. On the 3rd of December a *dhow* was sighted flying French colours. In such cases it was not Captain Brownrigg's custom to board, but only to go alongside to see that the papers were correct. He therefore ordered the boat's crew to be careful not to board without direct orders, intending a mere cursory examination, and no detention whatever, as he did not arm the boat's crew, and directed the time alongside to be noted.

He went alongside without hailing or stopping the *dhow* in any way, the wind being light and the craft scarcely forging ahead.

Prior to getting alongside he sent the coxswain forward to make a hook, with a chain and rope attached, fast to the *dhow*, his object in doing so seemingly being to prevent the necessity of the vessel stopping, and to enable him to converse with the captain and to quietly verify her papers. He took the tiller himself, and was alone, with the exception of his steward (a Goanese) and a native interpreter, in the after-part, which is separated from the rest of the boat by a standing canopy, over which one has to climb to get fore or aft. It was still more cut off by the fact of the main-boom having been raised to the height of the top of the ensign staff on the mainmast, and over it the after-part of the rain-awning was spread, being loosely gathered back towards the mast.

When the boat was quite close to the *dhow*, a man, supposed to be the captain of her, stood up aft with a bundle or roll of papers in his hand, and said something as he unfolded them, and pointed to the French flag. What he exactly said is unknown.

There were then visible on board the *dhow* four men, two aft and two forward, all armed with the usual Arab swords and *creeses*. The forecastle sun-awning was spread at the time from the foremast to a stanchion shipped abaft the stern-piece, and under it were two bluejackets and the writer, the leading stoker was at the engines, whilst the two stokers appear to have been sitting on the inside of the gunnel of the well, *i.e.* the space for boilers and engines.

As the coxswain was standing on the stem of the boat, in the act of making fast with the hook rope, he caught sight of some eight or ten men crouched in the bottom of the boat with guns at the "ready" position. He sang out to the captain aft, when they rose up and fired; he flung the hook at them, and closed with one, both falling overboard together.

The Arabs, the number of whom is variously estimated at from fifteen to twenty-five, then jumped into the pinnace with drawn swords and clubbed guns. As their first fire killed one man (a stoker) outright, mortally wounded another, and severely wounded two others of the boat's crew, the Arabs found but little difficulty in driving the rest, unarmed as they were, overboard.

Captain Brownrigg and his steward were the only two left,

and both were in the after-part of the boat. He seized a rifle, and at the first shot knocked an Arab over; but before he could reload three or four of them rushed aft to attack him, getting on the top of the canopy and at the sides, but he, clubbing his rifle, kept them at bay, fighting with a determination that filled the survivors, who were then in the water unable to get on board, with the greatest admiration, they describing him as "fighting like a lion."

He knocked two of his assailants over, but was unable to get at them properly, owing to the awning overhead, whilst they were above him on the canopy cutting at him with their long swords, but fearing to jump down and close with him. As he knocked one over, another took his place.

The first wound that seems to have hampered him in the gallant fight was a cut across the forehead, from which the blood, pouring over his face, partially blinded him. He was then cut across the hands, the fingers being severed from the left and partially so from the right one, and, badly wounded in both elbows, he could no longer hold the rifle.

He then appears to have tried to get hold of any of his foes or of anything wherewith to fight on, but, blinded as he was, his efforts were in vain. He fought thus for upwards of twenty minutes, keeping his face to his assailants, and having no thought, or making no effort, to seek safety by jumping overboard. At length he was shot through the heart and fell dead, having, besides the fatal one, received no less than twenty wounds, most of them of a severe, and two of a mortal nature.

During this time, of the men in the water, Thomas Bishop, seaman, was badly wounded, and was supported to the dinghy astern of the pinnace by William Venning, leading stoker, who was himself slightly wounded in the head by a slug. There he held on, but the Arabs, hauling the boat up alongside the pinnace, cut him over the head until he sank.

Samuel Massey, A.B., was severely wounded, and was supported to the shore, a distance of about 700 yards, by Alfred Yates, leading seaman, and William Colliston, ordinary; the remaining stoker swam there by himself, as also did the interpreter. The writer (third class), John G.T. Aers, having been mortally wounded at the first fire, there was left on board the pinnace only the captain's steward, who lay quiet, pretending to be dead.

The Arabs then left the boat and sailed away in their *dhow*, when the leading stoker got on board of her,—he having been in the water all the time,—got up steam, and picked up the men on the beach.

CHAPTER 25

# The Egyptian Campaign
## 1882

The bombardment of Alexandria, which commenced the war in Egypt, was of the highest interest to naval men; for here, for the first time, ironclad ships, armed with new and heavy ordnance, attacked forts mounted with the heaviest guns. A bloodless revolution had taken place in Egypt. The army, headed by Arabi Pasha, had quietly pushed aside the authority of the Khedive, and had become supreme in Egypt. The people at large were with the army, and regarded the movement as a national one; its object being to emancipate the country from foreign control. England was unable to behold the change without apprehension; the Khedive was her own nominee, and had from the commencement of the trouble with the army acted entirely in accordance with the advice of the representative of England. We had a large stake in the country from the numerous loans which had been raised for the most part in England; but we were principally affected by the fact that the rebels would have it in their power to stop the canal, and so to block the highway to our Eastern possessions.

The Egyptians began to manifest a hostile spirit towards foreigners, and an attack was made upon the Europeans in Alexandria; a large number were killed, and the rest compelled to take shelter on board a ship. A powerful English fleet was assembled in the port of Alexandria; the attitude of the Egyptians became more and more threatening, and they proceeded to throw up batteries to command the British fleet. Admiral Seymour, who was in command, peremptorily called upon them to desist; but in spite of his threat to open fire upon them they continued to work upon the forts; the fleet therefore prepared for action. All neutral ships were warned to withdraw from the harbour, and the fleet then steamed out and took up its position facing the outer forts.

At seven o'clock on the morning of the 5th of July 1882, the signal to engage the batteries was made on board the admiral's ship the *Invincible*; and the *Invincible, Monarch*, and *Penelope* immediately opened fire on the forts known as the Mex batteries; while the *Sultan, Alexandria, Superb*, and *Inflexible*, at the same moment, opened fire on the forts at Pharos Point and Ras-el-Tin. The Egyptians were standing at their guns, and instantly replied to the fire. The gunboats were lying in a second line behind the line of battle-ships, but the sailors who manned them were not content to remain idle, and, though without orders to engage, the *Cygnet* soon crept in close enough to use her guns. The *Condor* steamed away to the west, and engaged alone and unsupported the Marabout Fort. The admiral, seeing the disproportion of force between the Egyptian fort and the little gunboat, signalled the *Bittern* and *Beacon* to join her. The *Decoy* went of her own accord, and the other gunboats and the *Cygnet* also moved off to aid in pounding the Marabout Fort.

The roar of the heavy guns of the fleet and batteries was tremendous, and on both sides cannon of vastly heavier metal than had ever before been used in war were sending their deadly messengers. The Egyptians stuck to their guns with the greatest bravery, but their skill was far from being equal to their courage, and the greatest portion of their shot flew high over the vessels; this was especially the case with the heavy guns, the lighter and more manageable pieces were better aimed, and the round shot continually struck the men-of-war but failed to penetrate their iron sides. On the other hand, the huge shot and shell of the ironclads committed terrible devastation on the batteries. These were for the most part constructed of stone, which crumbled and fell in great masses under the tremendous blows of the English shot and shell.

After an hour's continued firing the return from the forts began to slacken. Many of the guns were dismounted, and rugged gaps appeared in their walls; but it was not for three hours later that the Egyptian gunners were driven from their pieces. Even then they continued to fire steadily from several of their forts. At one o'clock the gunboats had silenced the fire of the Marabout Fort, and proceeded to aid the *Invincible, Monarch,* and *Penelope* in their bombardment on the Mex batteries; and the *Temeraire*, which had hitherto been engaged with a fort commanding the Boghaz Channel, joined the *Alexandria, Sultan,* and *Superb*, and their fire completely silenced the Pharos forts and blew up the enemy's powder magazine. By four o'clock in the afternoon, the enemy's fire ceased altogether, but for another hour and a half the fleet continued to pound the forts.

The action was decisive; almost every Egyptian gun was dismounted, the forts were riddled with holes and reduced to ruins, and the slaughter of the Egyptian artillery was very great, while on the English side the casualties amounted to only 5 killed and 28 wounded. So tremendous was the effect produced by the fire of the British guns, that the Egyptian soldiers entirely lost heart, and although the fleet carried no force capable of effecting the capture of the town, if staunchly defended, the Egyptians at once evacuated Alexandria. The European quarter was plundered and fired by the mob of the town, and an enormous amount of damage done.

As soon as the place was found to be evacuated, a strong body of marines and bluejackets landed and took possession of it, and speedily restored order, and held the city until the arrival of the troops from England. Sir Archibald Alison came out and took command of the force on shore, and, sallying out with 600 men, captured the waterworks at Ramleh—an important position between the sea and the canal, and facing the camp of Arabi's army some four miles distant; here, for some time, artillery duels from time to time went on between the guns of the two armies.

Captain Fisher of the Royal Navy took possession of a railway train and made of it a moving battery. Its armament consisted of two heavy guns and some Gatlings; the trucks were protected by sand-bags, and the battery was manned by sailors. This train did great service, as the line of railway ran from Alexandria through the rebel camp, and when reconnaissances were made the movable battery accompanied the troops, and by its fire greatly facilitated the operation.

Until the end of July the principal part of the work of defending Alexandria and checking the army of Arabi fell upon the Naval Brigade, but by that time so large a number of troops had arrived that the services of the sailors on shore were no longer required, and, with the exception of those serving in Captain Fisher's battery, they returned to their respective ships. The marines, however, remained on shore and took part in a sharp engagement which took place on the 5th of August. Sir Archibald Alison was desirous of discovering the exact position and force of Arabi's advance line of defences, and a reconnaissance, composed of six companies of the 60th Rifles, four companies of the 38th, and four of the 46th, were told off for the service; and seven companies of marines under Colonel Tewson were ordered to advance along the railway embankment in company with the ironclad train. The Rifles were to march by the canal, and the two parties would join at the point where the canal and railway approach closely to each other. The ground between the line taken by the two columns consisted of fields and marshy swamps.

No sooner had the advance begun than a movement was visible in the enemy's lines, and the Egyptians were soon seen extending in skirmishing order 1000 yards in front of the 60th. They took up their position in a deep ditch which crossed the British line of advance, and behind which was a thick jungle, and opened a heavy fire upon the Rifles. The troops advanced steadily in skirmishing order, opening fire upon their almost invisible foes, whose heads only could be seen when they raised them to discharge their muskets. The Egyptians fired high, and although a hail of bullets swept over the heads of the advancing troops there were but few casualties. When the Rifles approached the ditch, the supports were brought up and a rush was made, when the Egyptians at once forsook their position and fled through the jungle.

In the meantime, the marines, advancing along the embankment, had been met by a hot fire from the enemy, whose main position here was a large house, surrounded by entrenchments on which some guns were mounted. The forty-pounder on the moving battery kept up a steady fire on this position; while the marines, pushing forward, were hotly engaged with the enemy's infantry. The two columns advanced abreast until they reached a point some 600 yards from the spot where the railway and canal come together; the embankment was strongly held by the Egyptians, but the marines charged them with fixed bayonets and drove them before them—bayoneting and shooting great numbers.

By this time the enemy were coming up in great strength from their camps. The marines were now unsupported, for Colonel Thackwell, who commanded the other column, had received orders to advance to the White House. There were two white houses on the canal, and he stopped at the first, whereas the second was the one intended; the marines having pushed on farther, were therefore entirely without support, and the enemy, massing in great numbers, threatened them on both flanks. The order was therefore given to fall back, but in order to check the enemy while the movement was being carried out, Major Donald with 50 marines advanced boldly close up to the Egyptian position, and kept up so hot a fire that the enemy's advance was checked, while the main body of the marines retired steadily across the fields to the embankment, keeping perfect order in spite of the tremendous fire which was poured into them, and bringing off every wounded man as he fell.

The enemy had now brought up several batteries of artillery, which opened from a distance, and under this cover pressed hotly upon the marines; these, however, retired in alternate companies, turning round and facing their pursuers, and aided by the musketry fire of the sailors in the train as well as by their machine guns and forty-pounder.

Darkness was fast coming on, and as the batteries at the waterworks now opened fire upon the Egyptians, the latter ceased to press the retiring troops, who withdrew without further molestation to their position at Ramleh.

When the main body of troops from England reached Alexandria, with Sir Garnet Wolseley in supreme command, steps were taken to remove the scene of war to Ismailia—half-way along the Suez Canal—in order to advance upon Cairo from that place, and to avoid the necessity for attacking the formidable works which Arabi had erected facing Alexandria. The plan was kept a profound secret: the troops were placed on board the transports, and, escorted by the fleet, steamed away to Port Said at the mouth of the Suez Canal, and then up the canal to Ismailia.

In spite of the efforts of the sailors, upon whom the burden of the operation of disembarkation fell, there was considerable delay before the troops were in a position to advance, and Arabi was able to collect a large army at Tel-el-Kebir, on the line by which the army would have to advance. While the preparations for a forward movement were going on, a portion of the British troops pushed forward; and a brigade, among whom was a battalion of the marines, occupied Kassassin, a few miles distant from the Egyptian position.

On the 10th of September, Arabi, seeing how small was the force which had taken up its post near him, determined to attack them, with the intention of crushing them first, and then advancing and destroying one by one the small bodies of British troops at the posts on the line down to Ismailia. He advanced with a powerful force, and so quickly did he push forward that the British had scarcely time to get under arms when the Egyptian shell began to fall fast in the camp. The little force fell in with the greatest coolness, and the marines and 60th Rifles advanced in skirmishing order to meet the vastly superior numbers of the Egyptians. So staunchly and steadily did they fight, that they were able to keep their assailants at bay until the English cavalry came up from the next post, and, falling upon the Egyptians in flank, completely routed them. At the battle of Tel-el-Kebir, where Arabi's army was completely defeated and the rebellion finally crushed, the marines, who had hitherto borne the brunt of all the fighting which had taken place, were not in the front line of attack, and bore but little share in the fighting, which was done almost entirely by the Highland Brigade.

### Campaign Against the Mahdi—1883-1885

After the English had broken up the Egyptian army, and had, for a time at least, practically assumed the direction of affairs there, they found themselves face to face with an insurrection under a fanatic who assumed the title of the Mahdi. The followers of this man had overrun the whole of the Soudan, shutting up the various Egyptian garrisons in the towns they occupied. One of the chiefs of the Mahdi, named Osman Digma, was threatening the port of Suakim, on the Red Sea, and had besieged the Egyptian garrisons in the towns of Sinkat and Tokar. Admiral Hewett was ordered to protect Suakim, and with the *Ranger, Sphinx, Euryalus,* and *Decoy* took his station off that town.

Several times Osman Digma's followers came close up to the place, but, whenever they did so, the bluejackets and marines from the four English ships were landed, and the men-of-war opened a fire over the town upon the ground which the rebels must cross to reach it. Thus they succeeded in defending Suakim from any serious attack until Baker Pasha, who was in command of a miscellaneous force known as the Egyptian Police, came down with some thousands of newly-raised troops. These men had received but little drill, and were scarce worthy the name of soldiers; but, as the garrisons of Sinkat and Tokar still held out, although sorely pressed by hunger, Baker Pasha determined to make an effort to relieve them, although he and his officers were well aware of the wholly untrustworthy nature of the force at his command. There were plenty of English troops doing nothing in Egypt, and had but one regiment been sent down to Baker Pasha it would have been worth all the armed rabble he had under him; but the English Government could not at the time bring itself to acknowledge its responsibility for the safety of the Egyptian garrisons.

Baker's force was conveyed down the coast to Trinkatat; Admiral Hewett with some of the ships going down with him. The force was landed and marched towards Tokar; on the way it was attacked by the tribesmen who had embraced the cause of Osman Digma. The undisciplined levies of Baker broke at once when attacked; their English officers fought gallantly; many were killed, and the greater portion of the Egyptians massacred almost unresistingly; the rest fled to Trinkatat. The rebels, fearing to come within range of the guns of the English ships, ceased from their pursuit, and the survivors of Baker's force were able to get on board the vessels in safety.

The result of this defeat was that the garrison of Sinkat, who had held out heroically, finding themselves without a hope of relief, and their provisions being wholly exhausted, marched out and tried to cut their way through the besieged town to the coast. They were, however, exterminated, not a man making his way through to tell the tale.

Tokar also fell into the Mahdists' hands, its garrison having accepted terms of surrender; and thus Osman Digma was left free to attack Suakim itself, which but for the presence of the fleet must have fallen into his hands.

### Battle of El Tab

In the meanwhile the British Government, under the leadership of Mr Gladstone, had come to the conclusion that the advanced posts of the Egyptian Government in the Soudan could no longer be held, and pressed upon that Government the necessity of withdrawing the garrisons. The Egyptians reluctantly accepted the advice of their powerful "ally," but were unable of themselves to execute its purpose. The British Government then applied to General Gordon, who had been formerly governor of the Soudan, and who had more influence over the Arab tribes than any other European of modern times, to undertake the task of the evacuation of Khartoum, the civil population of which numbered about 11,000. General Gordon at once responded to the call of his country, and set out for

Khartoum, which he reached with General Stewart as his sole companion on the 16th of February. At first all seemed well, and Gordon was able to send down some widows and children, 2500 in all, to Korosko, but the events above related at once destroyed all hope of a peaceful retreat; and it became evident that help from without would become necessary if the population were to be saved; but the two British officers never doubted that their country would aid them in their time of need.

The sensation caused in England by the events around Suakim now became so great that Mr Gladstone's Government could no longer evade their responsibility, and now took the step which, had it been taken six weeks earlier, would have saved thousands of lives. English troops were set in motion from Egypt, some regiments were stopped on their way home from India up the Red Sea, and a force was assembled at Suakim under General Graham; when these were collected they were taken down to Trinkatat by sea, and the disembarkation there began on the 23rd of February 1884.

As usual, all the hard work to be done fell upon the sailors, who worked incessantly—landing stores through the surf, working up to their necks in water. On the 26th, having accomplished this work, a Naval Brigade, consisting of all the marines and sailors who could be spared from the men-of-war, was landed to take part in the expedition, taking with them several Gatlings and light ship guns; all of which were dragged by them through the deep sand, no means of transport being available. Two or three days now elapsed before the advance commenced, as some of the troops had not yet arrived; but on the 65th Regiment coming into port in the *Serapis* transport, orders were given for the advance to commence. As soon as the 65th landed, they crossed a lagoon, or shallow salt-water lake, which lay behind Trinkatat, and joined the main body, who had already taken post on the other side.

The column consisted roughly of 3000 infantry, 750 cavalry and mounted infantry, 115 men of the Naval Brigade, and about

200 artillery and engineers; of these 150 were left at Trinkatat, and 200 men at the camping ground across the lagoon, which had been entrenched by General Baker and bore his name. The troops advanced in a hollow square. The Gordon Highlanders formed the front face, the Irish Fusiliers the right face, the 65th the left, and the 42nd Highlanders formed the rear of the square. The Rifles marched inside the square next to the Fusiliers, the marines next to the Rifles, the sailors, with six Gatling guns, were stationed to the left of the Gordon Highlanders; while the eight seven-pounder guns belonging to the fleet, which had been transferred to the camel battery, were in the centre of the square in reserve. Two squadrons of cavalry were to scout far out on the front and flanks, the rest of the cavalry were to remain in readiness for action in the rear of the square.

Soldiers and sailors were alike in good spirits, and longing to meet the foe and to avenge the massacre of Baker's troops on the very ground across which they were about to march; but they knew that the work would be no child's play, and that the greatest steadiness would be needed to resist the tremendous rush of the fanatics. The march began in the morning, and the enemy's scouts were seen falling back as the cavalry dashed out ahead. Their main position was in the neighbourhood of some wells. It was marked by a number of banners floating in the light air on a low ridge which was swarming with men; guns could be seen in position at various points along the position, which extended about a mile in length.

As the column approached the ridge, the natives took up their post behind it; but, as in a direct advance against it, the column would be swept by the fire of their guns and musketry, without being able to make any adequate return against the concealed foes, General Graham determined to turn it by working round its flank. Accordingly, after a halt, the column continued its march in an oblique direction across the face of the position.

At a few minutes before eleven, the cavalry scouts moved away from the front of the column and left it face to face with the enemy, who were now but a few hundred yards away. Their heads could be seen popping up behind the bushes and earthworks, and every moment it was expected that they would rise from their hiding-places and charge down upon the column which was marching past their front at a distance of about 400 yards.

The assault did not come, but a sudden fire of musketry broke out from the face of the position, and the Krupp guns, captured from Baker's force, in their batteries opened fire on the column. The effect was at once visible, several men in the square fell out from the ranks wounded; but fortunately the enemy fired high, and the storm of shot and shell, for the most part, passed harmlessly over the column. Without returning a shot, the column moved steadily on in the line which would soon place them across the end of the enemy's position, and enable them to take it in the rear.

It was very trying to the nerve of the troops to march on without firing while pelted with such a storm of missiles. General Baker was badly wounded in the face by a bullet from a shell, and many men were struck, but by this time the column had reached the desired position; they had passed round the enemy's line, and were almost in their rear. They halted now, and the men lay down, while the sailors opened fire upon the enemy with the Gatlings, and the men of the camel battery with their seven-pounders,—six guns of the enemy replying. These were well handled and aimed, for the garrison of Tokar had three days before surrendered, and were now fighting in the ranks of their captors, whose guns were all worked by the Egyptian artillerymen.

By twelve o'clock the English guns had silenced those of the enemy, and the word was given for an advance against their position; the bagpipes struck up, the men sprang to their feet cheering, and the column, still keeping its formation as a square, marched straight at the enemy's position. The Arabs ceased firing as the British approached, and when the column was close at hand they leapt to their feet and charged furiously down.

The change of the direction of the march had altered the position of the column, the flank of the square was now its front, and the brunt of the attack fell on the 42nd, 65th, and the Naval Brigade. Groups of twenty and thirty Arabs rushed fiercely down upon them, but they were swept away by the fire of the musketry and the machine guns; but in some places the Arabs came to close quarters, but were unable to break through the line of bayonets.

The column had now reached the position, and with a cheer rushed over the bank of sand. From every bush around them the Arabs leapt up and flung themselves upon the troops. Admiral Hewett himself led the sailors and joined in the hand-to-hand fight. A party of fanatics nearly succeeded in breaking in between the sailors and the 65th, but Captain Wilson, of the *Hecla*, threw himself into the gap, and, fighting desperately, drove back the assailants.

There was a short halt when the post was captured, to re-form the column before moving forward to the attack of the main position of the enemy, of which we were now well in rear; and after a short artillery duel the column again advanced. The whole ground was covered with trenches and innumerable little rifle-pits, all hidden by the close growing bushes, and every foot was contested, the Arabs leaping from their defences and dashing recklessly on the British bayonets. Great numbers of them were slaughtered; and they fought with a desperate courage which extorted the admiration of our soldiers.

At last the column, which was now extended into line, passed across the whole of the position occupied by the enemy and emerged in front; the main body of the enemy withdrawing sullenly. Of the Naval Brigade two men were killed, and Lieutenant Royds and six sailors wounded.

No more fighting took place; a portion of the column advanced to Tokar, which the enemy evacuated at their approach, and brought off such of the townspeople as wished to leave. The force then marched down to Trinkatat, and, re-embarking, were conveyed in the transports back to Suakim, and marched out to attack Osman Digma. The Naval Brigade took part in the advance.

### BATTLE OF TAMANIEB—1884

When the column arrived within half a mile of the position occupied by the main force of Osman Digma, they encamped for the night. At eight in the evening, Commander Rolfe, RN, performed a most daring action; he started alone to reconnoitre the camp of the enemy, and made his way close up to their fires, and was able to bring back the news that the enemy were quiet and evidently meditated no immediate attack; the men were therefore able to lie down quietly and sleep for a while. At one o'clock, however, the enemy gathered round the position and kept up a fire all night.

The next day the advance was made, not in squares as before, but in two brigades. In the first of these, with the 42nd and 65th, were the marines and Naval Brigade. As the brigade advanced, the enemy swarmed down to the attack, and the soldiers with their rifles, and the sailors with their machine guns, opened a tremendous fire upon them; but the Arabs still came on with desperate bravery. The brigade was in square, and the 42nd, who were in front, charged the enemy at the double, cheering loudly; but this movement left a gap between them and the 65th, who formed the right face of the square, and, before the gap could be closed up, great hordes of Arabs charged down and burst into the square.

For a while all was confusion. The 65th fell back on the marines. The Naval Brigade, surrounded by the broken soldiers, were unable to use their guns, and, as the confused mass fell back, had to leave these behind them; but with great coolness they removed portions of the machinery, so that when the guns fell into the hands of the enemy they were unable to use them against us.

Wildly the Arabs pressed down upon the retreating troops, but the second brigade, under General Buller, came up in splendid order, their volleys sweeping away the enemy. This gave the retreating troops time to reform their ranks, and they at once advanced again in line with Buller's brigade; and the enemy were put to flight, after suffering a loss of over 5000 men.

Amongst those who fell in this action were Lieutenant Montresor, RN, Lieutenant Almack, RN, and Lieutenant Houston, RN, with seven of their men who were killed at their guns.

CHAPTER 26.

# Wars in South Africa

In 1879 Great Britain became involved in war with Cetewayo, chief of a powerful race of savages on the north-eastern border of the colony of Natal in South Africa, and two years after in a short conflict with the Boers, or Dutch farmers, in the Transvaal; and in both of these wars a Naval Brigade took part. From this time onward, South Africa has held a position of increasing importance in our colonial history, and is likely to continue to do so for many years to come; it will be well therefore before considering the wars referred to, to give a general view of the position of the British, the Dutch, and the Zulu at the date of their commencement.

Cape Colony was originally founded by the Dutch about the middle of the seventeenth century; it was seized by Great Britain during the wars with France in 1806, and finally annexed to the British Empire by virtue of the Treaty of Vienna in 1815.

A great proportion of the colonists, and especially of the farmers in the districts farthest from the coast and from civilisation, did not take kindly to British rule; and in 1835 and succeeding years a great number crossed the Orange River—at that time the boundary of the colony on the north—with the intention of setting up independent Dutch communities. To this movement, known as the Great Trek, the occupation by the Dutch Boers (*i.e.* farmers) of the territories, since known as the Orange Free State and the Transvaal, or South African Republic, is due.

At that time the limits of the British colony were, on the north, the Orange River; and, on the east, the Fish River. Beyond this, on the east, was territory occupied by hostile Kaffir tribes, afterwards called British Kaffraria, and now annexed to Cape Colony, and still farther to the east of these lay the fertile land of Natal.

A large section of the trekking Boers, after passing the Orange and going north, crossed the mountains, and descended upon Natal. There were a few English hunters and traders settled upon the coast, but the country had been depopulated of its original inhabitants by a ferocious and warlike race of superior physique, whom we call the Zulu. These had been trained to a high state of military and athletic perfection by a succession of sanguinary chiefs, and had broken and massacred every tribe with whom they had come in contact, so that in this district of Natal alone it is computed that over a million had perished, and but five or six thousand of the original inhabitants remained lurking in caverns and amid the dense bush.

The first leader of the Boers, Retief, and some 70 persons, were treacherously murdered by Dingaan, the chief or king of the Zulus, at his *kraal*, which they had visited at his request in February 1838; and the chief made a sudden attack with his armies upon the isolated bands of farmers, and killed a great many of them. After many bloody fights, in which large numbers of Zulus were killed, the Boers drove Dingaan and his armies across the Tugela, and occupied the country.

The British Government, however, declined to recognise the right of its colonists to leave the colony, wage war upon the native tribes, and set up as independent republics, and therefore, after overcoming the resistance of the Boers, occupied Natal, and eventually made it into a separate colony. After some trial of British rule, the bulk of the Dutch recrossed the mountains, and joined their fellow-countrymen in the Orange Free State, or in the land beyond the Vaal.

At length in 1852 the British Government, having enough to do with native wars on the Cape frontier, found it expedient to concede independence to the Transvaal Boers; and two years afterwards abandoned the territory between the Orange and Vaal

Rivers to its inhabitants, the Dutch farmers, who thus founded the Orange Free State.

The Dutch of the Free State were of much the same type and education as the Cape Dutch, and soon settled down and arranged their affairs, and evolved an almost ideal form of republican government, under which, after having at great sacrifice and courage overcome the native difficulties on their borders, they lived a happy and contented existence, with increasing prosperity, no public enemy, perfect civil and religious equality, and, except for railways and public works, no public debt, until in 1899 that wonderful loyalty to race which is so remarkable a trait in the Dutch African involved them in the ambitions and the ruin of the South African Republic.

With the Transvaal Boer it was far otherwise. Amongst the leaders of the Voor-trekkers, as the original emigrants from Cape Colony are called, were leaders of whom colonists of any race might be proud, such as Pretorius, Potgieter, Uys, and Retief, and, no doubt, among their followers were many like them; but it was the most discontented and the most uncivilised and turbulent, as a rule, that crossed the Vaal originally; and there they lived isolated lives, far away from any white being but those of their own family, without books, without intercourse with the outer world, surrounded only by their wives and children and Kaffir servants, or rather slaves; and thus the Transvaal Boer, to whom alone we ought to apply the name, became more sullen, obstinate, bigoted, and ignorant than his cousins farther south.

Very little good could such people, with few exceptions little above the average of an English farm-labourer, do with independence. Many years were wasted in quarrelling and even fighting among themselves, every leader of a district with a few scattered farms claiming independence, before all were united under one government. There was constant war with natives on the border, no means of collecting taxes or providing for public works, and by the year 1877 it seemed as though the State must collapse and the Transvaal be overrun by its enemies. The Boers were defeated by Sekukuni, chief of the Bapedi; they had an open dispute with Cetewayo about territory which they had annexed from his country, and he was preparing for war; the tribes in the north had driven back the farmers; the State was bankrupt, and all was confusion. The more settled members of the community in the towns called for firm government, but the president had no power at his back to enforce it.

Such a state of things encouraged a general native rising, and was a menace to the safety of all the whites in South Africa. The Cape Government watched the situation with anxiety, and at length the British Government intervened, and on 12th April 1877 proclaimed the Transvaal to be annexed to the British dominions.

At the time it was believed that the majority of the burghers were in favour of this step, which met with no serious opposition. Subsequent events, however, proved that this belief was not well founded. It is, however, tolerably certain that it saved the Transvaal an attack from the thirty or forty thousand Zulus collected by Cetewayo on its frontier.

Chapter 27

# The Zulu War

Cetewayo had for many years been training a large army of warriors, and had intended, unquestionably, to use them for an attack upon his neighbours the Boers of the Transvaal, who, indeed, had given him more than sufficient cause, by constantly violating the frontier, squatting upon Zulu territory, and committing raids upon Zulu cattle. Upon our taking over the Transvaal, however, the prospect of great plunder and acquisition of territory vanished, and the king and his warriors remained in a state of extreme discontent. So large and threatening was his army, that Sir Bartle Frere, the Governor of the Cape, considered it absolutely necessary to bring matters to a crisis. A commission sat upon the disputed frontier question between the Zulus and the Boers. They had also to investigate charges of a raid into Natal territory by some Zulu chiefs. Their decision was in favour of the Zulus against the Boers; and, in respect of the raids, they ordered that a fine should be paid and the offenders given up.

At the time that this decision was announced to the Zulus, Sir Bartle Frere called upon Cetewayo to disband his army, to abandon the custom of universal conscription, and of the refusal of marriage to the young men until they had proved their prowess in battle. To this demand Cetewayo returned an evasive answer, and an ultimatum was then sent to him.

Preparations were made to enforce the British demands, and, as the British force in Natal was not large, the ships of war on the coast were asked to furnish a contingent. Sailors being always ready for an expedition afloat or ashore, the demand was gladly complied with, and a brigade with rockets and Gatling guns was at once organised. This brigade was attached to the column which, under the command of Colonel Pearson, was to advance by the road nearest to the coast.

On the 12th of January, no answer having been received to the ultimatum, the column crossed the Tugela. The sailors had been at work at this point for some time. They had established a ferry-boat worked by ropes, and by this they transported across the river the stores and ammunition needed for the expedition. The column advanced slowly and carefully, and upon the 23rd they were attacked at the Ebroi River by the enemy. These had placed themselves upon high ground, and opened a heavy fire. The sailors at once got the Gatlings and rockets to work, and so great was their effect that the rush of the Zulus was checked, and they were unable to carry out their favourite tactics of coming to close quarters. Three hundred of them were killed, and the rest retired.

The column now marched on to Ekowe, and upon reaching that place a messenger from the rear brought the news of the terrible disaster which had befallen Lord Chelmsford's column at Isandhlwana. The British camp at that place had on the advance of the main body been rushed by a large Zulu force, and the whole of the British and native troops, numbering over 1000, were killed, only a few, scarce 50 escaping. It was a hand-to-hand combat against thousands, and from the Zulus themselves, for no white man saw the end, come the accounts of how firmly the soldiers stood. The Zulus, who had a keen appreciation of gallantry, tell many tales of how our men stood fighting till the last. "How few they were and how hard they fought," they said; "they fell like stones, each man in his place."

There was only one sailor in the camp. He belonged to HMS *Active*, and throughout the terrible fight displayed the utmost courage. At last, when all was nearly over, he was seen in a corner of the *laager*, leaning against a wagon wheel, keeping the Zulus at bay. One after another fell as he stabbed them with his cutlass. The savages themselves were lost in admiration at his stern resistance. At last a Zulu crept round at the back of the wagon, and stabbed him through the spokes of the wheel.

It would have been the height of rashness to have advanced farther, as the column would now have been exposed to the whole force of the Zulus. Colonel Pearson determined, therefore, to fortify Ekowe, and to maintain himself there until reinforcements came up. The cavalry and the native contingents who had accompanied the column were therefore sent back, the sailors being retained to assist the regular troops in holding the place.

The first step was to erect fortifications, and, as the enemy attempted no attack, these were made strongly and massively. Here for many weeks the little garrison held out. The Zulus surrounded the place closely, but never ventured upon any sustained attack upon it. The garrison, however, suffered severely from fever, heat, and the effects of bad food and water. For some time they were cut off entirely from all communication with Natal; but at length an officer, upon the top of the church, observed one day, far among the hills to the south, a twinkling light. From the regularity with which it shone and disappeared, he came to the conclusion that it was caused by signallers endeavouring to open communications. The flashes were watched, and were found to be in accordance with the Morse alphabet; and the joyful news was spread that their friends were telegraphing to them.

After some trouble, a mirror was fixed and signals returned, and from that time, until relief, regular communication was kept up by this means. There was disappointment at first when it was found that some time must elapse before a relieving column could advance; but as the news came of the arrival of ship after ship, laden with troops from England, confidence was felt that relief would arrive before the exhaustion of the stock of provisions. The garrison on their part were enabled to send to their friends accurate information of the state of their stores, and the time which they would be able to hold out.

At length, on the 28th of March, the news arrived that the column would advance upon the following day. The relieving force was attacked at Gingihlovo, near the River Inyanzi, and there the Zulus were defeated with great loss. With this relieving column was another Naval Brigade, consisting of men of the *Shah* and *Tenedos*. The *Shah* was on her way to England when, upon arriving at Saint Helena, the news of the massacre at Isandhlwana reached her. Captain Bradshaw, who commanded, at once determined to take upon himself the responsibility of returning to Natal, where his arrival caused the liveliest satisfaction, as at that time none of the reinforcements from England had reached the spot, and strong fears were still felt of the invasion of the colony by the Zulus. The Naval Brigade bore their part in the fight at Gingihlovo, and were with the relieving force when it entered Ekowe. The garrison of this place, small as they were, had been prepared upon the following day to sally out to effect a diversion in favour of the column, should it again be attacked in its advance to Ekowe.

The garrison was now relieved. Few of those who had formed part of it were fit for further service. Ekowe was abandoned, and the Naval Brigade returned to Natal. The brigade took part in the further advance after the arrival of Sir Garnet Wolseley; but the defeat of the Zulus at Ulundi occurring a few days after the start had been made, hostilities ceased, and the Naval Brigade were not called upon for further exertions.

CHAPTER 28
# The Boer War
*1881*

Two years after the conclusion of the Zulu war, when the troops who had been hurried from England to take part in that campaign had for the most part returned, and the country was almost deserted of troops, the Boers, saved by our arms from all danger of a native rising, longed again for independence, and they determined to have it. They had, in fact, never acquiesced in the act of annexation. At the time, the residents in the towns had desired it for the sake of law and order, and in the general helplessness of the State many of the country Boers acquiesced, and to many it seemed the only way to save the country from the Zulu. But it was expected and promised that some form of self-government would be left to the Dutch community. As time went on, the discontent grew, and it was fomented by the speeches of party leaders in England, where the Liberal party were violently attacking the colonial policy of Lord Beaconsfield; and Mr Gladstone, referring to the Boers' country, actually said, that if the acquisition was as valuable as it was valueless, nevertheless he would repudiate it. When Mr Gladstone came into office, the Boers, who did not understand the ethics of election campaigns, expected him to reverse an act which he repudiated; and when they found that though he disapproved the act he did not intend to revoke it, they saw that they must take up arms, thinking that their cause would have many supporters among the English, who would put pressure upon the Government to give way,—a view which subsequent events proved to be correct.

The burghers have always objected to paying taxes even to their own republic, and naturally the opposition to our rule presented itself, in the first place, by a resistance to the payment of taxes. Meetings assembled, at which rebellious speeches were uttered; and the rising commenced by an attack upon the English at Potchefstroom, the investment of the garrisons of Pretoria, Leydenburg, Standerton, and other positions, and by an attack upon a column of the 94th on their way from Leydenburg to Pretoria, ending with the slaughter or captivity of the whole force. The instant the news arrived at Pietermaritzburg, the capital, Sir George Colley, the governor, commenced preparations for marching to the frontier, and the ships in harbour were called upon to furnish a naval contingent. A hundred and fifty bluejackets and marines were landed and marched rapidly to Newcastle, an English town within a few miles of the frontier of Natal.

At the attack upon the Dutch lines at Laing's Nek, the Naval Brigade were in reserve, and took no active part in the engagement. But on the 26th of February a portion of them accompanied General Colley on his night march to Majuba Hill. This mountain was situate on the flank of the Boer position. The Dutch were in the habit of occupying it during the daytime with their videttes, but these at night fell back, leaving the place open to the British assault.

All through the night the troops, who with the bluejackets numbered between 500 and 600 men, laboured across an extremely difficult country; but, after encountering immense fatigue and difficulty, they reached the top of Majuba Hill before sunrise. It was not until two hours later that the Boer videttes, advancing to occupy their usual look-out, found the English in position. The Boers at once perceived the danger, as their position was made untenable by the possession of Majuba Hill by the English. Had the force left in camp been sufficiently strong to threaten a direct attack at this moment, the Boers would doubtless have fled: but the paucity of numbers there prevented any demonstration being made in favour of the defenders of Majuba Hill, and the Dutch were able to use their whole force against these.

Surrounding the hill, and climbing upwards towards the precipitous summit, they kept up for some hours a heavy fire upon the defenders. Presently this lulled, and the garrison thought that the attack had ceased. The Dutch were, however, strongly reinforcing their fighting line, creeping among the bushes and gathering a strong force on the side of the hill, unseen by the British. Suddenly these made an attack, and this in such force that the defenders at the threatened point fell back in haste before they could be reinforced from the main body, who were lying in a hollow on the top of the small plateau which formed the summit of the mountain.

The first to gain the summit were rapidly reinforced by large numbers of their countrymen, and these, covering their advance with a tremendous fire of musketry, rushed upon the British position. The defence was feeble. Taken by surprise, shot down in numbers by the accurate firing of the Boers, attacked on all sides at once, the garrison failed to defend their position, and in a moment the Boers were among them. At this point a bayonet charge would have turned defeat into a victory, but there were no officers left to command, all had been picked off by the accurate shooting of the Boers, and the soldiers were panic-stricken. All cohesion became lost, and in a few minutes the whole of the defenders of the position were either shot down or taken prisoners, with the exception of a few who managed to make their escape down the side of the hill and to lie concealed among the bushes, making their way back to camp during the night. Sir George Colley stood still, and was shot down at close range as the men ran down the hill.

This was the only affair in which the Naval Brigade were engaged during the war, as, shortly afterwards, just as they were hoping to retrieve the disasters which had befallen the force,—the reinforcements from England having now come up to the spot,—peace was made, the Transvaal was surrendered to the Boers, and the sacrifices made and the blood which had been shed were shown to have been spent in vain. The intense disappointment of the troops at this summary and unexpected termination of the campaign was fully shared by the bluejackets and marines.

The defeat at Majuba Hill was a great blow to British prestige, but it was one that, in the course of the war which all the world expected to follow, could have been speedily retrieved, but the effect upon the Dutch must have remained. It seemed, indeed, as if in fighting for freedom they were truly invincible, and as if they could withstand the power of Great Britain, and defeat it, just as their fathers, a few hundred in number, had withstood Dingaan and defeated his thousands of warriors. This impression was greatly strengthened by the action of the British Government.

The Liberal party in England had undertaken the war with very little fervour, to many the cause of the Boer was the cause of freedom, and the sight of a small peasant nation, armed as it then was only with rifles, rising against the power of Great Britain, appealed to the sentiment of many people, to whom the great popular orator had repeatedly declared that the act of annexation was an act of tyranny.

Still the war was the act of their great leader, and had therefore been supported; moreover, regarded as a military matter only, the defeat was of no importance; the various British garrisons in the country were manfully holding their own; Sir Evelyn Wood was gathering sufficient force to take action; he held, he said, the Boers in the hollow of his hand,—so the war must go on, and Sir F (now Lord) Roberts was sent out to take command.

Mr Gladstone now suddenly changed his mind; further prosecution of the war, he said, would be "sheer blood-guiltiness."

He gave the Boers their independence, but they and all the world noted that he did not discover the blood-guiltiness of the war before the defeat, and they drew their inferences; and to their dislike of British rule, added a contempt for British courage, which led their leaders into a course of action which culminated in an ambition to substitute Dutch for British throughout South Africa, and thus brought down upon the two republics the ruin and disasters of the great war of 1899-1901.

CHAPTER 29
# The Boer War
## 1900

### THE SIEGE OF LADYSMITH

Early in the year 1899 the differences between Mr Kruger, President of the South African Republic, and the British Government, upon the position of the foreign population in his territory, began to assume an acute phase. A petition to Her Majesty, setting out their grievances and asking for protection for her subjects in the Transvaal, was very largely signed, and the British High Commissioner stated his opinion that the position of the non-burgher population was intolerable, and that this was an overwhelming case for intervention. For many weeks negotiations were carried on between London and Pretoria, the British Government making very little preparation for a war which it hoped to avoid; while Mr Kruger, on the other land, proceeded to arm his burghers and make every preparation for a war which, if he made no concessions, he knew to be inevitable if the British Government did not retire from the position they had taken.

At length, everything being ready on his side, on 9th October President Kruger issued an ultimatum, demanding the withdrawal of Great Britain's troops within forty-eight hours. This was a declaration of war. War immediately followed, and armed Boers, previously assembled on the frontier, poured in thousands into Natal, crossing the frontier both on the north and on the west on the 12th of October, and gradually overran the north of the colony, converging upon Ladysmith. The British force in that part was small, and though in the various actions at Talana Hill—in which the situation of Majuba Hill may be said to have been reversed—Elandslaagte, and Rietfontein, portions of the Boer forces had been met and defeated, it became evident that their numbers and their mobility had been absurdly underestimated, and that when once concentrated they far outnumbered the forces at the disposal of Sir George White, who therefore decided to entrench and await reinforcements at Ladysmith,—not a strong position, for it was commanded by hills on all sides, but it had been a great depot of military stores which could not be removed.

By 2nd November the railway and telegraph connecting Ladysmith with the south was cut, and the strict siege began. The Boers brought into position on the neighbouring hills guns of far greater calibre than any of those possessed by the garrison and its defences, and kept up a heavy bombardment out of range of their guns.

Most fortunately HMS *Powerful*, then at Durban, was armed with 4.7-inch guns of as great range as any of the "Long Toms" of the assailants. A land carriage for these had been designed by Captain Percy Scott, and rapidly constructed by the ship's engineers, and the guns sent up by rail just before the line was cut, together with a Naval Brigade of bluejackets from the ship under the command of Captain Hon. H. Lambton. These guns, the two 4.7-inch and four 12-pounders, were of the greatest value to the defence, for they were the only guns capable of equalling the big guns of the Boers, and the firing was so accurate that during the whole of the siege they succeeded in keeping the enemy's siege guns at a distance, with so little waste of ammunition, the supply of which was of course limited, that when the siege was raised on 20th February 1900 it was not yet exhausted.

On the 30th of October Lieutenant Egerton, RN, of the *Powerful*, was struck by a shell and died of his wounds a few days after; he had been at once promoted to commander for his services, and received intelligence of this before his death.

The most serious fight during the siege took place on 6th January, when the enemy made a most determined and as it proved final attempt to carry Ladysmith by storm. Every part of the position was attacked, but the chief assault was upon Cassar's Camp and Wagon Hill. On the former was a detachment of the Naval Brigade with a 12-pounder gun and some Natal Naval Volunteers, as well as the 1st Battalion Manchesters and 42 Battery, RA; and on Wagon Hill, in addition to its usual garrison, a 12-pounder gun and a 4.7-inch had arrived the day before. The fighting was very severe and at close quarters, and the Boers were only finally driven off after 15 hours' battle, our losses being 14 officers and 135 men killed, 31 officers and 244 wounded. The Boers lost much more heavily, and made no further attempt.

The sufferings of the garrison and inhabitants during this memorable siege were very severe, and the losses by disease amounted to 12 officers and 529 men.

In addition to those engaged in the defence of Ladysmith, naval brigades with guns from various ships of war on the South African station accompanied the various columns engaged in the movement through the Orange Free State and the Transvaal, which republics have since become the Orange River Colony and the Transvaal Colony.

CHAPTER 30
# Fighting in China
*1900*

The early part of 1900 saw an outbreak of religious and anti-foreign fanaticism in China which rapidly assumed alarming proportions. A sect or society known as the Boxers, founded in 1899 originally as a patriotic and ultra-conservative body, rapidly developed into a reactionary and anti-foreign, and especially anti-Christian organisation. Outrages were committed all over the country, and the perpetrators shielded by the authorities, who, while professing peace, encouraged the movement. Thousands of native Christians were massacred, and the protests of the ministers of Christian powers disregarded or answered by lies and denials, and at length Peking itself became no longer safe to Europeans.

### First Attempt to Relieve the Legations at Peking

On the 30th of May Sir E.H. Seymour, the British admiral on the China station, received a telegram from Sir Claude Macdonald, the British minister at Peking, stating that the situation there had become very grave, the China soldiers mutinous, the people very excited, and that European life and property were in danger. Guards were immediately despatched by train to Peking, and these, numbering 337 of all nations, among them 79 men and 3 officers of the British Marines, arrived unopposed on the 31st. The position of the legations, however, soon became extremely difficult, and on the 9th of June another telegram was received by the admiral, stating that if relief did not reach the Europeans in Peking very soon, it would be too late.

The admiral at once put in motion all his available men, and the foreign naval officers commanding on the station cooperated with him. By the 11th, four trains had reached Lofa station, some distance out of Tientsin, containing over 2000 men, namely, 915 British (62 officers, 640 bluejackets, and 213 marines), 25 Austrians, 40 Italian, 100 French, 450 German, 54 Japanese, 112 Russians, and 112 Americans, all under the command of the British admiral.

From this time onward there was continuous fighting. About six p.m., three miles outside Langfang, Boxers attacked Number 1 train, but were repulsed. The next day, after repairing the line, the force advanced to Langfang, but beyond this the line was found to be cut up and bridges destroyed; and, as the necessary repairs would occupy some time, Lieutenant Smith, RN, of HMS *Aurora*, was sent forward with 3 officers and 44 men to prevent further damage if possible. He occupied a village on the line next morning, and was at once attacked by Boxers. After being driven off three times, they made a final and determined attack, and about 450 charged in line with great bravery, but were again repulsed with heavy loss; this fighting, however, had so reduced the ammunition of his party that Lieutenant Smith was compelled to return to the main body.

The next day, 14th June, the outposts came running in, closely followed by Boxers, who made a determined attack upon the first train, with so much courage that some of them, notwithstanding a tremendous fire, actually reached the train before they were killed. An unfortunate picket of five Italians on outpost duty were cut off and killed by this party.

Meantime the Boxers were also gathering in the rear and damaging the line from Tientsin, and attacked the guard left to protect the line at Lofa. These succeeded in beating them off, and on the arrival of reinforcements, sent back to their assistance, cut them up as they retreated. All was of no avail, for while the force remained at Langfang repairing the road forward, the enemy was busy in the rear breaking up the line, and so cutting off communication with Tientsin, and it now became clear that the attempt to reach Peking must fail, as provisions and ammunition were running short and it became necessary to protect the rear.

The expedition was, in fact, now in a very critical position. All attempts to send couriers back to Tientsin had failed, and it was cut off from all communication with the outer world, the lines were broken up in front and rear, the whole country was overawed by Boxers, and no supplies could be obtained from the inhabitants. It was therefore decided to desert the trains and march by the left bank of the river to Tientsin, putting the wounded on board of some junks which had been captured by the Germans. The latter had been unexpectedly attacked on the 18th at Langfang by some 5000 of the enemy, some of whom were undoubtedly imperial troops acting with the Boxers, thus exploding the idea that the Chinese Government would assist the Europeans against the latter. The Chinese on this occasion, though armed with the latest type of magazine rifle, were driven off with a loss of 400 killed, the allies losing only 6 killed and 48 wounded.

The retreat commenced on the afternoon of the 19th June, and it was necessarily slow, as the junks could not be got along very fast, our men not being accustomed to the craft, and the river shoals making the passage in places difficult. The Chinese harassed and obstructed the advance of the column on shore as much as possible, and villages *en route* had to be taken by the bayonet, and so persistent was the resistance that on the 21st the column did not advance more than six miles, and was brought to a dead stop at a place called Peitang, where the enemy were in such a strong position that by the evening they had not been dislodged from it.

It now appeared to be becoming doubtful whether the column, embarrassed with the wounded, and with no reserves of ammunition, would succeed in getting through to Tientsin; it was therefore determined, after a rest, to make a night march, and, wearied with a continuous day's battle, the column started again at one a.m. on the 22nd.

After it had gone about one and a half miles, the column was heavily attacked from a village, but the bayonets of the marines soon cleared this, not, however, without a serious loss. The junk which carried the field-guns was sunk by a shot, and all but the Maxim guns lost.

This disaster was, however, destined to be retrieved in a very unexpected manner. At four a.m. the force found itself opposite the Imperial Chinese Armoury, near Hsiku; the allies were not at war with the Imperial Government, by whom officially the Boxers were called rebels, nevertheless the guns from the armoury opened fire upon them. Major Johnstone, Royal Marines, with a party of bluejackets and marines, crossed the river at a point where they were under cover of a village, then, appearing suddenly with a cheer and with the sheen of glittering bayonets, put the Chinese to flight, and captured two Krupp guns. At the same time the Germans crossed over lower down, with similar results, and the Armoury was taken. The Chinese, recovering from their panic, made a determined attempt to retake the position by assault, under cover of artillery fire, but were driven off with loss; but at the same time the allies suffered severely also.

The force now settled down in the Armoury, which could easily be defended and was well supplied with guns and ammunition, and the sick and wounded were now in quarters which, compared with the holds of the junks, must have seemed luxurious; and, but for the question of rations, the force was now safe, but of these latter only enough for three days and that at half allowances remained. Anxiety on this last account was happily set at rest the next day, 23rd June, when, besides immense stores of ammunition, which included war material of the newest pattern, 15 tons of rice were discovered.

All danger was now past. Several efforts had been made to communicate with Tientsin, only five miles distant, but none of the native runners had got through, till the 24th, when a force at once set out under the Russian Colonel Shrinsky, who led a force of 1000 Russians; 600 British, under Captain Bayly, and 300 of other nationalities then arrived at daylight on the

25th. The arsenal, said to contain three million pounds worth of military stores, was set on fire, and the united forces returned to Tientsin the next day without further incident.

So ended the first expedition to relieve the legations in Peking. The failure was owing to the destruction of the railway and the fact that the Imperial Chinese army, so far from assisting or even standing neutral, took the side of the Boxers and opposed the expedition. That it was not a disaster was owing to the wonderful manner in which officers of no less than eight nationalities worked together, and the courage and endurance of their men. The thought of the Chinese habit of torturing their captives must have added to the natural anxiety of depression on board the junks and to the terrible strain upon the commander.

### The Capture of the Taku Forts

Soon after the admiral's departure it became clear to the commanders of the ships off Taku that the Chinese Government were preparing to bring down an army upon Tongku, the terminus of the railway, and that the communication with Tientsin was threatened, and that the Taku forts were being provisioned and manned. It was therefore decided to occupy the forts, and notice was given to the Chinese of the intention to do so at two a.m. of 17th June.

Taku is situate at the mouth of the Peiho River, which was until the railway was built, and, if this were interrupted, would become again the principal approach from the sea to Peking, about 80 miles by river, and to Tientsin 44 miles. The entrance, which runs east and west, is strongly guarded by a series of forts on the north and south sides, the principal fort being the north, which is very strong and mounts some 50 guns of all sizes, and connected with this by a covered way is another on the same side but farther up the river with 30 guns. On the south side there is a series of strong forts and batteries for about a mile along the shore, mounting about 120 guns of various patterns, the greater part being quite modern. Some distance inland is another fort and the magazines. These forts, designed to protect the sea-front, are therefore very formidable, and well manned with competent gunners would constitute a real danger to any ships entering the river. The bar of the river is 5 miles off, and is so shoaly that vessels drawing 20 feet have to lie 5 miles off that, that is 10 miles from the forts, and it was at this point that the fleet of the various nations was at this time lying at anchor, the British being *Centurion*, flagship, *Barfleur, Orlando, Endymion, Aurora.*

The only vessels that could therefore enter the river and bombard the forts were gunboats and destroyers; of these the Russians had three, *Bobr, Koreelah,* and *Gilyak*; the French, the *Lion*; the British, the *Algerine*, steel despatch boat with six 4-inch guns, and two destroyers, the *Whiting* and *Fame.* These two last captured four perfectly equipped modern destroyers, whose crews bolted; properly handled, they might have destroyed all the attacking ships, who without them found sufficient work to do in keeping down the fire of the forts.

The plan arranged by the others was that, after an effective bombardment, a landing party should attack the north-west and north forts and the other forts in succession.

The Chinese, however, had no intention of letting the Westerns have it all their own way, but at a quarter to one a.m. on the morning of the 17th opened the ball by firing upon the *Algerine*, who promptly replied, and the battle became general. A terrific bombardment on both sides roared through the night, the gunboats in addition to the fire of their big guns keeping up a continuous hail from their quick-firing guns in their tops. The Chinese were equally determined, and stuck to their guns through it all, but they were very poor gunners, and their shells did not burst, and so for six hours the gunboats' targets for two miles of forts and some 200 or more guns escaped serious injury.

As daylight came, however, the Chinese made better practice, and the position became more serious for the allies, and it seemed as though the attack was going to fail. The Russian ship *Gilyak* was hit by a shell, and lost several men. She could not leave her moorings in consequence, and suffered severely from rifle fire from the shore, her losses during the action being the heaviest in the fleet, 2 officers and 10 men killed and 47 wounded.

The tide now rising, the ships boldly steamed amid a storm of shot and shell close under the forts. The German *Itlis* was seen constantly in the post of danger, and the gallantry with which she was fought evoked the admiration of all.

HMS *Algerine*, commander R.H. Stewart, greatly contributed to the final success, which at one time was so doubtful. She was always in the thick of the fight, but escaped with only slight damage to cowls and rigging, and received no shot in her hull, largely owing to the fact that her commander put her so close into the forts that they could not be brought to bear on her, and the shot passed over. She had only 1 officer wounded and 3 men killed.

Still the battle continued, and the Chinese kept doggedly at it, and succeeded in bursting their shells. Fortunately about seven a.m. an awful explosion occurred, the chief magazine blew up, and the Chinese lost heart, and soon after all firing ceased. Meantime the storming-parties had seized the north-west fort.

The landing party consisted of British, 23 officers and 298 men, from the Alacrity, Barfleur, and *Endymion*; German, 3 officers and 130 men; Japanese, 4 officers and 240 men; Russian, 2 officers and 157 men; Italian, 1 officer and 24 men; Austrian, 2 officers and 20 men,—total, 904 officers and men. The command was confided to Commander Craddock, RN. These landed under heavy shell fire in the dark by 2:30 a.m. with no loss, and at 4:30, when the ships' guns had silenced those of the forts, advanced upon the north-west fort. In the firing line were men from the *Alacrity* and *Endymion* on the right, Russians on the left, and Italians on the right flank; the *Barfleur*'s men supported the charge, and the rest of the force were in support. The Japanese, however, were not to be restrained, and as soon as the charge sounded, raced with the British for the west gate, and both nations climbed the parapet together. Their commander was first in, and the English commander a good second, the former unfortunately being killed. The remaining forts were easily taken, and with small loss to the allies. The Chinese garrison was estimated at 3000, of whom one-third was killed.

### THE CAPTURE OF TIENTSIN CITY

During the absence of the admiral and his force, the Chinese had kept our force defending the foreign settlement at Tientsin sufficiently busy, and did everything in their power to prevent trains with reinforcements going forward even before the 14th June, when the rails were torn up. Captain Bayly, RN, of HMS *Aurora*, had been left in charge of the British forces, and was joined on the 11th June by Commander Beattie, of HMS *Barfleur*, with 150 bluejackets and marines, and later by between 1600 and 1800 Russians, with cavalry and artillery. The Boxers made their first attack upon the settlement upon 16th June, and from that time, until the capture of the Chinese city, there was almost continual fighting, in the course of which the Naval Brigade lost several officers and men.

The native city began to bombard the settlement on the 17th, and on the 25th a 12-pounder gun from the *Terrible*, one of those mounted on Captain Percy Scott's system, which had done such service in South Africa, arrived and shelled the forts.

The *Terrible* had also brought to Tongku a military force consisting of Royal Welsh Fusiliers, 7 officers and 328 men, some engineers, and other details, under Major Morris; these with a naval force of about 150, under Captain Craddock, RN, of the *Alacrity*, together with 1500 Russians with 4 guns and 100 American marines, made on the 23rd June an attack upon the military school, a strong position commanding the settlements. A great deal of bayonet-fighting took place in clearing the villages on the way, but the position itself was easily taken and the settlement relieved. The approximate total of the forces of all nations at Tientsin after this reinforcement was 4500, of whom about 1400 were British.

On 27th June a force of British seamen under Commander Craddock, and marines under Major Johnstone, the whole

THE JAPANESE RACED WITH THE BRITISH FOR THE WEST GATE

about 600 strong, under the command of Captain Burke, joined with the Russians in an attack upon the Chinese arsenal. The Russians took the centre and right face, our men being ordered to advance parallel to the left face. At 200 yards they were met with a heavy fire, and had to advance for some space over a flat piece of ground until they could turn and face the arsenal, and when they advanced received the fire of a field-gun at the left corner. However, fixing bayonets, the bluejackets charged with a cheer, the enemy quickly bolted, and were met with the fire of the marines, who had been left outside for that purpose. The Russians also drove out the enemy at their end, and destroyed the arsenal. Our losses were 7 killed and 21 wounded.

On 28th June and the following day messages came in from Peking, dated 24th June, "Our case is desperate; come at once." *Terrible* news indeed for the allies; it was but two days since the expedition which had set out for Peking had returned, and now the Tientsin settlement itself was in danger, besieged and bombarded daily by the Chinese forts. No attempt even at relief was at this time possible, and there was an awful anxiety both here and in Europe as to what the fate of the embassies might be.

On the 4th of July the Chinese made an attack upon the railway station, and were repulsed; and on the same day two additional 12-pounder guns from the *Terrible* arrived, and also two Krupp guns taken from the Taku forts, a most important access of strength to the Naval Brigade, for up to this time the only guns had been the 12-pounder of the *Terrible*, two 9-pounder marine field-guns, and three 6 pounder Hotchkiss.

The next two days the forts in the native city were heavily bombarded by the *Terrible's* guns, assisted by French and Japanese field-guns. Several of the Chinese guns were silenced, but others, difficult to locate owing to the use of smokeless powder, replied with spirit and made good practice. A gallant attempt was made on the afternoon of the 6th by Major Bruce of the 1st Chinese Regiment to silence a 9-pounder which had been pushed up to within short range, and appeared to be aiming at the waterworks. The admiral lent him a 9-pounder gun, and Commander Beattie, of the *Barfleur*, with 70 men. No cover could be found, and the 9-pounder could not be brought into action owing to the heavy rifle fire, and the attempt had to be abandoned. The force lost 2 killed and 5 wounded, among the latter being Major Bruce and Mr F. Esdaile, midshipman of the *Barfleur*, the latter mortally.

The Chinese for some days had gradually been pushing their lines round to the west and south of the native city, with a view to cutting the communication by river and also placing the battery of the British naval guns under a fire from the rear as well as front. Moreover, the Chinese gunners were improving daily in their practice, and evidently had knowledge from spies of the exact position and ranges of the barracks. It became therefore necessary to clear the enemy out of their position.

It was accordingly arranged that a combined movement should be made at daybreak on 9th July to drive the enemy out of their position, and by a wide flanking movement to converge upon and capture the west arsenal. The command was entrusted to the Japanese General Fukushima, whose force consisted of about 1000 infantry and 150 cavalry, with 150 American 9th Infantry Regiment. The British sent 1000 men, namely, two companies 2nd Battalion Royal Welsh Fusiliers, half company Hong-Kong Regiment, two companies Chinese Regiment, and 400 bluejackets and marines under General Dorward as supports; and the Russians a reserve of 400.

The force moved off before daylight on the 9th. The bulk of the fighting fell upon the Japanese, but there was very little of that, for though the Chinese artillery replied briskly for some time, when once the guns were silenced and the infantry through the line of fire, the Chinese fled precipitately. The Japanese cavalry charged and dispersed a body of Boxers, killing about 200, and the infantry advancing captured four Krupp guns. The arsenal was taken with a rush by the Japanese, and found to be deserted, but being commanded by rifle fire was found to be untenable. The place was therefore set on fire, and the forces returned, having most thoroughly effected their purpose. The naval casualties among the British were 1 killed and 3 wounded.

This reverse, severe though it was, did not weaken the determination of the Boxers, for early in the morning of the 11th they made a most determined attack upon the railway station, an important position for them, from which they could bombard the settlement as well as destroy the rolling stock. The fight lasted three hours, and was stubbornly contested. The Chinese got to close quarters and even crossed bayonets with the allies. They were at length driven out with very heavy loss. The allies also lost heavily, 150 killed and wounded, principally Japanese and French. The British loss was very slight.

At this time the number of the enemy attacking was estimated at 20,000, while of the allies the total force was 12,170, namely, 50 Austrians, 2160 French, 1420 British, 400 Germans, 40 Italians, 3090 Japanese, 4450 Russians, and 560 Americans. The bombardment of the settlement by the Chinese was inflicting daily losses. Hitherto their artillery had been superior to ours, but by the arrival of two 4-inch guns, one from HMS *Algerine*, and another from HMS *Phoenix*, the position was altered and it was at length decided to make a general attack upon the enemy on the 18th, with a view to capturing the native city and finally relieving the foreign settlement. In this action the British naval guns were assigned a prominent part, and to their very accurate shooting the success was mainly due. The plan arranged was that under cover of the naval guns on the east the Russians and Germans should take the Chinese batteries to the north-east of the city, while the Japanese and British should at the same time deliver their attack upon the city to facilitate the capture of the batteries by the Russians. The Japanese were under their own general, the rest of the allies under General Donvard. The forces consisted of 1500 Japanese, under General Fukushima; 800 British, of whom 300 were naval; 900 Americans, 30 Austrians, 900 French, and about 3000 Russians and 400 German marines.

After about an hour's bombardment the main attack was delivered, the French on the right, the British on the left, and the Japanese in the centre, which was the point of greatest danger, for they were to advance upon the south gate and blow it up to effect an entrance. The Americans were ordered to support the left of the Japanese, and to their left were the Welsh Fusiliers. The Americans unfortunately soon became involved in a very exposed position, whence they could neither retreat nor advance, their colonel was killed and they lost very heavily, and 100 men of the Naval Brigade under Lieutenant Phillimore were sent to their aid.

Meantime the naval guns were keeping up a constant and accurate fire, keeping down the fire from the city walls. Still, however, the day wore on; the Japanese were unable to reach the gate, and the city, which it was expected to enter by noon, was not yet taken, and the Japanese general decided to hold his position through the night and to resume the attack in the morning.

Under fire of the naval guns the Fusiliers and American marines were withdrawn with very slight loss, and then the unfortunate 9th Regiment with the company of the Naval Brigade. This was a very delicate business, for they were in danger of being themselves hit by the guns, but so accurate was the fire that it was performed without accident. Splendid work had meantime been done by our men in getting in the American wounded, nearly all of whom they brought in under fire.

The Russians, of whom nothing had been heard during the day, had been thoroughly successful, although their attack had been delayed. In the end they completely routed the Chinese and captured 11 guns, but not without heavy fighting, in which they lost 120 in killed and wounded.

The next morning the Japanese, who in the night had made a bridge across the canal, crossed over at three a.m., blew in the gate, and in less than an hour the city was taken. The British seized a number of junks and a steamer and 8 guns, which had kept up such a fire on the preceding day. The total loss of the allies concerned in the attack on the south gate was— British, naval, 6 men killed, among whom was Captain Lloyd of the marines, and 38 wounded; military, 12 killed, 38 wounded; Americans, 9 killed, 119 wounded; French, no killed and wounded; Japanese, 400.

The effect of the naval guns was remarkable, and is thus reported by General Dorward:

> The success of the operations was largely due to the manner in which the naval guns were worked by Lieutenant Drummond, RN, the accuracy of their fire alone rendering steady fire on the part of the troops possible against the strong Chinese position, and largely reducing the number of casualties. The delicate operation of withdrawing troops from advanced positions at nightfall to strengthen other parts of the line, and the bringing back of the wounded, could not have been effected without the aid of the well-directed fire of the guns. I desire to place on record my appreciation of the gallantry and fine spirit of the men, and to join in their regret for the heavy loss in killed and wounded, and particularly with the Royal Marines in regret for the death of Captain Lloyd.
>
> The Naval Brigade had their full share in the fighting at the centre and right of the position, and had the honour of being among the first troops to enter Tientsin. The succour they brought under a heavy fire to the hard-pressed American troops on the right was highly appreciated by the 9th Regiment United States Infantry, who found themselves unexpectedly under the heaviest fire of the day, and were much heartened by the arrival of Lieutenant Phillimore, RN, and his men.

## A Young V.C.

During the fighting on 13th July a midshipman, Basil John Douglas Guy, displayed great coolness and bravery in stopping with and attending to a wounded seaman, under an excessively hot fire, eventually assisting to carry him across a fire-swept force. When it is remembered what kind of treatment the Chinese dealt out to all who fell into their hands, and the brutalities of which they were guilty, the heroism of the above act stands out all the more sharply and unmistakably. For the action thus described in the *Gazette* Mr Guy was awarded a Victoria Cross.

## The Siege of Peking

The foreign guard that arrived in Peking on the evening of 31st May and following days numbered only 18 officers and 389 men, far too few for the defence, and ridiculously inadequately supplied with guns and ammunition. The British brought one old type Nordenfeldt; the Austrians, one quick-firing gun; while the Russians brought a supply of 12-pound shell, but left their gun behind. It seemed as if the powers only contemplated a demonstration, whereas this little force was destined to sustain a siege that will rank amongst the most memorable in history, and to hold—against Krupp guns and hordes of Chinese, firing at close quarters modern magazine rifles—gardens and buildings occupying some ten acres of ground, surrounded by a high wall, but in other respects before the commencement of the siege utterly unprotected.

The superior number of the enemy and the daily bombardment was not the greatest danger they had to meet. One compound was crowded with women and children and native refugees; famine and failure of ammunition daily approached; the only hope of relief from these was the arrival of a relieving force. The thought of the horrors that must follow if this failed, and the awful fate at the hands of the fanatic and cruel Chinese soldiery which must befall the women and children, was ever before each member of the force, as day by day, for over nine weeks, day and night he guarded his post, cut off from the world outside and with hardly a hope of rescue.

The British party consisted of 75 non-commissioned officers and men of the Royal Marines, under Captains Strouts, Halliday, and Wray. There were also present of other nations—American, 3 officers and 52 men; Austrians, 5 officers and 30 men; French, 2 officers and 45 men; German, 1 officer and 51 men; Italian, 1 officer and 28 men; Japanese, 1 officer and 24 men; Russian, 2 officers and 79 men. The British brought an old-fashioned five-barrel Nordenfeldt, the Italians one small gun and 120 rounds, the Americans a machine gun with good supply of ammunition; but the supply of small arm ammunition was very scanty, ranging from 300 to 100 rounds per man.

In addition to these trained men the embassies supplied of students and others 85 men, of whom 31 were Japanese armed with any rifle or weapon that they could find; and these men shared in all the fatigues of the siege, and added greatly to the strength of the garrison. At this time fearful and indescribable horrors were occurring in the Chinese city, thousands of Chinese Christians were cruelly tortured and killed. Reports came in daily of the murder of missionaries, of railway stations destroyed, and the gradual isolation of Peking. Missionaries and their families and native Christians took refuge in the legations, and rescue parties were sent out to bring in others, and these reported the most terrible scenes of massacre and indescribable cruelty.

The Paitang, the great Roman Catholic cathedral, saved some thousands of Christians. These with the priests and sisters, assisted by 30 French marines, were enabled to keep the attacking forces at bay till the city was taken by the allies. The guard lost 10 killed, and some 200 of the people died also, but the rest must have soon perished of starvation when the supplies collected with wonderful prudence by Bishop Favier, who foresaw what was coming, had been exhausted.

All this time Peking was in the hands of the Boxers, with the Imperial soldiers looking on, assisting, but the Chinese Government officially professing great solicitude for the safety of the legations. This did not prevent the Boxers firing, and upon the 17th June Imperial soldiers were observed doing the same. Upon 19th June the storm burst; the Government had heard of the attack upon the Taku forts, and gave the ambassadors notice to leave Peking within twenty-four hours. To have done so would have been to leave all the thousands of Chinese Christians to their fate, and to have ensured a massacre; nevertheless some of the embassies at once prepared to move, and began to pack up. The British decided to remain and hold the legation at all hazards, and the course of events next day decided for the others.

The German minister, Baron von Ketteler, went unattended with his secretary to the Yamen. On the way he was murdered and his secretary wounded by Imperial troops.

The same day the Yamen withdrew the ultimatum, and requested the ministers to remain in Peking, as the country was so disturbed. This expression of anxious care for the welfare of the Europeans was a blind, for at four o'clock, the hour fixed in the ultimatum, fire was opened upon the legations, and the siege began.

All the women and children were brought in to the legation compound, and it was decided to hold the British Embassy as the last line of defence, the supreme command being assigned to Sir Claude Macdonald, the commanding officer of each guard being in command of their several legations.

Three sides of the legation compound were surrounded by Chinese buildings, and these constituted a very grave danger, as attempts were made, by setting them on fire, to burn out the legation buildings; and on the 22nd June one of these attempts nearly succeeded, the fire was got under, and the building destroyed under a hail of bullets.

Just outside the legation and only a few feet away was the Hanlin Academy. This was the most venerated and ancient building in Peking, and contained a priceless collection of books and ancient Chinese manuscripts, which could never be replaced. These buildings were a source of great danger if fired; the Europeans hesitated to destroy such a building; not so the Chinese, and on the 23rd it was found to be in flames, with a strong wind blowing towards the legation buildings. Fortunately, the wind changed, or these could not have been saved.

On the discovery that the building was on fire, a party of British and American marines and volunteers rushed in and drove out the Chinese, killing a good many; but it was too late to save the library, and only a few of its manuscripts were rescued. Thus the Chinese in their fury against the foreigner had destroyed a collection which for many centuries had been the pride of their literati.

The buildings had to be demolished on all sides as they were successively set on fire, and at length the legation buildings were safe from this source of danger, but the work was carried out under a continuous rattle of rifle fire, and there were numerous casualties.

On 24th June Captain Halliday with 30 marines was sent to clear out a party of the enemy who had set fire to the State buildings of the British legation, and were taking cover in the buildings. A hole being made in the legation wall, Captain Halliday followed by his men crept through, and at once came upon the enemy, and before he was able to use his revolver received a serious wound from a rifle at point-blank range, the bullet breaking his shoulder and entering the lung; notwithstanding, he shot three of the enemy and walked back unaided to the hospital. For this gallant action Captain Halliday was awarded the V.C. Captain Strouts then took charge, and driving back the enemy captured some rifles, and, what was most valuable, a large quantity of ammunition.

Danger from incendiarism was now removed, but a new peril appeared. The enemy on the 26th opened fire at 1000 yards with a Krupp 2.7-inch gun; this was silenced by rifle fire, and the next day, when a sortie was made to take it, it had been withdrawn. As, however, it was known that there were ten more in Peking, all hands turned to making bomb-proof shelters, and on the 28th the enemy mounted another gun at 300 yards, but soon withdrew it when a sortie was made to take it.

It was at length found possible to make some reply, for an old smooth-bore gun was found, and the projectiles the Russians had brought were made use of, and a 1-pounder gun, which the enemy had posted but 100 yards off, was silenced after the ninth round. What a curious instance of our Western ways this incident affords; the Chinese firing upon our own people with the latest artillery made by ourselves, while they are left to improvise a gun from a relic found in an old iron store!

The enemy now began to give up their attempt to get into the British legation, and to devote their attention to the Italians, Japanese, French, and Germans, who protected most of the Chinese converts, against whom they were increasingly savage; consequently the British marines had to reinforce all the posts outside the legation.

On 16th July, Captain Strouts was killed—a very great loss

to the defence—and Captain Halliday being wounded, Captain Wray took command of the marines and Sir Claude Macdonald of the legation.

On the 17th the Chinese Imperial authorities were getting frightened, no doubt affected by the fall of Tientsin, and till the 4th of August, except for occasional sniping practice, suspended hostilities, and again made suggestions that the embassies should retire under escort to Tientsin, and leave the native Christians to the Government, who promised them protection; but, nevertheless, the firing continued after 4th August, especially at night, and there were many casualties, but beyond this there was no serious fighting.

On 14th August the sound of guns was heard, and shells were seen bursting against the gates of the Tartar city, and the besieged knew that relief was at hand, and so it proved. At three p.m. the British native troops, followed by General Gaselee and staff, entered the legation, and the siege was at an end.

The relief and thankfulness felt in Great Britain and throughout the empire at the conclusion of this memorable siege could not be better expressed than in the words telegraphed by Queen Victoria to the officer commanding the marine guard:

"I thank God that you and those under your command are rescued from your perilous situation. With my people I have waited with the deepest anxiety for the good news of your safety and a happy termination of your heroic and prolonged defence. I grieve for the losses and sufferings experienced by the besieged."

The casualties among the British garrison amounted to 6 killed and 21 wounded, among the latter being Dr Morrison, the *Times* Chinese correspondent, the total amongst all the defenders being 65 killed and 160 wounded, although 4000 shells fell in the legation during the siege. The relief arrived only just in time, as there were but three days' rations left, and the Chinese were attacking with increasing rigour towards the end.

## The Relief of Peking

In Europe and in America, cut off from all reliable sources of information about what was happening at the embassies, the suspense was very great. In July rumours came of the fall of the legation, and the massacre of all the Europeans. Even in official circles the news was accepted as true; obituary notices of the members of the legation appeared in the daily press, and arrangements were made for a public funeral service at Saint Paul's Cathedral.

It was some time after the arrival of this report in Europe that the allies found themselves able to start from Tientsin, being equally uncertain as to what they would find to be the state of the embassies, if they themselves should arrive there; happily, though late, it proved not too late.

On 3rd August the allied generals arrived at a resolution to commence the advance the next day with, approximately, 20,000 men, namely, 10,000 Japanese, with 24 guns; 4000 Russians, with 16 guns; 3000 British, with 12 guns; 2000 Americans, with 6 guns; 800 French, with 12 guns; and 300 Germans, Austrians, and Italians.

Among the British contingent the navy was well represented, the Naval Brigade, under the command of Captain Gallaghan of the *Endymion*, consisted of 125 bluejackets with four 12-pounders from the *Barfleur*, *Terrible*, *Endymion*, *Phoenix*, and *Algerine*, and 278 marines under Major Luke; there were also two more naval 12-pounders manned by Hong-Kong artillery under Major Saint John; there started on the same day the junks which had been captured from the enemy.

The principal Chinese position was at Peitsang, where they were strongly entrenched on both sides of the river. This position was attacked and stormed by the Japanese, supported by the British, on the morning of the 5th, the brunt of the action being borne by the Japanese, who lost 200 in killed and wounded, the British only 25, of whom 21 were Indian. The force pressed on day after day, driving the enemy before them, the Japanese bearing the brunt of the fighting all the way up. Peking was reached on the 14th, and about 2:45 General Gaselee had the good fortune to enter the legation first of all the generals. In these actions very little fighting fell to the Naval Brigade, but the marines under Major Luke co-operated in the relief of the cathedral the next day.

# ALSO FROM LEONAUR
## AVAILABLE IN SOFTCOVER OR HARDCOVER WITH DUST JACKET

**AFGHANISTAN: THE BELEAGUERED BRIGADE** *by G. R. Gleig*—An Account of Sale's Brigade During the First Afghan War.

**IN THE RANKS OF THE C. I. V** *by Erskine Childers*—With the City Imperial Volunteer Battery (Honourable Artillery Company) in the Second Boer War.

**THE BENGAL NATIVE ARMY** *by F. G. Cardew*—An Invaluable Reference Resource.

**THE 7TH (QUEEN'S OWN) HUSSARS** *by C. R. B. Barrett*—Uniforms, Equipment, Weapons, Traditions, the Services of Notable Officers and Men & the Appendices to All Volumes—Volume 4: 1688-1914.

**THE SWORD OF THE CROWN** *by Eric W. Sheppard*—A History of the British Army to 1914.

**THE 7TH (QUEEN'S OWN) HUSSARS** *by C. R. B. Barrett*—On Campaign During the Canadian Rebellion, the Indian Mutiny, the Sudan, Matabeleland, Mashonaland and the Boer War Volume 3: 1818-1914.

**THE KHARTOUM CAMPAIGN** *by Bennet Burleigh*—A Special Correspondent's View of the Reconquest of the Sudan by British and Egyptian Forces under Kitchener—1898.

**EL PUCHERO** *by Richard McSherry*—The Letters of a Surgeon of Volunteers During Scott's Campaign of the American-Mexican War 1847-1848.

**RIFLEMAN SAHIB** *by E. Maude*—The Recollections of an Officer of the Bombay Rifles During the Southern Mahratta Campaign, Second Sikh War, Persian Campaign and Indian Mutiny.

**THE KING'S HUSSAR** *by Edwin Mole*—The Recollections of a 14th (King's) Hussar During the Victorian Era.

**JOHN COMPANY'S CAVALRYMAN** *by William Johnson*—The Experiences of a British Soldier in the Crimea, the Persian Campaign and the Indian Mutiny.

**COLENSO & DURNFORD'S ZULU WAR** *by Frances E. Colenso & Edward Durnford*—The first and possibly the most important history of the Zulu War.

**U. S. DRAGOON** *by Samuel E. Chamberlain*—Experiences in the Mexican War 1846-48 and on the South Western Frontier.

AVAILABLE ONLINE AT **www.leonaur.com**
AND FROM ALL GOOD BOOK STORES

## ALSO FROM LEONAUR
### AVAILABLE IN SOFTCOVER OR HARDCOVER WITH DUST JACKET

**THE 2ND MAORI WAR: 1860-1861** *by Robert Carey*—The Second Maori War, or First Taranaki War, one more bloody instalment of the conflicts between European settlers and the indigenous Maori people.

**A JOURNAL OF THE SECOND SIKH WAR** *by Daniel A. Sandford*—The Experiences of an Ensign of the 2nd Bengal European Regiment During the Campaign in the Punjab, India, 1848-49.

**THE LIGHT INFANTRY OFFICER** *by John H. Cooke*—The Experiences of an Officer of the 43rd Light Infantry in America During the War of 1812.

**BUSHVELDT CARBINEERS** *by George Witton*—The War Against the Boers in South Africa and the 'Breaker' Morant Incident.

**LAKE'S CAMPAIGNS IN INDIA** *by Hugh Pearse*—The Second Anglo Maratha War, 1803-1807.

**BRITAIN IN AFGHANISTAN 1: THE FIRST AFGHAN WAR 1839-42** *by Archibald Forbes*—From invasion to destruction-a British military disaster.

**BRITAIN IN AFGHANISTAN 2: THE SECOND AFGHAN WAR 1878-80** *by Archibald Forbes*—This is the history of the Second Afghan War-another episode of British military history typified by savagery, massacre, siege and battles.

**UP AMONG THE PANDIES** *by Vivian Dering Majendie*—Experiences of a British Officer on Campaign During the Indian Mutiny, 1857-1858.

**MUTINY: 1857** *by James Humphries*—Authentic Voices from the Indian Mutiny-First Hand Accounts of Battles, Sieges and Personal Hardships.

**BLOW THE BUGLE, DRAW THE SWORD** *by W. H. G. Kingston*—The Wars, Campaigns, Regiments and Soldiers of the British & Indian Armies During the Victorian Era, 1839-1898.

**WAR BEYOND THE DRAGON PAGODA** *by Major J. J. Snodgrass*—A Personal Narrative of the First Anglo-Burmese War 1824 - 1826.

**THE HERO OF ALIWAL** *by James Humphries*—The Campaigns of Sir Harry Smith in India, 1843-1846, During the Gwalior War & the First Sikh War.

**ALL FOR A SHILLING A DAY** *by Donald F. Featherstone*—The story of H.M. 16th, the Queen's Lancers During the first Sikh War 1845-1846.

AVAILABLE ONLINE AT **www.leonaur.com**
AND FROM ALL GOOD BOOK STORES

## ALSO FROM LEONAUR
### AVAILABLE IN SOFTCOVER OR HARDCOVER WITH DUST JACKET

**THE FALL OF THE MOGHUL EMPIRE OF HINDUSTAN** *by H. G. Keene*—By the beginning of the nineteenth century, as British and Indian armies under Lake and Wellesley dominated the scene, a little over half a century of conflict brought the Moghul Empire to its knees.

**LADY SALE'S AFGHANISTAN** *by Florentia Sale*—An Indomitable Victorian Lady's Account of the Retreat from Kabul During the First Afghan War.

**THE CAMPAIGN OF MAGENTA AND SOLFERINO 1859** *by Harold Carmichael Wylly*—The Decisive Conflict for the Unification of Italy.

**FRENCH'S CAVALRY CAMPAIGN** *by J. G. Maydon*—A Special Correspondent's View of British Army Mounted Troops During the Boer War.

**CAVALRY AT WATERLOO** *by Sir Evelyn Wood*—British Mounted Troops During the Campaign of 1815.

**THE SUBALTERN** *by George Robert Gleig*—The Experiences of an Officer of the 85th Light Infantry During the Peninsular War.

**NAPOLEON AT BAY, 1814** *by F. Loraine Petre*—The Campaigns to the Fall of the First Empire.

**NAPOLEON AND THE CAMPAIGN OF 1806** *by Colonel Vachée*—The Napoleonic Method of Organisation and Command to the Battles of Jena & Auerstädt.

**THE COMPLETE ADVENTURES IN THE CONNAUGHT RANGERS** *by William Grattan*—The 88th Regiment during the Napoleonic Wars by a Serving Officer.

**BUGLER AND OFFICER OF THE RIFLES** *by William Green & Harry Smith*—With the 95th (Rifles) during the Peninsular & Waterloo Campaigns of the Napoleonic Wars.

**NAPOLEONIC WAR STORIES** *by Sir Arthur Quiller-Couch*—Tales of soldiers, spies, battles & sieges from the Peninsular & Waterloo campaingns.

**CAPTAIN OF THE 95TH (RIFLES)** *by Jonathan Leach*—An officer of Wellington's sharpshooters during the Peninsular, South of France and Waterloo campaigns of the Napoleonic wars.

**RIFLEMAN COSTELLO** *by Edward Costello*—The adventures of a soldier of the 95th (Rifles) in the Peninsular & Waterloo Campaigns of the Napoleonic wars.

AVAILABLE ONLINE AT **www.leonaur.com**
AND FROM ALL GOOD BOOK STORES

# ALSO FROM LEONAUR
### AVAILABLE IN SOFTCOVER OR HARDCOVER WITH DUST JACKET

**AT THEM WITH THE BAYONET** *by Donald F. Featherstone*—The first Anglo-Sikh War 1845-1846.

**STEPHEN CRANE'S BATTLES** *by Stephen Crane*—Nine Decisive Battles Recounted by the Author of 'The Red Badge of Courage'.

**THE GURKHA WAR** *by H. T. Prinsep*—The Anglo-Nepalese Conflict in North East India 1814-1816.

**FIRE & BLOOD** *by G. R. Gleig*—The burning of Washington & the battle of New Orleans, 1814, through the eyes of a young British soldier.

**SOUND ADVANCE!** *by Joseph Anderson*—Experiences of an officer of HM 50th regiment in Australia, Burma & the Gwalior war.

**THE CAMPAIGN OF THE INDUS** *by Thomas Holdsworth*—Experiences of a British Officer of the 2nd (Queen's Royal) Regiment in the Campaign to Place Shah Shuja on the Throne of Afghanistan 1838 - 1840.

**WITH THE MADRAS EUROPEAN REGIMENT IN BURMA** *by John Butler*—The Experiences of an Officer of the Honourable East India Company's Army During the First Anglo-Burmese War 1824 - 1826.

**IN ZULULAND WITH THE BRITISH ARMY** *by Charles L. Norris-Newman*—The Anglo-Zulu war of 1879 through the first-hand experiences of a special correspondent.

**BESIEGED IN LUCKNOW** *by Martin Richard Gubbins*—The first Anglo-Sikh War 1845-1846.

**A TIGER ON HORSEBACK** *by L. March Phillips*—The Experiences of a Trooper & Officer of Rimington's Guides - The Tigers - during the Anglo-Boer war 1899 - 1902.

**SEPOYS, SIEGE & STORM** *by Charles John Griffiths*—The Experiences of a young officer of H.M.'s 61st Regiment at Ferozepore, Delhi ridge and at the fall of Delhi during the Indian mutiny 1857.

**CAMPAIGNING IN ZULULAND** *by W. E. Montague*—Experiences on campaign during the Zulu war of 1879 with the 94th Regiment.

**THE STORY OF THE GUIDES** *by G.J. Younghusband*—The Exploits of the Soldiers of the famous Indian Army Regiment from the northwest frontier 1847 - 1900.

AVAILABLE ONLINE AT **www.leonaur.com**
AND FROM ALL GOOD BOOK STORES

## ALSO FROM LEONAUR
### AVAILABLE IN SOFTCOVER OR HARDCOVER WITH DUST JACKET

**ZULU: 1879** *by D.C.F. Moodie & the Leonaur Editors*—The Anglo-Zulu War of 1879 from contemporary sources: First Hand Accounts, Interviews, Dispatches, Official Documents & Newspaper Reports.

**THE RED DRAGOON** *by W.J. Adams*—With the 7th Dragoon Guards in the Cape of Good Hope against the Boers & the Kaffir tribes during the 'war of the axe' 1843-48'.

**THE RECOLLECTIONS OF SKINNER OF SKINNER'S HORSE** *by James Skinner*—James Skinner and his 'Yellow Boys' Irregular cavalry in the wars of India between the British, Mahratta, Rajput, Mogul, Sikh & Pindarree Forces.

**A CAVALRY OFFICER DURING THE SEPOY REVOLT** *by A. R. D. Mackenzie*—Experiences with the 3rd Bengal Light Cavalry, the Guides and Sikh Irregular Cavalry from the outbreak to Delhi and Lucknow.

**A NORFOLK SOLDIER IN THE FIRST SIKH WAR** *by J W Baldwin*—Experiences of a private of H.M. 9th Regiment of Foot in the battles for the Punjab, India 1845-6.

**TOMMY ATKINS' WAR STORIES: 14 FIRST HAND ACCOUNTS**—Fourteen first hand accounts from the ranks of the British Army during Queen Victoria's Empire.

**THE WATERLOO LETTERS** *by H. T. Siborne*—Accounts of the Battle by British Officers for its Foremost Historian.

**NEY: GENERAL OF CAVALRY VOLUME 1—1769-1799** *by Antoine Bulos*—The Early Career of a Marshal of the First Empire.

**NEY: MARSHAL OF FRANCE VOLUME 2—1799-1805** *by Antoine Bulos*—The Early Career of a Marshal of the First Empire.

**AIDE-DE-CAMP TO NAPOLEON** *by Philippe-Paul de Ségur*—For anyone interested in the Napoleonic Wars this book, written by one who was intimate with the strategies and machinations of the Emperor, will be essential reading.

**TWILIGHT OF EMPIRE** *by Sir Thomas Ussher & Sir George Cockburn*—Two accounts of Napoleon's Journeys in Exile to Elba and St. Helena: Narrative of Events by Sir Thomas Ussher & Napoleon's Last Voyage: Extract of a diary by Sir George Cockburn.

**PRIVATE WHEELER** *by William Wheeler*—The letters of a soldier of the 51st Light Infantry during the Peninsular War & at Waterloo.

AVAILABLE ONLINE AT **www.leonaur.com**
AND FROM ALL GOOD BOOK STORES

# ALSO FROM LEONAUR
### AVAILABLE IN SOFTCOVER OR HARDCOVER WITH DUST JACKET

**OFFICERS & GENTLEMEN** *by Peter Hawker & William Graham*—Two Accounts of British Officers During the Peninsula War: Officer of Light Dragoons by Peter Hawker & Campaign in Portugal and Spain by William Graham.

**THE WALCHEREN EXPEDITION** *by Anonymous*—The Experiences of a British Officer of the 81st Regt. During the Campaign in the Low Countries of 1809.

**LADIES OF WATERLOO** *by Charlotte A. Eaton, Magdalene de Lancey & Juana Smith*—The Experiences of Three Women During the Campaign of 1815: Waterloo Days by Charlotte A. Eaton, A Week at Waterloo by Magdalene de Lancey & Juana's Story by Juana Smith.

**JOURNAL OF AN OFFICER IN THE KING'S GERMAN LEGION** *by John Frederick Hering*—Recollections of Campaigning During the Napoleonic Wars.

**JOURNAL OF AN ARMY SURGEON IN THE PENINSULAR WAR** *by Charles Boutflower*—The Recollections of a British Army Medical Man on Campaign During the Napoleonic Wars.

**ON CAMPAIGN WITH MOORE AND WELLINGTON** *by Anthony Hamilton*—The Experiences of a Soldier of the 43rd Regiment During the Peninsular War.

**THE ROAD TO AUSTERLITZ** *by R. G. Burton*—Napoleon's Campaign of 1805.

**SOLDIERS OF NAPOLEON** *by A. J. Doisy De Villargennes & Arthur Chuquet*—The Experiences of the Men of the French First Empire: Under the Eagles by A. J. Doisy De Villargennes & Voices of 1812 by Arthur Chuquet.

**INVASION OF FRANCE, 1814** *by F. W. O. Maycock*—The Final Battles of the Napoleonic First Empire.

**LEIPZIG—A CONFLICT OF TITANS** *by Frederic Shoberl*—A Personal Experience of the 'Battle of the Nations' During the Napoleonic Wars, October 14th-19th, 1813.

**SLASHERS** *by Charles Cadell*—The Campaigns of the 28th Regiment of Foot During the Napoleonic Wars by a Serving Officer.

**BATTLE IMPERIAL** *by Charles William Vane*—The Campaigns in Germany & France for the Defeat of Napoleon 1813-1814.

**SWIFT & BOLD** *by Gibbes Rigaud*—The 60th Rifles During the Peninsula War.

AVAILABLE ONLINE AT **www.leonaur.com**
AND FROM ALL GOOD BOOK STORES

## ALSO FROM LEONAUR
### AVAILABLE IN SOFTCOVER OR HARDCOVER WITH DUST JACKET

**ADVENTURES OF A YOUNG RIFLEMAN** by Johann Christian Maempel—The Experiences of a Saxon in the French & British Armies During the Napoleonic Wars.

**THE HUSSAR** by Norbert Landsheit & G. R. Gleig—A German Cavalryman in British Service Throughout the Napoleonic Wars.

**RECOLLECTIONS OF THE PENINSULA** by Moyle Sherer—An Officer of the 34th Regiment of Foot—'The Cumberland Gentlemen'—on Campaign Against Napoleon's French Army in Spain.

**MARINE OF REVOLUTION & CONSULATE** by Moreau de Jonnès—The Recollections of a French Soldier of the Revolutionary Wars 1791-1804.

**GENTLEMEN IN RED** by John Dobbs & Robert Knowles—Two Accounts of British Infantry Officers During the Peninsular War Recollections of an Old 52nd Man by John Dobbs An Officer of Fusiliers by Robert Knowles.

**CORPORAL BROWN'S CAMPAIGNS IN THE LOW COUNTRIES** by Robert Brown—Recollections of a Coldstream Guard in the Early Campaigns Against Revolutionary France 1793-1795.

**THE 7TH (QUEENS OWN) HUSSARS** by C. R. B. Barrett—During the Campaigns in the Low Countries & the Peninsula and Waterloo Campaigns of the Napoleonic Wars. Volume 2: 1793-1815.

**THE MARENGO CAMPAIGN 1800** by Herbert H. Sargent—The Victory that Completed the Austrian Defeat in Italy.

**DONALDSON OF THE 94TH—SCOTS BRIGADE** by Joseph Donaldson—The Recollections of a Soldier During the Peninsula & South of France Campaigns of the Napoleonic Wars.

**A CONSCRIPT FOR EMPIRE** by Philippe as told to Johann Christian Maempel—The Experiences of a Young German Conscript During the Napoleonic Wars.

**JOURNAL OF THE CAMPAIGN OF 1815** by Alexander Cavalié Mercer—The Experiences of an Officer of the Royal Horse Artillery During the Waterloo Campaign.

**NAPOLEON'S CAMPAIGNS IN POLAND 1806-7** by Robert Wilson—The campaign in Poland from the Russian side of the conflict.

AVAILABLE ONLINE AT **www.leonaur.com**
AND FROM ALL GOOD BOOK STORES

# ALSO FROM LEONAUR
## AVAILABLE IN SOFTCOVER OR HARDCOVER WITH DUST JACKET

**OMPTEDA OF THE KING'S GERMAN LEGION** *by Christian von Ompteda*—A Hanoverian Officer on Campaign Against Napoleon.

**LIEUTENANT SIMMONS OF THE 95TH (RIFLES)** *by George Simmons*—Recollections of the Peninsula, South of France & Waterloo Campaigns of the Napoleonic Wars.

**A HORSEMAN FOR THE EMPEROR** *by Jean Baptiste Gazzola*—A Cavalryman of Napoleon's Army on Campaign Throughout the Napoleonic Wars.

**SERGEANT LAWRENCE** *by William Lawrence*—With the 40th Regt. of Foot in South America, the Peninsular War & at Waterloo.

**CAMPAIGNS WITH THE FIELD TRAIN** *by Richard D. Henegan*—Experiences of a British Officer During the Peninsula and Waterloo Campaigns of the Napoleonic Wars.

**CAVALRY SURGEON** *by S. D. Broughton*—On Campaign Against Napoleon in the Peninsula & South of France During the Napoleonic Wars 1812-1814.

**MEN OF THE RIFLES** *by Thomas Knight, Henry Curling & Jonathan Leach*—The Reminiscences of Thomas Knight of the 95th (Rifles) by Thomas Knight, Henry Curling's Anecdotes by Henry Curling & The Field Services of the Rifle Brigade from its Formation to Waterloo by Jonathan Leach.

**THE ULM CAMPAIGN 1805** *by F. N. Maude*—Napoleon and the Defeat of the Austrian Army During the 'War of the Third Coalition'.

**SOLDIERING WITH THE 'DIVISION'** *by Thomas Garrety*—The Military Experiences of an Infantryman of the 43rd Regiment During the Napoleonic Wars.

**SERGEANT MORRIS OF THE 73RD FOOT** *by Thomas Morris*—The Experiences of a British Infantryman During the Napoleonic Wars-Including Campaigns in Germany and at Waterloo.

**A VOICE FROM WATERLOO** *by Edward Cotton*—The Personal Experiences of a British Cavalryman Who Became a Battlefield Guide and Authority on the Campaign of 1815.

**NAPOLEON AND HIS MARSHALS** *by J. T. Headley*—The Men of the First Empire.

AVAILABLE ONLINE AT **www.leonaur.com**
AND FROM ALL GOOD BOOK STORES

## ALSO FROM LEONAUR
### AVAILABLE IN SOFTCOVER OR HARDCOVER WITH DUST JACKET

**COLBORNE: A SINGULAR TALENT FOR WAR** *by John Colborne*—The Napoleonic Wars Career of One of Wellington's Most Highly Valued Officers in Egypt, Holland, Italy, the Peninsula and at Waterloo.

**NAPOLEON'S RUSSIAN CAMPAIGN** *by Philippe Henri de Segur*—The Invasion, Battles and Retreat by an Aide-de-Camp on the Emperor's Staff.

**WITH THE LIGHT DIVISION** *by John H. Cooke*—The Experiences of an Officer of the 43rd Light Infantry in the Peninsula and South of France During the Napoleonic Wars.

**WELLINGTON AND THE PYRENEES CAMPAIGN VOLUME I: FROM VITORIA TO THE BIDASSOA** *by F. C. Beatson*—The final phase of the campaign in the Iberian Peninsula.

**WELLINGTON AND THE INVASION OF FRANCE VOLUME II: THE BIDASSOA TO THE BATTLE OF THE NIVELLE** *by F. C. Beatson*—The final phase of the campaign in the Iberian Peninsula.

**WELLINGTON AND THE FALL OF FRANCE VOLUME III: THE GAVES AND THE BATTLE OF ORTHEZ** *by F. C. Beatson*—The final phase of the campaign in the Iberian Peninsula.

**NAPOLEON'S IMPERIAL GUARD: FROM MARENGO TO WATERLOO** *by J. T. Headley*—The story of Napoleon's Imperial Guard and the men who commanded them.

**BATTLES & SIEGES OF THE PENINSULAR WAR** *by W. H. Fitchett*—Corunna, Busaco, Albuera, Ciudad Rodrigo, Badajos, Salamanca, San Sebastian & Others.

**SERGEANT GUILLEMARD: THE MAN WHO SHOT NELSON?** *by Robert Guillemard*—A Soldier of the Infantry of the French Army of Napoleon on Campaign Throughout Europe.

**WITH THE GUARDS ACROSS THE PYRENEES** *by Robert Batty*—The Experiences of a British Officer of Wellington's Army During the Battles for the Fall of Napoleonic France, 1813 .

**A STAFF OFFICER IN THE PENINSULA** *by E. W. Buckham*—An Officer of the British Staff Corps Cavalry During the Peninsula Campaign of the Napoleonic Wars.

**THE LEIPZIG CAMPAIGN: 1813—NAPOLEON AND THE "BATTLE OF THE NATIONS"** *by F. N. Maude*—Colonel Maude's analysis of Napoleon's campaign of 1813 around Leipzig.

AVAILABLE ONLINE AT **www.leonaur.com**
AND FROM ALL GOOD BOOK STORES

## ALSO FROM LEONAUR
### AVAILABLE IN SOFTCOVER OR HARDCOVER WITH DUST JACKET

**BUGEAUD: A PACK WITH A BATON** *by Thomas Robert Bugeaud*—The Early Campaigns of a Soldier of Napoleon's Army Who Would Become a Marshal of France.

**WATERLOO RECOLLECTIONS** *by Frederick Llewellyn*—Rare First Hand Accounts, Letters, Reports and Retellings from the Campaign of 1815.

**SERGEANT NICOL** *by Daniel Nicol*—The Experiences of a Gordon Highlander During the Napoleonic Wars in Egypt, the Peninsula and France.

**THE JENA CAMPAIGN: 1806** *by F. N. Maude*—The Twin Battles of Jena & Auerstadt Between Napoleon's French and the Prussian Army.

**PRIVATE O'NEIL** *by Charles O'Neil*—The recollections of an Irish Rogue of H. M. 28th Regt.—The Slashers—during the Peninsula & Waterloo campaigns of the Napoleonic war.

**ROYAL HIGHLANDER** *by James Anton*—A soldier of H.M 42nd (Royal) Highlanders during the Peninsular, South of France & Waterloo Campaigns of the Napoleonic Wars.

**CAPTAIN BLAZE** *by Elzéar Blaze*—Life in Napoleons Army.

**LEJEUNE VOLUME 1** *by Louis-François Lejeune*—The Napoleonic Wars through the Experiences of an Officer on Berthier's Staff.

**LEJEUNE VOLUME 2** *by Louis-François Lejeune*—The Napoleonic Wars through the Experiences of an Officer on Berthier's Staff.

**CAPTAIN COIGNET** *by Jean-Roch Coignet*—A Soldier of Napoleon's Imperial Guard from the Italian Campaign to Russia and Waterloo.

**FUSILIER COOPER** *by John S. Cooper*—Experiences in the 7th (Royal) Fusiliers During the Peninsular Campaign of the Napoleonic Wars and the American Campaign to New Orleans.

**FIGHTING NAPOLEON'S EMPIRE** *by Joseph Anderson*—The Campaigns of a British Infantryman in Italy, Egypt, the Peninsular & the West Indies During the Napoleonic Wars.

**CHASSEUR BARRES** *by Jean-Baptiste Barres*—The experiences of a French Infantryman of the Imperial Guard at Austerlitz, Jena, Eylau, Friedland, in the Peninsular, Lutzen, Bautzen, Zinnwald and Hanau during the Napoleonic Wars.

AVAILABLE ONLINE AT **www.leonaur.com**
AND FROM ALL GOOD BOOK STORES

# ALSO FROM LEONAUR
### AVAILABLE IN SOFTCOVER OR HARDCOVER WITH DUST JACKET

**CAPTAIN COIGNET** *by Jean-Roch Coignet*—A Soldier of Napoleon's Imperial Guard from the Italian Campaign to Russia and Waterloo.

**HUSSAR ROCCA** *by Albert Jean Michel de Rocca*—A French cavalry officer's experiences of the Napoleonic Wars and his views on the Peninsular Campaigns against the Spanish, British And Guerilla Armies.

**MARINES TO 95TH (RIFLES)** *by Thomas Fernyhough*—The military experiences of Robert Fernyhough during the Napoleonic Wars.

**LIGHT BOB** *by Robert Blakeney*—The experiences of a young officer in H.M 28th & 36th regiments of the British Infantry during the Peninsular Campaign of the Napoleonic Wars 1804 - 1814.

**WITH WELLINGTON'S LIGHT CAVALRY** *by William Tomkinson*—The Experiences of an officer of the 16th Light Dragoons in the Peninsular and Waterloo campaigns of the Napoleonic Wars.

**SERGEANT BOURGOGNE** *by Adrien Bourgogne*—With Napoleon's Imperial Guard in the Russian Campaign and on the Retreat from Moscow 1812 - 13.

**SURTEES OF THE 95TH (RIFLES)** *by William Surtees*—A Soldier of the 95th (Rifles) in the Peninsular campaign of the Napoleonic Wars.

**SWORDS OF HONOUR** *by Henry Newbolt & Stanley L. Wood*—The Careers of Six Outstanding Officers from the Napoleonic Wars, the Wars for India and the American Civil War.

**ENSIGN BELL IN THE PENINSULAR WAR** *by George Bell*—The Experiences of a young British Soldier of the 34th Regiment 'The Cumberland Gentlemen' in the Napoleonic wars.

**HUSSAR IN WINTER** *by Alexander Gordon*—A British Cavalry Officer during the retreat to Corunna in the Peninsular campaign of the Napoleonic Wars.

**THE COMPLEAT RIFLEMAN HARRIS** *by Benjamin Harris as told to and transcribed by Captain Henry Curling, 52nd Regt. of Foot*—The adventures of a soldier of the 95th (Rifles) during the Peninsular Campaign of the Napoleonic Wars.

**THE ADVENTURES OF A LIGHT DRAGOON** *by George Farmer & G.R. Gleig*—A cavalryman during the Peninsular & Waterloo Campaigns, in captivity & at the siege of Bhurtpore, India.

AVAILABLE ONLINE AT **www.leonaur.com**
AND FROM ALL GOOD BOOK STORES

## ALSO FROM LEONAUR
### AVAILABLE IN SOFTCOVER OR HARDCOVER WITH DUST JACKET

**THE LIFE OF THE REAL BRIGADIER GERARD VOLUME 1—THE YOUNG HUSSAR 1782-1807** *by Jean-Baptiste De Marbot*—A French Cavalryman Of the Napoleonic Wars at Marengo, Austerlitz, Jena, Eylau & Friedland.

**THE LIFE OF THE REAL BRIGADIER GERARD VOLUME 2—IMPERIAL AIDE-DE-CAMP 1807-1811** *by Jean-Baptiste De Marbot*—A French Cavalryman of the Napoleonic Wars at Saragossa, Landshut, Eckmuhl, Ratisbon, Aspern-Essling, Wagram, Busaco & Torres Vedras.

**THE LIFE OF THE REAL BRIGADIER GERARD VOLUME 3—COLONEL OF CHASSEURS 1811-1815** *by Jean-Baptiste De Marbot*—A French Cavalryman in the retreat from Moscow, Lutzen, Bautzen, Katzbach, Leipzig, Hanau & Waterloo.

**THE INDIAN WAR OF 1864** *by Eugene Ware*—The Experiences of a Young Officer of the 7th Iowa Cavalry on the Western Frontier During the Civil War.

**THE MARCH OF DESTINY** *by Charles E. Young & V. Devinny*—Dangers of the Trail in 1865 by Charles E. Young & The Story of a Pioneer by V. Devinny, two Accounts of Early Emigrants to Colorado.

**CROSSING THE PLAINS** *by William Audley Maxwell*—A First Hand Narrative of the Early Pioneer Trail to California in 1857.

**CHIEF OF SCOUTS** *by William F. Drannan*—A Pilot to Emigrant and Government Trains, Across the Plains of the Western Frontier.

**THIRTY-ONE YEARS ON THE PLAINS AND IN THE MOUNTAINS** *by William F. Drannan*—William Drannan was born to be a pioneer, hunter, trapper and wagon train guide during the momentous days of the Great American West.

**THE INDIAN WARS VOLUNTEER** *by William Thompson*—Recollections of the Conflict Against the Snakes, Shoshone, Bannocks, Modocs and Other Native Tribes of the American North West.

**THE 4TH TENNESSEE CAVALRY** *by George B. Guild*—The Services of Smith's Regiment of Confederate Cavalry by One of its Officers.

**COLONEL WORTHINGTON'S SHILOH** *by T. Worthington*—The Tennessee Campaign, 1862, by an Officer of the Ohio Volunteers.

**FOUR YEARS IN THE SADDLE** *by W. L. Curry*—The History of the First Regiment Ohio Volunteer Cavalry in the American Civil War.

AVAILABLE ONLINE AT **www.leonaur.com**
AND FROM ALL GOOD BOOK STORES

## ALSO FROM LEONAUR
### AVAILABLE IN SOFTCOVER OR HARDCOVER WITH DUST JACKET

**LIFE IN THE ARMY OF NORTHERN VIRGINIA** by *Carlton McCarthy*—The Observations of a Confederate Artilleryman of Cutshaw's Battalion During the American Civil War 1861-1865.

**HISTORY OF THE CAVALRY OF THE ARMY OF THE POTOMAC** by *Charles D. Rhodes*—Including Pope's Army of Virginia and the Cavalry Operations in West Virginia During the American Civil War.

**CAMP-FIRE AND COTTON-FIELD** by *Thomas W. Knox*—A New York Herald Correspondent's View of the American Civil War.

**SERGEANT STILLWELL** by *Leander Stillwell*—The Experiences of a Union Army Soldier of the 61st Illinois Infantry During the American Civil War.

**STONEWALL'S CANNONEER** by *Edward A. Moore*—Experiences with the Rockbridge Artillery, Confederate Army of Northern Virginia, During the American Civil War.

**THE SIXTH CORPS** by *George Stevens*—The Army of the Potomac, Union Army, During the American Civil War.

**THE RAILROAD RAIDERS** by *William Pittenger*—An Ohio Volunteers Recollections of the Andrews Raid to Disrupt the Confederate Railroad in Georgia During the American Civil War.

**CITIZEN SOLDIER** by *John Beatty*—An Account of the American Civil War by a Union Infantry Officer of Ohio Volunteers Who Became a Brigadier General.

**COX: PERSONAL RECOLLECTIONS OF THE CIVIL WAR--VOLUME 1** by *Jacob Dolson Cox*—West Virginia, Kanawha Valley, Gauley Bridge, Cotton Mountain, South Mountain, Antietam, the Morgan Raid & the East Tennessee Campaign.

**COX: PERSONAL RECOLLECTIONS OF THE CIVIL WAR--VOLUME 2** by *Jacob Dolson Cox*—Siege of Knoxville, East Tennessee, Atlanta Campaign, the Nashville Campaign & the North Carolina Campaign.

**KERSHAW'S BRIGADE VOLUME 1** by *D. Augustus Dickert*—Manassas, Seven Pines, Sharpsburg (Antietam), Fredricksburg, Chancellorsville, Gettysburg, Chickamauga, Chattanooga, Fort Sanders & Bean Station.

**KERSHAW'S BRIGADE VOLUME 2** by *D. Augustus Dickert*—At the wilderness, Cold Harbour, Petersburg, The Shenandoah Valley and Cedar Creek..

AVAILABLE ONLINE AT **www.leonaur.com**
AND FROM ALL GOOD BOOK STORES

# ALSO FROM LEONAUR
### AVAILABLE IN SOFTCOVER OR HARDCOVER WITH DUST JACKET

**THE RELUCTANT REBEL** by *William G. Stevenson*—A young Kentuckian's experiences in the Confederate Infantry & Cavalry during the American Civil War..

**BOOTS AND SADDLES** by *Elizabeth B. Custer*—The experiences of General Custer's Wife on the Western Plains.

**FANNIE BEERS' CIVIL WAR** by *Fannie A. Beers*—A Confederate Lady's Experiences of Nursing During the Campaigns & Battles of the American Civil War.

**LADY SALE'S AFGHANISTAN** by *Florentia Sale*—An Indomitable Victorian Lady's Account of the Retreat from Kabul During the First Afghan War.

**THE TWO WARS OF MRS DUBERLY** by *Frances Isabella Duberly*—An Intrepid Victorian Lady's Experience of the Crimea and Indian Mutiny.

**THE REBELLIOUS DUCHESS** by *Paul F. S. Dermoncourt*—The Adventures of the Duchess of Berri and Her Attempt to Overthrow French Monarchy.

**LADIES OF WATERLOO** by *Charlotte A. Eaton, Magdalene de Lancey & Juana Smith*—The Experiences of Three Women During the Campaign of 1815: Waterloo Days by Charlotte A. Eaton, A Week at Waterloo by Magdalene de Lancey & Juana's Story by Juana Smith.

**TWO YEARS BEFORE THE MAST** by *Richard Henry Dana. Jr.*—The account of one young man's experiences serving on board a sailing brig—the Penelope—bound for California, between the years 1834-36.

**A SAILOR OF KING GEORGE** by *Frederick Hoffman*—From Midshipman to Captain—Recollections of War at Sea in the Napoleonic Age 1793-1815.

**LORDS OF THE SEA** by *A. T. Mahan*—Great Captains of the Royal Navy During the Age of Sail.

**COGGESHALL'S VOYAGES: VOLUME 1** by *George Coggeshall*—The Recollections of an American Schooner Captain.

**COGGESHALL'S VOYAGES: VOLUME 2** by *George Coggeshall*—The Recollections of an American Schooner Captain.

**TWILIGHT OF EMPIRE** by *Sir Thomas Ussher & Sir George Cockburn*—Two accounts of Napoleon's Journeys in Exile to Elba and St. Helena: Narrative of Events by Sir Thomas Ussher & Napoleon's Last Voyage: Extract of a diary by Sir George Cockburn.

---

AVAILABLE ONLINE AT **www.leonaur.com**
AND FROM ALL GOOD BOOK STORES

# ALSO FROM LEONAUR
## AVAILABLE IN SOFTCOVER OR HARDCOVER WITH DUST JACKET

**ESCAPE FROM THE FRENCH** by Edward Boys—A Young Royal Navy Midshipman's Adventures During the Napoleonic War.

**THE VOYAGE OF H.M.S. PANDORA** by Edward Edwards R. N. & George Hamilton, edited by Basil Thomson—In Pursuit of the Mutineers of the Bounty in the South Seas—1790-1791.

**MEDUSA** by J. B. Henry Savigny and Alexander Correard and Charlotte-Adélaïde Dard —Narrative of a Voyage to Senegal in 1816 & The Sufferings of the Picard Family After the Shipwreck of the Medusa.

**THE SEA WAR OF 1812 VOLUME 1** by A. T. Mahan—A History of the Maritime Conflict.

**THE SEA WAR OF 1812 VOLUME 2** by A. T. Mahan—A History of the Maritime Conflict.

**WETHERELL OF H. M. S. HUSSAR** by John Wetherell—The Recollections of an Ordinary Seaman of the Royal Navy During the Napoleonic Wars.

**THE NAVAL BRIGADE IN NATAL** by C. R. N. Burne—With the Guns of H. M. S. Terrible & H. M. S. Tartar during the Boer War 1899-1900.

**THE VOYAGE OF H. M. S. BOUNTY** by William Bligh—The True Story of an 18th Century Voyage of Exploration and Mutiny.

**SHIPWRECK!** by William Gilly—The Royal Navy's Disasters at Sea 1793-1849.

**KING'S CUTTERS AND SMUGGLERS: 1700-1855** by E. Keble Chatterton—A unique period of maritime history-from the beginning of the eighteenth to the middle of the nineteenth century when British seamen risked all to smuggle valuable goods from wool to tea and spirits from and to the Continent.

**CONFEDERATE BLOCKADE RUNNER** by John Wilkinson—The Personal Recollections of an Officer of the Confederate Navy.

**NAVAL BATTLES OF THE NAPOLEONIC WARS** by W. H. Fitchett—Cape St. Vincent, the Nile, Cadiz, Copenhagen, Trafalgar & Others.

**PRISONERS OF THE RED DESERT** by R. S. Gwatkin-Williams—The Adventures of the Crew of the Tara During the First World War.

**U-BOAT WAR 1914-1918** by James B. Connolly/Karl von Schenk—Two Contrasting Accounts from Both Sides of the Conflict at Sea D uring the Great War.

AVAILABLE ONLINE AT **www.leonaur.com**
AND FROM ALL GOOD BOOK STORES

# ALSO FROM LEONAUR
### AVAILABLE IN SOFTCOVER OR HARDCOVER WITH DUST JACKET

**IRON TIMES WITH THE GUARDS** *by An O. E. (G. P. A. Fildes)*—The Experiences of an Officer of the Coldstream Guards on the Western Front During the First World War.

**THE GREAT WAR IN THE MIDDLE EAST: 1** *by W. T. Massey*—The Desert Campaigns & How Jerusalem Was Won---two classic accounts in one volume.

**THE GREAT WAR IN THE MIDDLE EAST: 2** *by W. T. Massey*—Allenby's Final Triumph.

**SMITH-DORRIEN** *by Horace Smith-Dorrien*—Isandlwhana to the Great War.

**1914** *by Sir John French*—The Early Campaigns of the Great War by the British Commander.

**GRENADIER** *by E. R. M. Fryer*—The Recollections of an Officer of the Grenadier Guards throughout the Great War on the Western Front.

**BATTLE, CAPTURE & ESCAPE** *by George Pearson*—The Experiences of a Canadian Light Infantryman During the Great War.

**DIGGERS AT WAR** *by R. Hugh Knyvett & G. P. Cuttriss*—"Over There" With the Australians by R. Hugh Knyvett and Over the Top With the Third Australian Division by G. P. Cuttriss. Accounts of Australians During the Great War in the Middle East, at Gallipoli and on the Western Front.

**HEAVY FIGHTING BEFORE US** *by George Brenton Laurie*—The Letters of an Officer of the Royal Irish Rifles on the Western Front During the Great War.

**THE CAMELIERS** *by Oliver Hogue*—A Classic Account of the Australians of the Imperial Camel Corps During the First World War in the Middle East.

**RED DUST** *by Donald Black*—A Classic Account of Australian Light Horsemen in Palestine During the First World War.

**THE LEAN, BROWN MEN** *by Angus Buchanan*—Experiences in East Africa During the Great War with the 25th Royal Fusiliers—the Legion of Frontiersmen.

**THE NIGERIAN REGIMENT IN EAST AFRICA** *by W. D. Downes*—On Campaign During the Great War 1916-1918.

**THE 'DIE-HARDS' IN SIBERIA** *by John Ward*—With the Middlesex Regiment Against the Bolsheviks 1918-19.

AVAILABLE ONLINE AT **www.leonaur.com**
AND FROM ALL GOOD BOOK STORES

## ALSO FROM LEONAUR
### AVAILABLE IN SOFTCOVER OR HARDCOVER WITH DUST JACKET

**FARAWAY CAMPAIGN** *by F. James*—Experiences of an Indian Army Cavalry Officer in Persia & Russia During the Great War.

**REVOLT IN THE DESERT** *by T. E. Lawrence*—An account of the experiences of one remarkable British officer's war from his own perspective.

**MACHINE-GUN SQUADRON** *by A. M. G.*—The 20th Machine Gunners from British Yeomanry Regiments in the Middle East Campaign of the First World War.

**A GUNNER'S CRUSADE** *by Antony Bluett*—The Campaign in the Desert, Palestine & Syria as Experienced by the Honourable Artillery Company During the Great War.

**DESPATCH RIDER** *by W. H. L. Watson*—The Experiences of a British Army Motorcycle Despatch Rider During the Opening Battles of the Great War in Europe.

**TIGERS ALONG THE TIGRIS** *by E. J. Thompson*—The Leicestershire Regiment in Mesopotamia During the First World War.

**HEARTS & DRAGONS** *by Charles R. M. F. Crutwell*—The 4th Royal Berkshire Regiment in France and Italy During the Great War, 1914-1918.

**INFANTRY BRIGADE: 1914** *by John Ward*—The Diary of a Commander of the 15th Infantry Brigade, 5th Division, British Army, During the Retreat from Mons.

**DOING OUR 'BIT'** *by Ian Hay*—Two Classic Accounts of the Men of Kitchener's 'New Army' During the Great War including *The First 100,000* & *All In It*.

**AN EYE IN THE STORM** *by Arthur Ruhl*—An American War Correspondent's Experiences of the First World War from the Western Front to Gallipoli-and Beyond.

**STAND & FALL** *by Joe Cassells*—With the Middlesex Regiment Against the Bolsheviks 1918-19.

**RIFLEMAN MACGILL'S WAR** *by Patrick MacGill*—A Soldier of the London Irish During the Great War in Europe including *The Amateur Army*, *The Red Horizon* & *The Great Push*.

**WITH THE GUNS** *by C. A. Rose & Hugh Dalton*—Two First Hand Accounts of British Gunners at War in Europe During World War 1- Three Years in France with the Guns and With the British Guns in Italy.

**THE BUSH WAR DOCTOR** *by Robert V. Dolbey*—The Experiences of a British Army Doctor During the East African Campaign of the First World War.

AVAILABLE ONLINE AT **www.leonaur.com**
AND FROM ALL GOOD BOOK STORES

# ALSO FROM LEONAUR
### AVAILABLE IN SOFTCOVER OR HARDCOVER WITH DUST JACKET

**THE 9TH—THE KING'S (LIVERPOOL REGIMENT) IN THE GREAT WAR 1914 - 1918** *by Enos H. G. Roberts*—Mersey to mud—war and Liverpool men.

**THE GAMBARDIER** *by Mark Severn*—The experiences of a battery of Heavy artillery on the Western Front during the First World War.

**FROM MESSINES TO THIRD YPRES** *by Thomas Floyd*—A personal account of the First World War on the Western front by a 2/5th Lancashire Fusilier.

**THE IRISH GUARDS IN THE GREAT WAR - VOLUME 1** *by Rudyard Kipling*—Edited and Compiled from Their Diaries and Papers—The First Battalion.

**THE IRISH GUARDS IN THE GREAT WAR - VOLUME 1** *by Rudyard Kipling*—Edited and Compiled from Their Diaries and Papers—The Second Battalion.

**ARMOURED CARS IN EDEN** *by K. Roosevelt*—An American President's son serving in Rolls Royce armoured cars with the British in Mesopatamia & with the American Artillery in France during the First World War.

**CHASSEUR OF 1914** *by Marcel Dupont*—Experiences of the twilight of the French Light Cavalry by a young officer during the early battles of the great war in Europe.

**TROOP HORSE & TRENCH** *by R.A. Lloyd*—The experiences of a British Lifeguardsman of the household cavalry fighting on the western front during the First World War 1914-18.

**THE EAST AFRICAN MOUNTED RIFLES** *by C.J. Wilson*—Experiences of the campaign in the East African bush during the First World War.

**THE LONG PATROL** *by George Berrie*—A Novel of Light Horsemen from Gallipoli to the Palestine campaign of the First World War.

**THE FIGHTING CAMELIERS** *by Frank Reid*—The exploits of the Imperial Camel Corps in the desert and Palestine campaigns of the First World War.

**STEEL CHARIOTS IN THE DESERT** *by S. C. Rolls*—The first world war experiences of a Rolls Royce armoured car driver with the Duke of Westminster in Libya and in Arabia with T.E. Lawrence.

**WITH THE IMPERIAL CAMEL CORPS IN THE GREAT WAR** *by Geoffrey Inchbald*—The story of a serving officer with the British 2nd battalion against the Senussi and during the Palestine campaign.

AVAILABLE ONLINE AT **www.leonaur.com**
AND FROM ALL GOOD BOOK STORES

www.ingramcontent.com/pod-product-compliance
Lightning Source LLC
Chambersburg PA
CBHW031616160426
43196CB00006B/157